Whys & Therefores

Whys & Therefores

A rational look
at the English language

William Rutherford

for Karen
with best wishes
Bill

equinox

SHEFFIELD OAKVILLE

Published by Equinox Publishing Ltd

UK: Unit S3, Kelham House, 3 Lancaster Street, Sheffield, S3 8AF
USA: DBBC, 28 Main Street, Oakville, CT 06779

www.equinoxpub.com

First published in 2011

British Library Cataloguing-in-Publication Data
A catalogue record for this book is available from the British Library.

ISBN 978-1-84553-651-0 (paperback)
    978-1-908049-90-2 (hardback)

Library of Congress Cataloging-in-Publication Data
Rutherford, William E.
  Whys & therefores : a rational look at the English language / William Rutherford.
    p. cm.
  Includes bibliographical references and index.
  ISBN 978-1-908049-90-2 (hb)— ISBN 978-1-84553-651-0 (pb)
  1. English language—Study and teaching. 2. English philology. 3. Language and languages—Study and teaching. I. Title. II. Title: Whys and therefores.
  PE1065.R88 2010
  428.0071—dc22
                        2010003589

Typeset by Ben Cracknell Studios
Printed and bound in the UK by the MPG Books Group

to Lynne

CONTENTS

CONTENTS

CONTENTS

PREFACE

Whys & Therefores: A Rational Look at the English Language has come into being in a way that seems very natural to me. The learning *about* one's own language in a school setting usually means having to identify the parts of speech, diagram sentences, memorize spellings, articulate long-held grammar rules, and so on. This is the way I was taught the "facts" of the English language in school more than six decades ago. Arising very rarely from us in school would be a "why" question about a grammar rule, a semantic principle, or a spelling convention … we usually assumed that these were unassailable tenets received from somewhere on high. The learning *about* one's own language was—and often still is—epistemologically similar to the learning of history, biology, or any of the other common school subjects.

It doesn't have to be that way. The workings of one's native language do not reside in an *external* hidden repository, the key to which can be the property only of the "expert," be that person schoolteacher, linguist, or language maven. The repository is in fact the *internal* property of the native speaker and figuring out a great deal of how the language works is therefore an enterprise readily accessible to that speaker through introspection. *Whys & Therefores* is my attempt to provide a scenario in which one kind of opportunity for such introspection might come into being. The format for this scenario is that of a series of Socratic dialogues between a mentor and a pupil. Each of these brief dialogues, one hundred of them, develops around some discrete aspect of English language organization that lends itself to grouping of this kind. The intended effects are, in essence:

- Appreciation of what it means to "know" a language

- Inducement of reliance upon native-language intuition

- Discovery of what one *didn't* know that one "knows" about the language

- Awareness of the use of *un*grammaticality as an empirical tool

- Healthy questioning of received "facts" about language from so-called "experts"

- Encouragement of critical thinking

- Realization that every person is at least potentially his or her own grammarian for whatever dialect or whatever variety of the language he or she speaks

- Usefulness of language "play"

PREFACE

Whys & Therefores is designed as a do-it-yourself book about aspects of English-language form and meaning that are adducible through rational inquiry. Cropping up throughout the material are conundrums such as *Why can there be no such thing as the longest word in the language?* How can the sentence *Who cares?* not be a question? What's so "possessive" about the *'s* in *today's news, a good night's sleep, the stock market's decline?* If from the verb *revise* we get the noun *revision*, why doesn't *divide* give us *dividion?* Why does the sentence *Mary's happy* sound fine but *I wonder how happy Mary's* doesn't? How can linguists claim that English spelling is 95% regular? Issues such as these and many others lie at the core of *Whys & Therefores* and can be engaged by the reader in several ways. The work may be read as a book, dipped into at random, expanded upon, even acted out (as exemplified in the accompanying CD). With the appendix of technical terms, the work may also serve as a reference source for all the language features treated here.

Interlocutors

The two characters taking part in the one hundred dialogues of the twenty chapters comprising *Whys & Therefores* are the same throughout. One serves as a "mentor," the other a "pupil" (or perhaps a teacher and a student). The mentor, "Marta Ramirez," is a young woman in her early thirties, a research assistant doing advanced graduate work in pursuit of a doctorate in linguistics. Marta, though a native speaker of English, is also fluent in Spanish, the native language of both her parents. The pupil, "Patrick O'Grady," is a nineteen-year-old undergraduate in his second year of university study who has chosen to satisfy one of his elective requirements with a tutorial in introductory English linguistics. Marta's work in mentoring undergraduates in their first study of English from a linguistically rational perspective satisfies one of her requirements for financial support from her institution. Patrick, an A student in high school, is supporting himself financially through an athletic scholarship. Both Marta and Patrick are very bright, full of curiosity, and possessed of a lively sense of humor.

Structure of Content

The one hundred dialogues of *Whys & Therefores* are each allotted a numbered "Day." Additional related material appears after every five Days and is labeled "PS." The book is thus divided into twenty chapters, each consisting of five days and a postscript. The material within each of the twenty chapters forms a linguistically coherent cluster (see Contents).

The overall coverage of general linguistic categories is as follows: Every third chapter, starting with Chapter 1, is devoted to an aspect of vocabulary and/or word formation; another third, starting with Chapter 2, is devoted to syntax; the final third, starting with Chapter 3, is devoted to one or another of the remaining areas: semantics, spelling, sounds, idiom, modification, spatial and temporal relations, etc. Selection of the linguistic coverage itself was largely determined by its suitability for the intended audience and its amenability to treatment in dialogue format.

The related Postscript (PS) material varies greatly; it may consist of:

- Headlines for decipherment and/or analysis (PS 4, PS 8)

- Prompting of a phonological rule (e.g., indefinite article use of *an*: PS 5)

- A small project involving word formation (PS 10)

- Assemblage of English words, some made up, from Greek roots (PS 15)

- A conundrum concerning the use of contractions (PS 17)

Solutions to PS problems can be found in the Notes and Solutions.

A recording of all one hundred spoken dialogues is available from the *Whys & Therefores* page at www.equinoxpub.com

ACKNOWLEDGEMENTS

There are many from whose comments, criticisms, suggestions, and general support I have benefited greatly in the writing of this book. For welcome encouragement along the way I wish to thank Marie Carbone, Paul Dahlin, Shadi Ganjavi, Ilai Gilbert, Carol Lord, Lorin Speltz, and MacMillan Thompson. Karen Santoro, in a close reading of much of the manuscript, has been very helpful. Norman Palley's computer expertise has rescued me on a number of occasions. Special thanks go to Sharon Klein for her very insightful commentary on a sizeable portion of the manuscript. I'm very grateful to Hiroyuki Oshita, a superb syntactician among other accomplishments, for his valuable indications of where more clarity and consistency have been called for. Margaret Thomas surrendered a portion of one of her summer vacations to render a detailed review of not only the content of *Whys & Therefores* at that point but also its internal structure. From David Crystal I have received encouragement and some valuable suggestions concerning the quest for permissions in the use of copyrighted material. Early in the manuscript's development Fusa Katada saw immediately the potential appeal of the book to a Japanese academic audience and volunteered herself for preparation of an edition annotated for the Japanese reader. Thanks go also to Sandra Margolies, my very fine copy-editor. Finally, there is my debt of profound gratitude to Lynne Hill for her constant encouragement, her copious insightful remarks of all kinds, and for putting up with me during these years of off-and-on attention to the task at hand. The book is dedicated to her.

CHAPTER ONE

WORDS ... WORDS ...

what we really "know" when we know a word; the difference between "content" words and "function" words; the semantic "rule" that we all routinely break and why it's OK

Day One **"drink"**

Day Two **content and function**

Day Three **open and closed**

Day Four **bricks and mortar**

Day Five **"so friendly to your taste"**

PS 1 **to know a word ...**

"drink"

All words are pegs to hang ideas on.

Henry Ward Beecher, *Proverbs from Plymouth Pulpit* (1887)

▶ M: Hi, Patrick ... Now that you've had time to think about what I asked—*words*—are you ready for our first session?

P: Yes, but I don't understand. What's the <u>big deal</u> about *words*, Marta? <u>Everybody</u> knows what they are ... You string a bunch of 'em together and you get a sentence.

M: That simple, huh?

P: Sure ... Take the word *drink*, for example. Stick it in between two other words—like *they* and *coffee*—and you get *They drink coffee*. Nothing could be simpler.

M: Seems so, doesn't it? OK, Patrick, tell me some things you already "know" about the word *drink* as you just used it. Is it an ADJECTIVE, a PRONOUN, a ...

P: It's a VERB ... obviously; and what you drink is a NOUN.

M: So can you say *They drink fright*, *They drink fog*, *They drink furniture* ...? These are NOUNS.

P: C'mon, Marta! ... It's not just <u>any</u> NOUN. What you drink has to be a <u>liquid</u> of some kind, unless you're some sort of weird poet.

M: All right ... But suppose the coffee drinking took place yesterday. Would it be *They drinked coffee*? I mean we do say *They sipped coffee*, *They tasted coffee*, and so on.

P: Nooo ... the PAST TENSE of *drink* is *drank*! Everybody knows that.

M: Looks like "knowing" that simple little word *drink* is starting to involve a lot of stuff. What's a word for someone who drinks?

P: ...*a drinker*?

M: OK ... and someone who drinks beer?

P: ...*a beer drinker.*

M: ...and if I say *They drink a lot*, what does that mean?

P: Well, I suppose it could mean that what they drink a lot of is something alcoholic ... but it doesn't have to ... the drink could be water ... anything, I guess.

M: Yes, so *They* **drink a lot** is AMBIGUOUS. But let's go on … What's another way of referring to **drink** where alcohol is concerned?

P: Umm … **alcoholic drink**?

M: No, I mean without using the word *alcoholic*.

P: Oh, **strong drink**?

M: And is someone who takes "strong drink" a **strong drinker**?

P: No … has to be **heavy drinker**!

M: So it's **strong drink** but **heavy drinker** … <u>not</u> **strong drinker** and **heavy drink**?

P: Ouch! Guess so, Marta … but why?

M: Well, there's really no easy answer to that, Patrick; you'd have to look for it in the history of the language.

P: I think I see what you've been getting at … I mean, what's involved in using just a simple word like **drink**.

M: Yes … knowing your "simple" word **drink** means knowing how to pronounce it and how to spell it, knowing it can be either a VERB or a NOUN, knowing that its NOUN OBJECT is **liquid**, knowing that it's AMBIGUOUS and that its PAST TENSE is the irregular **drank**, knowing the related NOUN form **drinker** and the expressions **heavy drinker** versus **strong drink**, and knowing lots of other stuff that we'll get into later.

P: Wow! Doesn't sound so "simple" any more … and I've been doing this all along …

M: …and without ever having to think about it. Let's go get something to **drink**!

Drink to me only with thine eyes,
And I will pledge with mine …
~
The thirst that from the soul doth rise
Doth ask a drink divine

Ben Jonson, from "The Forest" and "To Celia"

3

content and function

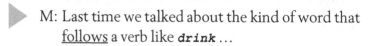
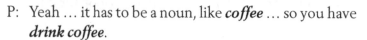

NAME TWO PARTS OF SPEECH.

"Umm ... your voice and your mouth."

© 1989. BIL KEANE, INC.
KING FEATURES SYNDICATE

M: Last time we talked about the kind of word that <u>follows</u> a verb like *drink* ...

P: Yeah ... it has to be a noun, like *coffee* ... so you have *drink coffee*.

M: Then what about *drink the water*?

P: What about it, Marta?

M: Well, the word following *drink* here is *the* ... Is *the* a noun?

P: Uh ... no ... it's an ARTICLE, I guess.

M: Yes, one of the so-called PARTS OF SPEECH ... and you just mentioned another.

P: I did? Oh ... NOUN.

M: So we've got the words *the* and *water*, an ARTICLE and a NOUN. Why do we have separate terms for them, Patrick?

P: Why? Because they're different!

M: In what way?

P: Oh, that's so obvious, Marta! For one thing, *water* you can look up in the dictionary.

M: But *the*'s in the dictionary too.

P: Sure, but how do you define it?

M: You're assuming that it <u>has</u> a definition ... a meaning.

P: How can it be in the dictionary if it doesn't have a meaning? How can it even be in the <u>language</u> if it doesn't have a meaning!

4

M: Well, you're a native speaker of English too, Patrick ... So tell me ... if *the* has a meaning, what is it?

P: I don't know ... something about being DEFINITE, I guess.

M: But where's the "definiteness" in phrases like, say, *the water*, *the stars*, *the library*, *the dinosaur*, *the end* ...? Does it really reside in the word *the*?

P: Sure ... 'cause if you take it away you get *water*, *stars*, *library*, etc. ... no more definiteness!

M: So *water*, *stars*, *library*, etc. become DEFINITE with the addition of *the*?

P: Looks like it.

M: Well, if adding *the* makes these words DEFINITE, then isn't it easier to talk about what *the* does, or how it FUNCTIONS, than about what it means?

P: I think I see where this is leading. So can you call *the* a FUNCTION WORD?

M: Yes, why not? But consider again that phrase *the water* ... If *the* performs a FUNCTION—making *water* DEFINITE—then *water* provides the CONTENT of the phrase, right, Patrick?

P: OK ... FUNCTION and CONTENT ... hmm ...

M: What are you thinking about?

P: Two kinds of words? ... FUNCTION WORDS and CONTENT WORDS?

M: Right on! And we'll see, as we move along, that it's a very important distinction for the rest of the language.

POLONIUS: What do you read, my lord?

HAMLET: Words, words, words.

Shakespeare, Hamlet, Act II, scene ii

open and closed

'Twas brillig, and the slithy toves
Did gyre and gimble in the wabe;
All mimsy were the borogoves,
And the mome raths outgrabe.

Lewis Carroll, "Jabberwocky"

M: We were talking last time about CONTENT WORDS and FUNCTION WORDS, and …

P: …sorry to interrupt, Marta, but actually <u>one</u> function word—*the*—and very few content words.

M: Right, Patrick, but we had to start somewhere. So now let's expand a bit. Take a look here at Lewis Carroll's "Jabberwocky" poem, Patrick … What do you notice right away, even sort of jumps out at you?

P: The strange words, I guess … *brillig, gimble, mimsy,* and so on … What an imagination!

M: Yes … Now take the first line and try substituting familiar words for the made-up "Jabberwocky" words.

P: Oh … let's see … "*'Twas* **bracing** … *and the … the* **puffy clouds** …"

M: Not bad! Go on …

P: Um … "*Did* **swoop** … *and* **swirl** … *in … in the* **wind***!*"

M: All right! Might as well finish it now.

P: OK … (*sigh*) Uhh …

> "All **fussy** were the … um … **turtledoves** …
> *And the … the …* **foot paths** … ooohh … **outgrew**"

M: "Outgrew," eh? Well, anyway, Mr. Carroll would have been amazed!

P: Yeah, sure … but why are you making me do this?

M: You'll see … Again, what are the two kinds of words we noted in the last session?

P: CONTENT WORDS and FUNCTION WORDS.

M: And which of the two figured in the substitutions you just made for the "Jabberwocky" words?

P: Well, content words, I guess.

M: What <u>kind</u> of content words … I mean what part of speech?

P: Um … let's see … I'm guessing NOUNS (*clouds, wind, turtledoves, foot, paths*), VERBS (*swoop, swirl, outgrew*), ADJECTIVES (*bracing, puffy, fussy*).

M: Of course those are just the CONTENT WORDS that you <u>happened</u> to pick, out of possibly millions! And if you leave them out, what's left?

P: OK …

Twas _____, and the _____ _____
Did _____ and _____ in the _____;
All _____ were the _____,
And the _____ _____ _____.

M: What've you got now? Could these have been turned into "Jabberwocky"?

P: Hard to imagine …

M: Why?

P: 'Cause we don't have whole bunches of words like *was* or *were*, like *and*, like *the, did, all* …

M: …words hardly anybody has to look up in the dictionary?

P: Yeah … oh … FUNCTION WORDS!

M: Yup. Think of it … along with *the* you have *a, an* … and *this, that* or *these, those*, maybe *some, many* … but that's about it. Likewise for *and, all, was, were*, and so on …

P: So zillions of substitutions for CONTENT WORDS but hardly anything for FUNCTION WORDS?

M: Well, I don't know about "zillions," Patrick, but you get the idea. Nouns, verbs, and adjectives are an OPEN CLASS of words: New words get added all the time and you can even make up your own, as Lewis Carroll did. And FUNCTION WORDS …?

P: CLOSED CLASS, obviously.

M: Obviously.

Parts of speech are metaphors because the whole of nature is a metaphor of the human mind.

Ralph Waldo Emerson, "Language," in Nature (1836), Chapter 4

7

bricks and mortar

> Bricks are the content words
> And function words the mortar.
> So the way you make a sentence
> Is to add a little wa(r)ter.
>
> with apologies to Ogden Nash

M: Patrick, remember your brilliant re-creation of the "Jabberwocky" poem last time?

P: What … you mean just substituting real words for jabberwocky words? You flatter me!

M: OK, but there's more in it than you realize. Let's lay out the original again without the jabberwocky …

```
' Twas _____ , and the _____ y _____ s
Did _____ and _____ in the _____ ;
All _____ y were the _____ s,
And the _____ _____ s out _____ .
```

…and what do we have?

P: Um … a bunch of FUNCTION WORDS … CLOSED CLASS?

M: Right! And if we do sort of the opposite—put in your clever substitutions and leave out everything else …

```
____ bracing, ___ ___ puffy clouds
___ swoop ___ swirl ___ ___ wind;
___ fussy ___ ___ turtledoves,
___ ___ foot paths ___ grew.
```

…what've we got now?

P: A bunch of CONTENT WORDS … all OPEN CLASS, of course.

M: And can you at least conjure up a picture of some kind from it?

P: Sure, Marta … puffy clouds swooping and swirling, and so on. And, of course, from the other set no picture at all … that's what you're getting at, right?

M: Yup. It reminds me a little of a rudimentary form of English called PIDGIN. Here's a sample I brought with me, with a rather free translation. The speaker is a Korean woman.

Picture marry.—I MARRIED THROUGH A PICTURE.

Husband picture me see girl-time Korea.—My husband saw my picture when I was a girl in Korea.

He like OK. Marry. Come Hawaii.—He liked it OK, so we got married and came to Hawaii.

Husband pay help husband better.—My husband's pay would help him better.

That's why Hawaii come.—That's why we came to Hawaii.

What do you make of it?

P: Easy … full of content words … mostly nouns and verbs … hardly anything on the function side.

M: Yes, and notice also the lack of inflection … another part of function.

P: What do you mean, Marta?

M: No past tense … no *married, saw, liked, came*; no possessive *'s* … no *husband's pay*; also hardly any pronouns … no *I, my, him, we*; and no prepositions: no *come to Hawaii*.

P: So hardly any grammar, it looks like …

M: Nice observation, Patrick.

P: …and yet a meaning of some kind comes across!

M: It sure does … and for the most part through content words alone, without inflection.

P: So the difference between Pidgin English and Standard English is the absence of all the function stuff.

M: Well, <u>one</u> of the differences … but probably the biggest. What we've noticed is that your "function stuff" holds the sentence together, so to speak …

P: Yea for grammar!

M: …and so you can think of sentences as little "buildings" made of bricks and mortar.

P: Cool! So the content words—the nouns, verbs, and adjectives—are the <u>bricks</u> and the function parts are the <u>mortar</u>!

M: I'd say so.

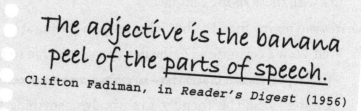

The adjective is the banana peel of the <u>parts of speech.</u>
Clifton Fadiman, in Reader's Digest (1956)

"so friendly to your taste"

"Oatmeal that <u>dares</u> to be different"

Advertisement for oatmeal

P: Marta, I've been thinking about something we got into on Day One.

M: Something about what it means to "know a word"?

P: Yeah ... like the kinds of words that can't come after other words—or at least they're not supposed to ...

M: ...like maybe with VERBS ... so the sentence, uh, **Fred chops wood** is OK but *Fred chops water* is not?

P: Sure ... what you chop has to be solid, at least for starters.

M: OK ... the object of *chop* must be something that <u>can</u> be chopped. Now what about, say, **Fire chops** *wood*?

P: Ridiculous, Marta! Fire can't do something like that ... you're treating "fire" like a person!

M: Yes ... chopping is a willful act, Patrick, so the SUBJECT of **chop** can't be "fire," or "dust," or "honesty" ... words like that. Is this the sort of thing you've been thinking about?

P: Right ... so wouldn't you be surprised if people did come out with weird stuff like with those **chop** examples?

M: Yes and no, my friend ... but what are you getting at?

P: Well, I saw a cigarette ad in the newspaper that ran something like:

[*call it*] COFFIN NAIL CIGARETTES – SO FRIENDLY TO YOUR TASTE

Cigarettes can't be "friendly" to anybody, or anything, let alone anybody's "taste."

M: Do you think it was a mistake?

10

P: I guess not ... probably deliberate.

M: And why?

P: To grab our attention ... They're trying to get us to buy something.

M: Can't argue with that, Patrick. Here's another for you:

> [Chintzy's] GIFTS FOR THE HOME TO PLEASE EVERYBODY AT
> PRICES TO PLEASE YOUR POCKETBOOK
> AND TERMS TO PLEASE YOUR BUDGET

P: Ha! As if pocketbooks and budgets can be made happy!

M: ...and another, advertising supposedly quality office furniture at bargain prices:

> **Only your checkbook will know the difference**

Are checkbooks capable of "knowing"?

P: [*laughter*] I'm sure I read more stuff like this all the time without noticing it.

M: ...and maybe unconsciously are led to go out and buy the product? Here's one more ad, directed at tourists in a fashionable part of town:

> **When shopping on [street with high-fashion stores],**
> **make sure you're wearing the right hotel.**

Can you "wear" a hotel?

P: No, but "wearing" a hotel is much more likely to catch your attention than "staying at" one.

M: Yes, so what we've seen here is <u>deliberate</u> violation of conventions associated with the use of CONTENT words: VERBS, NOUNS, and ADJECTIVES. But you can't violate them without knowing what they are to start with—part of what we mean when we talk about "**knowing a word.**"

Don't buy that!
It costs too much!
Don't make your
pocketbook angry!

PS ONE to know a word ...

Many features make up what we think of as "knowledge of a word." The kinds of knowledge entailed in fully "knowing" the English verb *drink*, as we've now seen, are at least the following:

PRONUNCIATION—drɪŋk

SPELLING—d-r-i-n-k

PART OF SPEECH—verb, noun

STRUCTURE—subject *drink* object

VERB FORMS—*drinks / drank / have drunk /*drinked*

DERIVATIVE—*drinker*

AMBIGUITY—*He drank a lot.*

COLLOCATION—*heavy/*strong drinker* vs. *strong/*heavy drink*

Choose several other verbs and try to determine, in similar fashion, what you already "know" about them. You could start, for example, with the verb *pour*.

CHAPTER TWO

TOGETHERNESS

the importance of what constitutes a "unit" or "constituent"; testing for constituency using "movement," "pro-form," "substitution," "focus and focalizing," "cleft sentence," "pseudo-cleft sentence"

Day Six **with a broom in his pajamas**

Day Seven **to my knowledge ...**

Day Eight **The able mentor met who?**

Day Nine **It was in the office that they met.**

Day Ten **What I want is . . . .** PS 2 **ambiguity**

with a broom in his pajamas

What's the difference between
"a tight-rope walker" and "a tight rope-walker"?
One walks on a tight rope;
the other's a rope-walker who's inebriated.

▶ P: [*reading, chuckling*]

M: What are you reading, Patrick?

P: It's an article about a guy trying to sleep who heard a noise around his trash can, grabbed a broom, and went outside in his pajamas to look.

M: And that's funny?

P: Well, it was a raccoon out there, and the article says "he chased the raccoon with a broom in his pajamas" … a broom in his pajamas? Can't you just picture that!

M: Do you think the writer meant that the broom was actually inside his pajamas?

P: No … 'course not, Marta. It's just the way the sentence came out.

M: So what made it "come out" like that, so to speak?

P: Must be the phrase **with a broom in his pajamas**.

M: And what's wrong with that?

P: Well … **in his pajamas** doesn't go with **broom** … it goes with **guy** … The guy was **in his pajamas**.

M: Fine! … But wasn't he also doing the chasing **with a broom**?

P: Sure … but there's got to be a better way of saying it, so you don't get **with a broom in his pajamas**! 'Cause they're not supposed to go together, at least in that sentence.

M: Yes. You want a version where you don't have the sequence *a broom in his pajamas*, which sounds like a unit, like a single CONSTITUENT. Any ideas, Patrick?

P: How about *The guy* was *in his pajamas* chasing the raccoon *with a broom* … or maybe even better *The raccoon was being chased by* ***a guy in his pajamas with a broom***.

M: Yes, better … so you've really collapsed two phrases into one: ***a guy in his pajamas*** and ***a guy with a broom***, each of which is …

P: …is what? Oh … each of them is a unit.

M: Patrick, what's the technical term?

P: Umm … oh, right … each is a CONSTITUENT.

M: And when you put them together you got …

P: …um … ***a guy in his pajamas with a broom***.

M: Which again is …

P: …what?

M: …in terms of CONSTITUENCY …

P: Oh … again … a CONSTITUENT … but a larger one.

M: Right on! We'll be looking some more at this sort of thing.

Constituent

Any of the main grammatical or morphological subdivisions of a sentence, phrase or word

The New Shorter Oxford English Dictionary (1993)

to my knowledge...

Late bus coordinator remembered

Headline in *Day* (New London, CT), April 10, 1985

▶ P: Yesterday in one of my classes I overheard the teacher mumble "Jodie doesn't have the answer to my question." Then a few seconds later he says, "She doesn't have the answer, to my knowledge". Isn't that weird, Marta?!

M: What's weird about it?

P: What's weird? ... *the answer to my question*? ... *the answer to my knowledge*?

M: Hmm ... and?

P: Well, for one thing, the two phrases differ by only one word—*question* vs. *knowledge*—and yet it seems like there's something going on that's much bigger than that.

M: Sure ... good intuition, Patrick ... but first of all, the *question/knowledge* contrast isn't the <u>only</u> difference between the two phrases, is it—at least the way you first said them, I mean?

P: Uuh ... oh ... you mean a little less emphasis with *to my knowledge*?

M: Yeah ... that'll do for now. But how would you go about discovering what's <u>really</u> going on?

P: I don't know, Marta.

M: I think you do. Try taking those contrasting phrases and moving them somewhere ... like to the front of the whole sentence.

P: OK ... like, uh ... *To my knowledge she doesn't have the answer* ... sounds fine to me.

M: ...and the other?

P: Umm ... *To my question she doesn't have the answer* ... a little odd, huh?

M: Yeah, but why, Patrick?

16

P: Well, … I think there's a different kind of connection.

M: What do you mean?

P: *To my question* "goes with" *the answer* … but *to my knowledge* doesn't.

M: So you mean *the answer to my question* "hangs together," so to speak?

P: Definitely!

M: By "hanging together," you mean one is a kind of unit and the other isn't?

P: Right!

M: But don't we have a new term now for "what hangs together as a unit"?

P: Um … OK, I remember … In that stuff that the teacher said in class, *the answer to my question* is a … a CONSTITUENT; *the answer to my knowledge* isn't.

M: Wonderful! And you reached that conclusion by applying that little test, right?

P: Right! … but what was it?

M: Oh, come on!

P: Uh … I guess I broke up the phrase by <u>moving</u> part of it to the front … which was OK in one example, but not so much in the other. I mean, it's a bit strange to say

> *To my question, she doesn't have the answer*.

M: Because …

P: Because I broke up a CONSTITUENT.

M: Yes! And MOVEMENT of that kind is one of the most common <u>tests</u> for CONSTITUENCY.

As a simple example of the new form for grammars associated with <u>constituent</u> analysis, consider the following: Sentence → NP + VP (noun phrase + verb phrase)

Noam Chomsky, *Syntactic Structures* (1957)

The able mentor met who?

What do your kids dream about?
... about ten hours a day!

M: So where were we, Patrick? ... Oh, yes, groups of words that go together, or don't go together ... units ... or ... what was that term?

P: CONSTITUENT!

M: Yes! And how do we know when a word group is a CONSTITUENT or not?

P: Well, we saw yesterday what can happen when you try to move something around in the sentence.

M: You're putting the cart before the horse, Patrick. What tells you that something is a CONSTITUENT is your own INTUITION as a native speaker. What the MOVEMENT test does is give <u>support</u> to that INTUITION. So MOVEMENT is one way. But there are others.

P: I thought so!

M: Here, let me show you. I'll make up a sentence ... something anybody might say, like *The able mentor met the eager pupil in the office right after lunch.*

P: Anybody might say that, Marta?

M: Of course. Now suppose for some reason you didn't catch the beginning of my sentence ... you heard only *thayblmntr met* ... you might ask ... you might ask ...

P: Oh! *Who met the eager pupil ...?* and so on ...

M: So *who* refers to what here?

P: *The able mentor*, of course.

M: ...and since *who* can, in a sense, substitute for it all, *the able mentor* is a ... a ...

P: ...a CONSTITUENT!

M: Yes! ... a NOUN PHRASE. Now, suppose it was a different part of my sentence that you didn't catch. You heard something like *The able mentor met thiygrpyupl in* ... You might say what now?

P: You mean *The able mentor met who in the office?* ... and *who* here refers to *the eager pupil*, another CONSTITUENT, another noun phrase ... right?

M: I'd say so! And notice also that the PRONOUNS *he* or *she* could substitute for *the able mentor* ... another test for CONSTITUENCY.

P: ...and *him* or *her* for *the eager pupil*, of course.

M: Yes! Good, Patrick! And you know what I'm leading up to next …

P: I sure do … You're going to garble the other parts of the sentence and see what I come up with.

M: Then let's just cut to the chase, so to speak. If you didn't catch the *office* part or the *lunch* part, you'd probably ask *met* …

P: …*met where*? … *met when*? … both substituting for CONSTITUENTS.

M: Yes, and so would the PRONOUNS *there* and *then*.

P: Right! *Met there*, *met then,* …

M: …which are ADVERBS, substituting for *in the office*, *right after lunch*, which are PREPOSITIONAL PHRASES. So, Patrick, what's the test for CONSTITUENCY we've been using in all this?

P: You mean making substitutions?

M: Yes … in these cases with WH-QUESTION words, with PRONOUNS, and with ADVERBS. But let's finish up with one more kind. Suppose I ask the question *Who met the eager pupil in the office right after lunch?* What would be a plausible response?

P: Umm … I guess *The able mentor*, no?

M: OK … but also *The able mentor did*, right?

P: Sure, I get it … so *did* here substitutes for the whole rest of the sentence:

met the eager pupil in the office right after lunch.

M: Which, of course, is again a CONSTITUENT, in this case a VERB PHRASE. So if you can replace whole stretches of language with forms like pronouns, question words, adverbs, *do/did* verb forms … you know you've got what?

P: CONSTITUENTS!

M: Go to the head of your class!

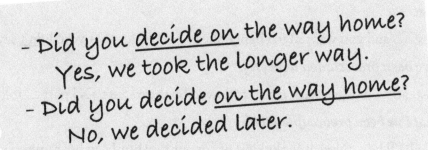

- Did you <u>decide on</u> the way home?
  Yes, we took the longer way.
- Did you decide <u>on the way home</u>?
  No, we decided later.

It was in the office that they met.

In beauty I'm not a great star;
Others are handsomer far.
But my face I don't mind it
Because I'm behind it;
It's <u>the folks out in front</u> that I jar!

Attributed to Abraham Lincoln

▶ M: Patrick, why the far-away look in your eyes … Been preoccupied with what's happening in the world?

P: No, it's all that CONSTITUENCY stuff that I've been preoccupied with.

M: You mean how you determine if a sequence of words is a CONSTITUENT or not?

P: Yes, those tests … like, if you can move it around, or if you can substitute a pronoun, an adverb, a question word, and so on.

M: Is that all?

P: That's all I can think of!

M: Interesting … A few seconds ago you said something that contains another very good test of constituency.

P: I did!

M: Yup … It was, let's see … oh yeah:

It's **all that constituency stuff** that I've been preoccupied with.

P: Well, Marta, that was right after you assumed I was absorbed with something else.

M: Yes! … and you wanted to change the FOCUS. Notice that you <u>didn't</u> say:

I've been preoccupied with [X].

Instead, you began with **It's** … followed by the FOCUSED [X] part … followed by

that I've been preoccupied with

P: Well, I'll be … Now it looks kind of convoluted but I can hear myself saying stuff like that all the time.

M: *It's **'stuff like that'** that we all say every day.*

P: We all say it?

M: Yes, *it's **you and I and everyone else** who say it.*

P: What's the point of all this, Marta? What's it got to do with CONSTITUENCY?

M: Everything! Take, for example, a variation of the sentence that we played around with in the last session:

The mentor met the pupil in the office right after lunch.

Suppose I mistakenly say, "*The <u>principal</u> met …*" and so on. You might correct me by saying …

P: Umm … "*No, it was **the mentor** who …*"

M: Fine … and if I mistakenly say, "*They met in the <u>library</u> …*"

P: I'd say, "*No, it was **in the office** that they met.*" So what gets the FOCUS has to be a CONSTITUENT? Is that what you're getting at, Marta?

M: Wouldn't you say so? Suppose I try to change the focus with something like

*It was **met the pupil** that the mentor in the office …*

P: Ow!

M: …or *It was **the pupil in** that the mentor met the office …*

P: Holy cow! I get the point!

*It's not **just any stretch of words** that can be a constituent.*

M: …and *it's not **everybody** who gets this as quickly as you do, Patrick!*

It's
<u>what you do when you have nothing
to do</u> that reveals what you are.

what I want is...

"They think what you want is some of their business."
"I think what I want is none of their business."

P: Marta, I overheard something in a conversation yesterday that intrigued me.

M: Oh? What was that?

P: Two guys were having an argument about fast food that went something like this … One says, "Eat one of those cheeseburgers and you'll gain five pounds." The other says, "It's the burger that puts on the pounds, not the cheese." Then the first guy says, "What puts on the pounds is the whole thing!"

M: What's intriguing about all that?

P: It's all the … what's that word … FOCALIZING that's going on.

M: What do you mean, Patrick?

P: Well, the sentence *It's **the burger** that puts on the pounds* is the kind we talked about in the last session, where ***the burger*** is the CONSTITUENT that gets the FOCUS, right, Marta?

M: Right.

P: But then you've got *What puts on the pounds is **the whole thing***. Isn't this another example of FOCUS, where the CONSTITUENT here is *the whole thing*?

M: Of course! Right again! Hadn't thought about that one. Nice observation! But how do you get it?

P: What do you mean?

M: Well, what's the corresponding sentence <u>without</u> the focus on ***the whole thing***?

P: Oh … OK, ***The whole thing puts on the pounds***?

M: Yes … which would be the appropriate thing to say if the notion of "putting on the pounds" is being mentioned for the first time. And *puts on the pounds*, of course, is a … a …

P: CONSTITUENT!

M: Can you keep the sentence *The whole thing puts on the pounds* and change the focus to the SUBJECT?

P: Uh … I guess it would be *The whole thing puts on the pounds*, with STRESS on *the whole thing*.

M: … which is pretty much the same as the derived sentence

What puts on the pounds is the whole thing.

P: So there are <u>two</u> possibilities here for where to make *the whole thing* the FOCUS.

M: …and in both cases it must be a …

P: CONSTITUENT! But isn't there still another way to show FOCUS with these examples?

M: I don't know … what are you thinking of?

P: I can turn it around, at least in my dialect … put *the whole thing* first and follow with *what puts on the pounds*.

M: Oh, right … I forgot about that. You're way ahead of me, Patrick! So what do you get?

P: *The whole thing is what puts on the pounds*.

M: …where again what you're moving around is a …

P: CONSTITUENT!

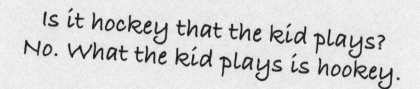

Is it hockey that the kid plays?
No. What the kid plays is hookey.

PS TWO ambiguity

Following are some humorous ambiguous newspaper headlines collected over the years by the *Columbia* [University] *Journalism Review*. The ambiguity arises from the assignment of two different possible CONSTITUENTS to the same sequence of words. For each example, identify the CONSTITUENTS in question.

ELIZABETH 3RD LONGEST REIGNING QUEEN
Los Angeles Times, December 26, 1981

SURPLUS STORE OWNER SENTENCED TO PRISON
Fayetteville, NC, Observer, May 14, 1985

LIFE MEANS CARING FOR HOSPITAL DIRECTOR
Hamilton, Ontario, Spectator, June 20, 1985

GARDEN GROVE RESIDENT NAÏVE, FOOLISH JUDGE SAYS
Orange County, CA, Register, July 2, 1985

CHAPTER THREE

BEING CREATIVE

malapropisms; mixed metaphors; spoonerisms; neologisms; punning; sniglets; how we create (often unconsciously) new words and expressions out of old ones

Day Eleven

worth a standing ovulation...

Day Twelve

a mirror into the future

Day Thirteen

souving the serp

Day Fourteen

hamburgers & infotainment

Day Fifteen

hair today, gone tomorrow

PS 3

glarpos & elbonics

worth a standing ovulation...

*"Be it ever so hovel,
there's no place like home."*

Goodman Ace

▶ P: Marta, can we go back to something we talked about earlier?

M: Fine with me, Patrick. What's on your mind?

P: I was thinking again about the odd uses of language you sometimes find in advertising ... slogans like, um ... "oatmeal that dares to be different."

M: Yes ... as if *oatmeal* could *dare* ... but clever, of course.

P: Well, the "oatmeal" example is a <u>deliberate</u> violation. What about when it's <u>not</u> deliberate? ... when it's accidental?

M: Like what?

P: Well, I was waiting to meet a friend of mine for coffee yesterday. After about ten minutes she finally shows up and says, "Sorry I'm late, but some people *conjugated* at my house."

M: [*chuckles*] That one's a little different. What do you think is going on?

P: Well, I guess she probably meant to say, "Some people *congregated* at my house."

M: But isn't *conjugate* a word in the language?

P: Yes, but it just doesn't fit that sentence, unless those people at her house maybe get their kicks by sitting around and *conjugating* ... um, Latin verbs!

M: [*laughter*] Confusion of that kind—substituting *conjugate* for *congregate*—is quite common. The term is MALAPROPISM ... been in use for a long time.

P: You mean people do this a lot?

M: Sure ... I know someone, for example, who doesn't use four-letter words, because he says his parents brought him up not to be *profound*.

P: Ah! ... not to be *profane*. Glad you did that on purpose, Marta!

M: Did you know that my father was a *veterinarian* of two wars?

P: Should be *veteran*, of course!

M: …and he had great **expectorations** for his daughter.

P: *Expectations*, unless maybe … no, that I could never believe!

M: You're doing very well … worth a standing **ovulation**!

P: *Ovation*!

M: So, in these MALAPROPISMS, is it just <u>any</u> word that can be substituted?

P: Well, **conjugate** for *congregate* … **profound** for *profane* … **ovulation** for *ovation* … and so on … No, I guess not.

M: Why?

P: For one thing, it looks like there has to see some—I mean be some—similarity in the <u>sounds</u> of the two words.

M: Interesting slip, by the way; we'll come back to that. OK … anything else?

P: Offhand, I can't think of anything.

M: How about the <u>meanings</u> of the two words?

P: Certainly very different.

M: What about part of speech?

P: Part of speech … hmm … oh, sure … the two should be of the same … uh, category. So, with **conjugate**/*congregate*, they're both VERBS. **Profound** and *profane* are ADJECTIVES … **ovulation** and *ovation* are NOUNS.

M: Good! *So keep your nose to the **brimstone**, explore every **revenue**, and stay the **curse**!*

P: *…and rise to higher **platitudes** of achievement!*

"In 1957, Eugene O'Neill won a pullet surprise."

From a student's paper in a class taught by Amsel Greene, as reported in the *Los Angeles Times*

a mirror into the future

His mounting ambition was bridled by a wave of opposition.

American Heritage Dictionary, under "mixed metaphor"

P: Speaking of howlers like *standing ovulation*, the other day I heard something else that sounded a bit similar.

M: And what was that, Patrick?

P: One guy's trying to settle an agreement without signing anything and the other says, "*A verbal agreement isn't worth the paper it's written on.*"

M: Pretty funny … but not a MALAPROPISM, of course, unless the guy said maybe *an herbal agreement*, or something like that. Still, very common though.

P: I can hear myself saying stuff like that.

M: So do I on occasion, like … um … while driving past a school today I was upset to see paper cups and candy wrappers scattered around, because throwing trash on the schoolhouse lawn *leaves a bad taste in the public eye.*

P: [*laughter*] … and it has *all the earmarks of an eyesore*!

M: Ha! That was quick, Patrick. I'm impressed! These are what we call MIXED METAPHORS, by the way.

P: I remember reading somewhere that former presidential candidate Robert Dole once said, "*This country is a boiling pot with open arms.*"

M: …and former president Gerald Ford: "*If Abraham Lincoln were alive today, he'd be turning over in his grave.*"

P: Is this sort of thing common with politicians, Marta?

M: Well, you might think so … I saw in today's paper this quote from some high government official: "*The smell of war has returned to Washington and this time I am listening seriously.*"

P: [*peals of laughter*]

M: But it's not just politicians … One of my esteemed colleagues recently finished chairing a particularly angry meeting with "*Next time we'll have to take the bull by the horns and open that can of worms*!"

P: You don't think it was deliberate?

M: Absolutely not! …You catch all kinds of people doing it in ordinary conversation or whenever there's little time for thinking ahead about what they're going to say. One that gets quoted all the time—I don't know where it came from—is "*A virgin forest is a place where the hand of man has never set foot.*"

P: I can imagine putting together a great comic routine.

M: Not surprising … some mixed metaphors have already been used in that way. But you don't have to look very far; newscasters are no different.

P: What do you mean?

M: Flash! This just in! "*The floodgates of famine and pestilence are stalking through the land*!"

P: What an image … stalking floodgates!

M: And some people get confused in the metaphorical use of *windows* and *mirrors*.

P: You mean like, uh … "*window into the future*"?

M: Yes, and of course the rear-view mirror in your car lets you see what's behind you, so *mirror* and *past* go together pretty well here.

P: I can guess what's coming next …

M: Yes, and I heard it recently … "*California is really a mirror into the future!*"

The world is emblematic.
Parts of speech are metaphors
because the whole
of nature is a metaphor of the
human mind.

Ralph Waldo Emerson, 'Language,' in Nature (1836), Chapter 4

souving the serp

"A slip of the tongue is no fault of the mind."

Proverbial (Irish)

▶ P: You know, Marta, most of the time what you say comes out the way you want to say it, but once in a while it doesn't.

M: You mean like MALAPROPISMS and MIXED METAPHORS?

P: No ... it's like, um ... it's like a weather forecaster I heard who said that tomorrow would be *coldy* and *winder*.

M: Great example! ... A SLIP OF THE TONGUE they call it, or SPEECH ERROR. People do it all the time, Patrick, including me, including you.

P: Me?

M: Yes, a couple of sessions ago, I remember. You meant to say, what was it ?... **has to be some similarity**, but it came out **has to see some similarity**.

P: Weird!

M: No, it's not. All you did was anticipate the *s* sounds in **some similarity** and change **be** to **see**. But you were aware of it, because you corrected yourself. Sometimes particular sounds in two adjacent words get <u>switched</u>.

P: Did I do that too, Marta?

M: Not that I noticed, but how about these ... A certain college professor intends to say to a hapless student **You have missed all my history lectures**, but he slips and instead says **You have hissed all my mystery lectures.** Then he follows up, intending to say **You have wasted the whole term**, but instead it comes out as **You have tasted the whole worm.**

P: That's hilarious!

M: Yes ... that particular kind of SPEECH ERROR is well known. They're called SPOONERISMS. Sometimes the errors create words that don't even exist ... for example, when **soup is served** comes out as **serp is souved.** What's happening in this one, by the way?

P: I guess the vowel portion of the two words **soup** and **serve** got switched.

M: Uh huh. And how about where it's just one word ... **pancakes** becoming **canpakes**, for example?

P: Easy ... **p** and **c** sounds get switched.

M: Noted somewhere is the attempt to say **My throat is sore** ... becoming **My sore is throat** instead.

P: Ah … interchanging <u>words</u> this time … *throat* and *sore*. And I just remembered … I recently heard one of my neighbors say the word *muddle* when he meant *mud puddle*.

M: And it gets even <u>more</u> interesting … How about this? There's documentation somewhere of the intended sentence *I cooked a roast* being rendered as *I roasted a cook*! See if you can figure out what's happened now.

P: Wow, Marta! Well, for one thing, *cook* and *roast* got switched … and, oh, both of them are <u>both</u> a noun and a verb … but with *cook* the verb becomes a noun and with *roast* the noun becomes a verb. Is that it?

M: Yes, but is that all? What can you say about the *-ed*?

P: Ah! Now that you mention it, it's like the *-ed* detaches from *cook* and "floats" over to attach to *roast*, which is how verb becomes noun and vice versa. That's incredible!

M: Yes, and the incredible part is what has to be going on in the speaker's head to produce an error like this. Do you think the speaker planned the sentence by starting with *I*, then adding *roasted*, and so on?

P: Couldn't be … more likely he, or she, had the <u>whole</u> sentence in mind before saying anything at all. Otherwise, how could some feature late in the sentence wrongly show up early?

M: Sure looks that way, Patrick. And speech errors of these kinds are strong evidence that this <u>is</u> exactly what is happening when we open our mouths to say something.

P: Amazing … what can come out of our mouths by mistake!

M: One of the <u>most</u> amazing examples ever recorded involves the intended utterance *Mary always dated shrinks*, "shrink" of course being slang for "psychiatrist." Want to guess how it came out?

P: I don't have a clue.

M: *Mary always date shranks*!

P: [*pause*] Holy mackerel!! I don't believe it! … So somehow the past tense *-ed* of *dated* gets detached, moves over to the plural <u>noun</u> *shrinks* and shows up as what would be the <u>irregular</u> past tense of the <u>verb</u> *shrink*. But *shranks* has to be a noun, because it has the plural *-s*!

M: How about that!

"I said they were lighting fires."
"Oh … I thought you said they were fighting liars!"

hamburgers
& infotainment

web (an interconnection of many things)
+ log (an account of many objects)
= weblog >>>>
weblog > blog > blogging blogger blogosphere

▶ P: You know, I thought at first, Marta, that some of those Jabberwocky words we played with a while back might have been slips of the tongue.

M: You mean you could actually imagine real words when you heard "'Twas brillig, and the slithy toves …"?

P: Hmm … guess not. "Jabberwocky" was just <u>made-up</u> words.

M: What do you mean "just"? The language is full of made-up words.

P: It is?

M: Yes, Patrick, and we use them every day. The technical name for them is NEOLOGISM. Didn't you say something about updating your online *blog*?

P: Right!

M: Well, where does *blog* come from, and how long do you think it's been around?

P: I guess it's a combination of *web* and *log* … and it can't have been around before we had the internet, and … ha! there's another one … *internet*!

M: See! The computer world especially is full of them … like *cyberspace*, *hard drive*, *download*, *flop* …

P: …*floppy disk*, *email*, *desktop*, *website*, *networking*, *online*, *workstation*, *logon* …

M: And it's all about the computer world, of course. What about the <u>rest</u> of the language, Patrick?

P: I wouldn't know where to start.

M: Well, what'd you have for lunch?

P: A *hamburger* … why?

M: It's another NEOLOGISM … *hamburger* derives from the German city of Hamburg, whose inhabitant is a "**Hamburger**," and **Hamburgers** are fond of eating a certain kind of sausage in a bun.

P: Plus *hamburger* has nothing to do with "ham." … I can see that too. But it's given rise to a bunch of offshoots like *cheeseburger*, *chiliburger*, *baconburger*, *veggieburger* … and I recently saw advertised a *thingburger*, if you can imagine eating such a "thing." I guess these are more … uh, what was it? … NEOLOGISMS.

M: Yes … and by the way, what do the Germans call an inhabitant of the city of *Frankfurt*?

P: Ah! *Frankfurter* … just like *hamburger* … and also the shortened form *frank* … and then, I guess, *hot dog*.

M: …all of which are?

P: **NEOLOGISMS!**

M: Someone said, "Yesterday's neologisms are often today's essential vocabulary."

P: OK, Marta, but all these examples have meaning; the Jabberwocky words don't and they're <u>not</u> part of the vocabulary.

M: Very observant! But there are <u>lots</u> of neologisms around that aren't <u>yet</u> part of the vocabulary.

P: Like what?

M: Well, *infotainment*—the combination of *information* and *entertainment*—is quite recent, but I just heard *irritainment* for the <u>first</u> time … annoying TV spectacles, like wrestling, that you can't stop watching.

P: I can hear myself coming up with words like that.

M: Yes, but of course some NEOLOGISMS do seem to appear one time only. Kids are a great source of these. I have a friend who remembers when she was a little girl using a word to describe how she felt upon waking up in the morning after not sleeping very well. Want to guess?

P: Not a chance!

M: She was *bed-raggled*!

Some winning entries from the Annual Neologism Contest in the <u>Washington Post</u>

lymph (verb) to walk with a lisp
balderdash (noun) a rapidly receding hairline
coffee (noun) the person upon whom one coughs
giraffiti (noun) vandalism spray-painted very, very high up

hair today, gone tomorrow

WE PRY HARDER

advertisement for television news organization

P: Marta, there is something I forgot to ask about last time when we were discussing the origins of words like *hamburger*, *frankfurter*, and so on.

M: Go on.

P: Well, I read somewhere about places that sell frankfurters ... places with names like **Uncle Frank's**, **Frankly yours**, **Franks-A-Lot** ... They all take off on the *frankfurter* NEOLOGISM but it's like they've gone beyond that.

M: Nice observation ... want to elaborate?

P: OK ... It's a matter of shortening *frankfurter* to *frank* and then having fun with it, especially the **Franks-A-Lot** example ... a take-off, I guess, on **Thanks** *a lot*.

M: Yes, Patrick! Do you know what this kind of "having fun" is called?

P: Um ... PUNNING?

M: Uh huh ... and what makes it a PUN is the **franks** / *thanks* similarity, an actual rhyme in this case.

P: Are there any rules where PUNS are concerned?

M: Good question. I wouldn't exactly call them rules ... more like characteristics. An ad for a house cleaner once read **Maid to order**, a pun on the phrase **made** *to order*. The words **maid**/*made*, by the way, are HOMOPHONES ... but more on that in a later session.

P: That's something like the name of a store I saw that sells dieting products: **Weight no longer!**

M: **Weight** and *wait* ... great! But sometimes it's just a switch in vowels. There's a laundromat that goes by the name of **The Washing Well**.

P: **Wishing** *well* ... I get it.

M: ...and a cleaning service for septic tanks called **The Wizard of Ooze**.

P: Ow!

M: …or other times it can be simply reversing two sounds or letters. Most of us are familiar with what we call a *farmers' market* … but there's a store selling picture frames called *Framer's Market*, a deliberate PUN, of course.

P: …and I saw a barber shop with a sign that said *Hair Today, Gone Tomorrow*.

M: Yes … turning on the *hair*/*here* correspondence in this case. And sometimes the PUN is created by <u>blending</u> two words or simply <u>adding</u> a letter or sound … A local pet supply store goes by the name of *Petcetera*.

P: …and that store might sell the puppy treat they call *pupperoni*!

M: That's terrific, Patrick! You really notice these things.

P: And what about license plates? I saw one a few days ago that I couldn't figure out till I got home: **2TH DR**. But the owner's obviously a dentist.

M: A dentist? I'm having trouble with this one. How do you get "dentist" out of …? Oh, now I see … It's **2**(two)+**TH** equals **TOOTH**, and **DR** is the abbreviation for **DOCTOR** …. **TOOTH DOCTOR**! With license-plate PUNS you have to be really inventive, because of the limited space available.

P: But, Marta, I've been thinking … haven't we already dealt with PUNNING in that session before on MALAPROPISMS? I mean, for example, when somebody says, "I performed my act and got a *standing ovulation*," isn't that a pun on *standing ovation*?

M: Hmm … hadn't thought about it that way. Very interesting … but certainly one difference has to be that PUNS are <u>intended</u>, whereas MALAPROPISMS are <u>un</u>intended. And of course not <u>all</u> PUNS are likely to be construed as MALAPROPISMS … the ones seen on license plates or in advertisements, for example, or the ones on store fronts or in fast-food outlets. In other words, wherever the word or expression's been planned or thought out. But you've really given me something to think some more about!

A man entered a local paper's pun contest. He sent in ten different puns, in the hope that at least one of them would win. Unfortunately, no pun in ten did.

PS THREE glarpos & elbonics

SNIGLET (SNIG' LIT) any word that doesn't appear in the dictionary, but should

GLARPO—"the juncture of the ear and skull where pencils are stored"

ELAVERSION—"avoiding eye contact with other people in an elevator"

CHARP—"the green mutant potato chip found in every bag"

ELBONICS—"the actions of two people maneuvering for one armrest in a movie theater"

HOZONE—"the place where one sock in every laundry disappears to"

Reprinted with the permission of Scribner, a division of Simon & Schuster, Inc., from Sniglets by Rich Hall. Copyright © 1984 Not the Network Company, Inc.

CHAPTER FOUR

THE END OF THE WORD

properties of inflectional and derivational suffixation; ordering of the two within a word; why there can be no such thing as "the longest word in the language"

Day Sixteen

curiosity, yes... furiosity, no

Day Seventeen

wait, waiting, waiter

Day Eighteen

lengthen and given

Day Nineteen

compute r iz ation s

Day Twenty

no longest word?

PS 4

Large church plans collapse

curiosity, yes…
furiosity, no

"Daddy, if <u>furious</u> comes from <u>fury</u> and <u>glorious</u> comes from <u>glory</u>, then what does <u>serious</u> come from?"

P: While dipping into *Alice in Wonderland* as part of a class project the other day, I was struck by some ADJECTIVE stuff that I never paid much attention to before.

M: And …

P: I'm trying to remember … Oh yeah, words like **curious**, **serious**, **notorious**, and … um … **furious**.

M: What about them, Patrick?

P: Well, if you want to turn them into, uh, <u>things</u> …

M: I guess you mean the corresponding NOUN.

P: Whatever. What I'm trying to say is the adjectives all end in **-ous** but your noun forms are all different.

M: How so?

P: OK, you got the adjective **curious** and the noun **curiosity**, right?

M: Yup.

P: But along with **serious** we don't have **seriosity**, and with **furious** we don't have **furiosity**, do we?

M: Certainly not, but what <u>do</u> we have?

P: Uh, **seriousness** and **fury**.

M: And what about the adjective **notorious**? Do you want nouns like **notoriosity**?

P: Ugh! It would be **notoriety**. So they're <u>all</u> different!

M: The ones <u>you</u> picked are, Patrick. But try some more. What's the noun form for **anxious**?

P: I guess it's **anxiety** … like **notoriety**.

M: And **conscious**?

P: **Consciousness** … like **seriousness**!

M: OK. Now think again about the adjective *furious* and the noun *fury*. Which comes from which?

P: It's obvious. From *fury* we get *furious*.

M: So would there be any <u>reason</u> to create a noun *furiosity* from the adjective *furious*, analogous to *curiosity* from *curious*?

P: No. I get it, Marta. There's no *furiosity* because *fury* already exists. And we do need something like *curiosity* because there's no noun *cury*.

M: Now you're cookin'. But why *curiosity*? Why not *curiousness*, like *seriousness*?

P: But *curiousness* doesn't sound bad at all.

M: Nice observation. There's really nothing wrong with *curiousness*. It's just that *curiosity* has been in use for a long time. These endings are all SUFFIXES and the *-ness* suffix is actually very productive. You can use it quite freely in forming nouns from adjectives, like the familiar *happy* (*happiness*), *kind* (*kindness*), and so on, but you can also create your own. What would you call "the quality of being nice"?

P: Hmm … *niceness*?

M: Why not? So what have we been looking at? Take the suffixes *-ness* and *-ity*. What are they actually doing?

P: What do you mean?

M: What's the part of speech of, say, *serious* and *curious*?

P: Oh, you mean like they're ADJECTIVES?

M: Yes. And *seriousness* and *curiosity*?

P: They're NOUNS, of course.

M: So what do the suffixes *-ness* and *-ity* do?

P: They change adjectives into nouns, obviously.

M: Phew! Now go back to your original observation. Can you conclude anything from even just these few suffixes that we've been talking about? Is it possible to determine from the form of the STEM what SUFFIX it takes?

P: I guess not, Marta.

M: Right. Now you've learned something.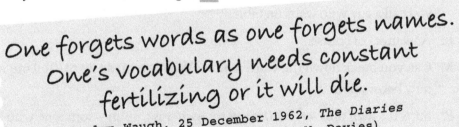

One forgets words as one forgets names. One's vocabulary needs constant fertilizing or it will die.

Evelyn Waugh, 25 December 1962, The Diaries
of Evelyn Waugh (ed. M. Davies)

wait, waiting, waiter

- These slow restaurants are funny places.
- Really? How so?
- They've got waiters, but we're the ones who do the waiting!

M: We talked a bit before about words with various SUFFIXES like *-ness* (*seriousness*), *-ity* (*curiosity*), *-ous* (*furious*). Remember what we said about them?

P: You mean that it's often hard to predict the suffix just from looking at what it's going to get attached to?

M: The STEM. Yes. What else, Patrick? What about the grammatical category— noun, adjective, and so on?

P: Oh, yeah. It changes from what it was before … like *serious* is an adjective but *seriousness* is a noun.

M: Right. We can say that *seriousness* DERIVES from *serious*. So, in other words, the *-ness* suffix is DERIVATIONAL. Some more examples … Take *argue*, a verb, add the suffix *-ment*, and what do you get?

P: A noun: *argument.*

M: And if you add *-ize* to *computer*, a noun?

P: You get the verb *computerize*. So are all suffixes like this?

M: What do you mean?

P: They make the new word have a different grammatical category?

M: You're asking if all suffixes are DERIVATIONAL. Good question! Let's find out. What do you call a guy who waits on tables?

P: A "waiter," of course.

M: Can you break down the word *waiter*? What's it made up of? Tell me what you now know about it.

P: Sure. It's *wait* plus *-er*. *Wait* is a verb; *waiter* is a noun—someone who "waits" … on tables, I guess.

40

M: OK. Now what about the word you just used—*waits*? How do you break <u>that</u> down?

P: Easy … *wait* plus *-s* … and, wait a minute! *Wait* is a verb, but so is *wait<u>s</u>*. No change.

M: Nice observation … important too. And what about *wait<u>ing</u>*, also *wait<u>ed</u>*?

P: Same thing. They're still verbs. So *-s*, *-ing*, *-ed* are all SUFFIXES that <u>don't</u> change the grammatical category of the stem?

M: Sure looks like it. But then, of course, we can't call them "derivational," can we? In fact, there's another term that applies here. These suffixes *-s*, *-ing*, *-ed* are all INFLECTIONAL. They're VERB INFLECTIONS.

P: Are there other kinds?

M: Yes, and you've just used one.

P: What do you mean, Marta?

M: What you just said a second ago: "Are there other kinds?" You can answer your own question.

P: Oh … *kinds*. Sure. The PLURAL of the noun *kind* with *-s*. So plural marking should be NOUN INFLECTION. It's getting clearer.

M: Yes, and right there's yet another bit of INFLECTION … what you just said!

P: You mean the word *clearer*? Hmm … yeah … *clear* plus *-er*.

M: So what <u>kind</u> of inflection is it?

P: *Clear*'s an adjective … got to be ADJECTIVE INFLECTION. And so would *clear<u>est</u>*.

M: Right on! Adjectives inflected with *-er* and *-est*, like *taller/tallest*, *smarter/smartest*, and so on, are what we call COMPARATIVE/SUPERLATIVE. We'll be looking more closely at this another day. But right now there's more to be explored concerning the properties of DERIVATIONAL and INFLECTIONAL suffixes. ■

I do not know which to prefer,
The beauty of inflections
Or the beauty of innuendoes …
Wallace Stevens, "Thirteen Ways of Looking at a Blackbird" (1923)

lengthen and given

Typing lessens,

Pay 10% less for the IBM Electronic 85

© International Business Machines Corporation

M: Let's look some more at what's going on with SUFFIXES. Remember the two kinds we identified last time?

P: Inflational? Denigrational?

M: Very funny! Get serious, Patrick.

P: OK … INFLECTIONAL and DERIVATIONAL … Couldn't resist. But I do remember the big difference between them concerning grammatical category.

M: Which is …?

P: Well, it's easier for me if I use examples. Take, say, the VERB *compute*. Add **-er** and you get **computer**, which is a NOUN. But add **-ed** and you get **computed**, which is a VERB again. So **-er** is a DERIVATIONAL SUFFIX and **-ed** is an INFLECTIONAL suffix. Right, Marta?

M: Good. But be careful. Think some more about the suffix **-er**. One of the examples we used was **waiter**. What does it mean?

P: What, you mean like "somebody who waits on tables"?

M: That'll do. How about coming up with some more words like **waiter** with SUFFIX **-er**?

P: That's easy … **teacher**, **worker**, **driver**, **player**, **drummer** … I could go on.

M: You don't need to. Think for a moment about the words with **-er** SUFFIXES we mentioned at the end of the last session: **clearer** and **taller**.

P: What about them?

M: Are they just more of the same?

P: No, they're ADJECTIVES, both before and after adding the **-er** SUFFIX.

M: So what does that tell you about **-er** concerning the <u>kind</u> of SUFFIX?

P: Oh … That there are two different **-er** SUFFIXES, one DERIVATIONAL and one INFLECTIONAL?

M: Exactly!

P: Is this some little weird quirk among the suffixes?

M: Let's find out. I'll give you some words and you break them down into STEM and SUFFIX, identify the suffix as INFLECTIONAL or DERIVATIONAL, and tell me why.

P: Sounds like a lot, Marta!

M: I'm sure you can do it. OK, here's the first one: **wooden**.

P: It's **wood**, a NOUN, plus **-en**, which makes **wooden**, an ADJECTIVE. So **-en** is DERIVATIONAL.

M: OK. How about **lessen**?

P: Another *-en* … and different … *less* is an ADJECTIVE and *lessen* is a VERB; so *-en* is DERIVATIONAL again.

M: And *lengthen*?

P: Wow, different again! *Length* is a NOUN and *lengthen* is a VERB, so yet another DERIVATIONAL *-en*.

M: Good. Now what about *given*?

P: You mean like in *given name*? It must be an ADJECTIVE because …

M: Hold on … *given* is <u>used</u> as an ADJECTIVE or modifier in *given name*, but take it back to something like *She's been **given** a name*. What is it now?

P: OK … *give* is a VERB and *given* is still a VERB of some kind, so …

M: Yes, it's a verb form called PAST PARTICIPLE, but you get the point. So what <u>kind</u> of SUFFIX is *-en* in *given*?

P: I guess it's INFLECTIONAL.

M: And what about *oxen*?

P: My god! *-en* here is the PLURAL SUFFIX on the noun *ox*, so another INFLECTIONAL. Where does it end, Marta?

M: Well, what about *heaven*?

P: What! Wait a minute! A breakdown to *heave* plus *-en*! That's hilarious!

M: [*chuckles*] Thought I might catch you there. So look at what we have now: three different DERIVATIONAL *-en* and two different INFLECTIONAL *-en* endings. I'll lay them out and you can add the grammatical categories: *wooden / lessen / lengthen / given / oxen*.

P: *wood* (NOUN) + *-en* → *wooden* (ADJECTIVE)
    less (ADJECTIVE) + *-en* → *lessen* (VERB)
    length (NOUN) + *-en* → *lengthen* (VERB)
    give (VERB) + *-en* → *given* (VERB)
    ox (NOUN) + *-en* → *oxen* (NOUN)

M: Bravo, Patrick! By the way, remember what we said before about predicting the SUFFIX if you know the STEM?

P: Yeah. You can't, at least a lot of the time. That was the point of the *seriousness/ curiosity* example.

M: Yes. So now what about predicting the grammatical category of the STEM if you know the SUFFIX, like *-er* and *-en*?

P: How could that be possible!

M: Right, at least not for the examples we've looked at. But we'll have some more to say about it.

Fallen, fallen, fallen, fallen,
And fallen from his high estate …
John Dryden, *Alexander's Feast*, ll.77-8

compute r iz ation s

M: Let's see … Where did we leave off last time?

P: Don't you remember, Marta? That INFLECTIONAL and DERIVATIONAL stuff?

M: Oh right. Let's go back a bit. In playing around with those two kinds of suffix we were actually starting to break certain words into their smaller parts.

P: You mean like the word *computers* is made up of *computer* + *s* and the word *computer* is made up of *compute* + *er*? Pretty obvious.

M: Well, maybe. So you've got the example of these two suffixes **-er** and **-s**, as in **compute** + **er** + **s**. Do they have to be in that order?

P: What do you mean?

M: Why not **compute** + **s** + **er**?

P: You mean **computeser**? That's ridiculous!

M: Why, Patrick? Just because we don't say it?

P: No … *compute* is a verb. Plural *-s* doesn't go on a verb; it goes on a noun: *computer* in this case.

M: Good! So we have **computers**. But suppose I want a verb that means "to store, say, some files using computers." What do I do to the files?

P: You **computerize** them?

M: Fine. What did you just do?

P: I took the noun **computer** and added **-ize**, which is a DERIVATIONAL SUFFIX, because the grammatical category changes. **Computerize** is a verb. Right?

M: Right, but it's more than one computer that we're using. So why didn't you say *computers* + *ize*?

P: What? **Computersize**! That's crazy! You got off track, talking now about the <u>size</u> of computers; but *size* is not *s-ize*!

M: Yes, but **computer** is a noun, and the plural adds an **-s**. So why can't we form a new word with **computers** + **ize**: **computersize**, meaning "performing some task using computer<u>s</u>"?

P: I don't know, Marta. Does it have something to do with the two kinds of SUFFIX you were talking about?

M: You're getting warm. Look at **computerize** again. What word would you use to refer to the "<u>act</u> of computerizing"?

P: I guess it could be **computerization**.

M: What part of speech is it?

P: It's a NOUN.

M: And how did you form it?

P: By taking **computerize** and adding **-ation**, I guess.

M: Fine. Now suppose that in performing our hypothetical task there's more than one way of doing it with a computer—in other words, several possible *computer* …

P: **Computerizations**?

M: Yes, so what's the breakdown now? You have

the <u>verb</u> *compute* …

the <u>noun</u> *comput* **-er**   DERIVATIONAL

the <u>verb</u> *computer* **-ize**   DERIVATIONAL

the <u>noun</u> *computeriz* **-ation**   DERIVATIONAL

the <u>noun</u> *computerization* **-s**   INFLECTIONAL

P: I can tell we're leading up to something.

M: We can even keep on going. Take *computerization* and make an ADJECTIVE out of it.

P: *Computerization***al**?

M: Yes, and you can even change <u>that</u> into a noun with the suffix *-ism* …

P: *Computerizational***ism**? Wow!

M: Not that you'd ever have an occasion to use it. And, of course, since it's a noun, somebody might actually refer to more than one kind—several *computerizationalism***s**.

P: What … once in a hundred years? But I think I know now what you're driving at.

M: Which is …

P: **That the inflectional suffix goes on last, after any derivational suffixes.**

M: Bravo, Patrick! That's good for starters. ■

> Let the singing singers
> With vocal voices, most vociferous,
> In sweet vociferation, out-vociferize
> Ev'n sound itself.
>
> Henry Carey, *Chrononhotonthologos* (1734),
> Act I, scene i

no longest word?

floccinaucinihilipilification [flaksɪ nawsɪ nɪhɪlɪ pɪlɪfɪkešn]
the action or habit of estimating as worthless

Oxford English Dictionary

M: There's something I wanted to call attention to at the end of our last session. I could tell from the look on your face, Patrick, that you were struck by the sheer length of a word like *computerizationalisms*.

P: "Struck," to say the least! Who would ever say it? <u>Why</u> would anyone ever say it?

M: That's not the point. If you look in any large English dictionary, you'll find plenty of words—big words, small words—that most people would never use, words they never even heard of.

P: Like what, Marta?

M: Oh … like, let's see, maybe *sequacious*, which means "lacking independence or originality of thought." Or how about *pseudohermaphroditism*, meaning "the condition of having the chromosomes of one sex and some anatomical characteristics of the other"?

P: I get it. But that *pseudoherm* … something word seems longer even than our *computerizationalisms*. I bet it's the longest word in the language!

M: You mean "longest word in the dictionary." Interesting concept … that there can be such a thing as the longest word in the <u>language</u>.

P: Seems pretty obvious to me. Just find the longest word in the biggest dictionary.

M: OK. Take that noun **pseudohermaphroditism**. It's pretty long and you can find it in the *Oxford English Dictionary*, or *OED*. Let's assume that it's actually the <u>longest</u> word you can find there. Now, suppose you want to use it in reference to "the <u>condition</u> of having the chromosomes," etc., in other words changing it into an adjective. What would you say?

P: I don't know.

M: Yes, you do, Patrick. What's the adjective formed from, say, the noun *spasm*?

P: You mean *spasmodic*?

M: Yes. So …

P: Uh … **pseudo** … **pseudohermaph** … **pseudohermaphro** …**ditism** …**ic**. My god!

M: Yes, *pseudohermaphroditismic*. Now suppose you want to MODIFY the word to mean something like "opposed to the condition of having the chromosomes," etc. What would you say now?

P: I'd attach *anti-* at the beginning. But please don't make me try to say it.

M: Don't worry; it's *antipseudohermaphroditismic*.

P: So what's the point, Marta?

M: Let me put it to you this way. As we've just seen, we can identify the longest word appearing in the *OED*. But, according to the rules of word formation that we've been looking at over several sessions, we can make that word still longer. So the longest possible word, whatever that means, doesn't even appear in the dictionary.

P: You mean any long word can always be made longer?

M: Well, not just any; they have to be words that can take DERIVATIONAL SUFFIXES, which means the major vocabulary categories of NOUN, VERB, and ADJECTIVE.

P: And the suffixation can go on forever?

M: Hardly, Patrick. Think of what a struggle you had just pronouncing that "little" word *antipseudohermaphroditismic*. Even in print it's hard to take in. I'm sure you can guess why we have so few words in the language that are anywhere near as long and complex.

P: That's not hard to figure out now. If the word's too long, I lose track of what's being said, or written.

M: Yes. If a word's internal structure becomes too complex through continuous suffixation, our brains can no longer do the necessary work of giving a meaning to that word. And you could also forget the beginning of such a long word before you even got to the end of it!

P: So words can't expand indefinitely.

M: Right. But not because the language prevents it. Nothing in the rules of word-formation tells us to stop after a certain number of applications.

P: OK. You mean **the language possibilities for word-length are maybe infinite, but limitations of another kind outside language keep it within bounds.**

M: I couldn't have said it better myself!

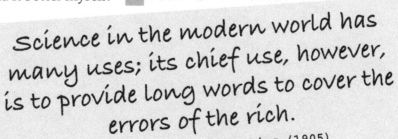

Science in the modern world has many uses; its chief use, however, is to provide long words to cover the errors of the rich.

G. K. Chesterton, *Heretics* (1905)

PS FOUR

Large church plans collapse

Headline in *Spectator* (Hamilton, Ontario)

Consider the above newspaper headline from Day Nineteen. Headlines like this are ambiguous in that one of the readings is the intended one, the other an unintended, usually humorous one. In this example the ambiguity hinges upon the word *plan*—whether it is being used as a verb (unintended) or a noun, and therefore whether the INFLECTIONAL suffix **-s** is the noun-plural marker or the marker of verbal third-person singular. Scan the following headline, determine how the inflectional suffix figures in the crux of the ambiguity, and cite the major grammatical categories (noun, verb) for both interpretations.

Downtown hogs grant cash

Headline in *Chicago Tribune*

The only interpretation for the following headline, which is <u>not</u> ambiguous, is surely not the intended one. What slight adjustment in INFLECTION will have the headline be understood as a complaint about there being too many dogs? Do you want to make any comments about subject–verb AGREEMENT?

More dogs bring complaints

Headline in *Martinsburg (WV) Evening Journal*

CHAPTER FIVE

THOSE LITTLE WORDS

count nouns, non-count nouns, and the use of the determiner; the partitive construction; definiteness; specific and non-specific; genericness

more this, a lot of that

"Waiter—could we have a little more table over here?"

▶ P: I've been noticing something in advertisements and newspaper captions that's a bit puzzling.

M: Really? How so?

P: Well, for example, the big print in a recent newspaper ad for one of the major airlines reads

More seat vs. more seats

I know what it's trying to say, Marta, but **more seat** sounds kind of strange.

M: Maybe we can figure out why. Is it strange to say *more chair*?

P: Yes, just as weird as *more seat*.

M: What about *more furniture*?

P: Fine! No problem.

M: So **more furniture** is good but **more chair** and *more seat* are weird … why?

P: Has to be **chairs** and **seats**, with an **-s**, 'cause they're plural.

M: So why don't we say **furnitures**, Patrick, since a room full of it probably contains lots of chairs or seats?

P: Well, for one thing, the idea of **furniture** by itself <u>includes</u> things like chairs, tables, sofas, and so on.

50

M: Yes. Think of them as things you can COUNT … *one chair, two chairs*, etc., but not *one furniture* … What part of speech are all of these, by the way?

P: Obviously they're all NOUNS.

M: And the ones that are countable you can call COUNT NOUNS. Since we can't say *a furniture* or *furnitures*, the noun *furniture* is therefore a NON-COUNT NOUN.

P: So what about *more seat*? I still don't understand why it sounds peculiar, Marta.

M: *More seat* gives you a problem but *more seats* doesn't. Think about it … What kind of noun, did we say, are *seat(s), chair(s), table(s)*, etc.?

P: COUNT NOUNS.

M: Right. And how does *more seat* differ from *more seats*?

P: *Seat* is SINGULAR and *seats* is PLURAL, obviously.

M: Therefore, *seat* is … is … is …

P: …a COUNT NOUN **in the** SINGULAR!

M: Bravo! So why is *__more seat__* giving you fits?

P: Because *more* doesn't go with SINGULAR COUNT NOUNS?

M: Really! What else besides *more* doesn't seem to "go with" singular count nouns? What about *many* … *many seat* …?

P: That one's actually bad. By comparison, *more seat* starts to sound pretty good.

M: That's because *many seat* is simply not the way standard English makes plurals … like *five seat* or *these seat*. But you said at the beginning that you knew what that ad was getting at—I mean

More seat vs. more seats

P: Yeah … the idea is a contrast between a <u>larger</u> *seat* and a <u>larger quantity</u> of *seats*. Somebody might also say something like *"**You get a lot of seat on that airline.**"*

M: Right on, Patrick! And for closers, here's another ad, this one from a computer manufacturer touting its technical support. Notice the nice ambiguity:

When you've got a [brand], You've got a lot of company.

piece o' cake

A persistence of pupils and a mania of mentors

with apologies to James Lipton

M: We left a few things hanging last time, Patrick.

P: We <u>always</u> seem to leave something hanging.

M: Come on! That's because language is so rich, vast, open-ended. We were talking before about nouns that don't have a plural and don't take *a* or *an*.

P: Oh yeah … like *furniture*, for example. You don't say *furnitures* or *a furniture*.

M: Right. But since furniture can include chairs, tables, and so on, how do we single something out regarding furniture?

P: Uh … you mean like ***a piece** of furniture*?

M: Why not? Interesting word, ***piece*** …

P: ***Piece*** seems pretty ordinary to me, Marta.

M: Think of it this way. We have all kinds of terms to refer, say, to a "token" or "part" of something—we call them PARTITIVES. Take NON-COUNT NOUNS, for example, like *grass, sand, wind, water, dirt.* Handy PARTITIVES for these might be ***blade of grass**, **grain of sand*** … You go on …

P: …***gust of wind**, **drop of water**, **clump of dirt*** …

M: You're getting the idea! But lots of other non-count nouns <u>don't</u> have handy related PARTITIVE terms … nouns like *equipment, luggage, clothing, machinery,* for example. So what do we do?

P: Ah! … ***piece of equipment**, **piece of luggage**,* and so on … like ***piece of furniture**!*

M: Yes, and you can keep on going. What about abstract items like *music, information, news, advice?*

P: ***Piece of*** … all of them!

M: Yes, and even in METAPHORS like ***piece of cake*** …

P: …and ***piece*** *of mind*!

M: Wait a minute!! The expression is ***p-e-a-c-e** of mind*! You did that on purpose!

P: Couldn't resist. So ***piece of*** is sort of like an "all-purpose" PARTITIVE?

52

M: For NON-COUNT NOUNS, and only up to a point. (When we finish, let's go have *a piece of coffee*!) But it's good enough for starters. Look for a moment now at COUNT nouns. What PARTITIVE would you stick onto the count-noun *birds*?

P: Umm … *a flock of birds*?

M: What about *bees*? *cattle*? *ants*? *puppies*? …

P: Stop, Marta! OK … er … *swarm of bees*? *herd of cattle*? *colony of ants*? *litter of puppies*?

M: These are certainly the conventional ones that easily come to mind. Also, maybe less common, *brood of hens*, *host of angels*, *plague of locusts*, *nest of vipers*. Writers often concoct more imaginative, even whimsical, ones. Name some occupations …

P: Plumber?

M: Just for fun, how about *a flush of plumbers*?

P: Butcher?

M: Maybe *a goring of butchers*.

P: Flute player?

M: OK … *a tootle of flutists*. You can make these up, you know. Try some yourself. How about *soldier*?

P: *An army of soldiers*!

M: Pretty unimaginative, Patrick … I'm thinking more like *a drill of soldiers*, *a menace of soldiers*, *a carousing of soldiers* … How about *painter*?

P: *A canvas of painters*?

M: Now you're cooking! How about *pupil*?

P: *A persistence of pupils*!

M: …and *mentor*?

P: *A mania of mentors*!

M: Walked right into it, didn't I?

a rash of dermatologists (p.93)
an embarrassment of twitches (p.135)
a conjunction of grammarians (p.101)

James Lipton, An Exaltation of Larks or, The Venereal Game, © Viking-Penguin 1968, 1977, 1991.

a sandwich and the cheese

© Wiltern Theatre Incorporated

P: Funny little word, *the*, don't you think?

M: What's funny about it, Patrick?

P: Well, for one thing it doesn't have any meaning.

M: Depends on what you mean by "meaning." If you looked *the* up in the dictionary, you'd get more about what it <u>does</u> than what it "means." That's why we call it a FUNCTION WORD. Didn't we talk about this a while back?

P: Yeah … but does it matter if you leave it out, I mean other than just breaking a little rule of grammar? If you say *she made the sandwich* and I say *she made sandwich*, what's the difference, except one sounds like what a non-native speaker might say?

M: Let me put it this way. Suppose we make them plural: *she made the sandwiches* vs. *she made sandwiches*. Now is there a difference? Did we break a little grammar rule again?

P: No … nothing broken; they're both OK this time, Marta, but the presence of *the* makes a difference.

M: How so?

P: Because with *she made the sandwiches*, it's like we already know what sandwiches are being mentioned.

M: Good observation … *the sandwiches* are, in a sense, "known," or "definite," not just any sandwiches. So your "funny little word" *the* makes all the difference. *The* is the part of speech termed ARTICLE … actually DEFINITE ARTICLE. We talked about this in the first week.

P: OK … and if there's a DEFINITE ARTICLE, then I bet there's got to be an <u>IN</u>DEFINITE ARTICLE!

M: How'd you guess? In fact, you just used it, Patrick! What was it?

P: OK … *there's **a** definite article* and *a* … no, ***an** indefinite article*.

M: Right, but you wouldn't say it like that in ordinary conversation. The articles aren't stressed; they don't convey information about the world.

P: Then why do we bother with them? Why not just leave them out?

M: Well, they <u>are</u> FUNCTION WORDS, you know … and let's assume we have them for a reason. If not, then they would never have entered the language. Common sense tells us that human language doesn't retain a feature that has no function at all.

P: OK … What's the reason, Marta? What's the function?

M: Certainly more than one, but you've <u>already</u> identified one of the most important ones.

P: I have?

M: Sure, when you said … What was it? … Oh yeah … "With *she made **the** sandwiches*, it's like we already know what *sandwiches* are being mentioned."

P: So the topic of "sandwich" had to come up before?

M: Right. Let's conjure up a little scenario here. Suppose I tell you that my friends and I had a jam session last night. The instruments included a saxophone, a clarinet, drums, a string bass, and a vibraphone. Pretend you were there, pick out one of these instruments and say something about it, like maybe it was hard to hear.

P: OK … The clarinet was hard to hear.

M: Now notice that I said, "The instruments included ***a clarinet***," and then you said, "***The clarinet*** was hard to hear"—*a clarinet, **the** clarinet* … Why the difference? Why the INDEFINITE article and then the DEFINITE?

P: No-brainer! It was ***a clarinet*** on the first mention and ***the clarinet*** on the second, and from then on, I suppose.

M: Pretty sensible, but let's take it a little further. I set up that little scenario with a hypothetical jam session: "I had **a** jam session last night." Then I continued with "**The** instruments included …" Why ***the*** here? Why not say ***some***, or nothing, since ***instruments*** is being mentioned for the first time?

P: Ah! You can't have a jam session without instruments, so the first mention of INDEFINITE "a jam session" is followed by DEFINITE "**the** instruments."

M: Right! So I can tell you that I bought, for example, ***a clarinet***, and then go on to say something about ***the** mouthpiece*, ***the** keys*, ***the** reed*, and so on.

P: And I've been doing this sort of thing all the time without realizing it!

M: So has everybody else! ▮

"I have to sell my car … I need the fifty dollars."

See a blue pencil?... it? ... one?

A penny for your thought.
John Heywood (1497–1580), *Proverbs*, II, 4

▶ M: Hmmm ... Where were we?

P: We were talking last time about the use of *a* and *the*.

M: Oh yeah, the ARTICLES: INDEFINITE and DEFINITE. Let's take another look. What do you think we mean when we say "indefinite"?

P: Seems kind of obvious ... If I tell you that *I saw a good movie last night*, it's the first mention of the movie, so it's *a*, INDEFINITE.

M: "Indefinite" for me but not for you!

P: That's not the point! You're doing that on purpose! There's supposed to be some kind of "collaboration" here ... Umm, it's kind of hard to explain.

M: You're doing very well, Patrick ... "collaboration" between speaker and hearer— you and me in this case. You're introducing "movie" into our discourse and are assuming that I don't know yet what movie you're talking about. I'd likely respond with something like "What's it about"?

P: And if I had said, "I saw **the** good movie last night," you would have answered with maybe "What movie?" or "Which movie?"

M: Absolutely! Now suppose I casually say to you, "I want to go see **a movie**, any movie; do you want to see [*blank*] too?" What comes to mind to fill in the blank?

P: "Do you want to see **one** too?"

M: OK. But suppose I say, "I want to go see **a movie**; they gave [*blank*] a pretty good review." What goes in the blank this time?

P: Hmm … "They gave **it** a pretty good review."

M: Why **one** in the first and **it** in the second, Patrick? They both refer to **a movie**.

P: I don't know. Maybe **a movie** by itself is sort of ambiguous.

M: That's an interesting way to put it. What does this tell us about the INDEFINITE ARTICLE **a**?

P: That "indefinite" isn't enough? That there's more to it than that?

M: Right on! The PRONOUN substitutions with **one** versus **it** are a pretty good clue. If I say, "I'm looking for **a red pencil**," it could be a <u>particular</u> red pencil or <u>any</u> red pencil. A follow-up then might be either "Can you help me find **it**?" or "Can you help me find **one**?" The **it** substitution identifies *a red pencil* as a SPECIFIC pencil; the **one** substitution identifies *red pencil* as NON-SPECIFIC.

P: **So the INDEFINITE ARTICLE is further divided into SPECIFIC and NON-SPECIFIC.**

M: Seems so, doesn't it?

Girl: I wonder if there really <u>is</u> a man for every woman in the world?

Guy: Yes, and I'm very busy; they have to make an appointment.

From the "Momma" comic strip by Mell Lazarus. Reprinted by permission of Mell Lazarus and Creators Syndicate, Inc.

a tiger, the tiger, tigers

A fool may talk, but a wise man speaks.
Ben Jonson, *Timber; or, Discoveries Made upon Men and Matter* (1640)

The fool thinks he is wise, But the wise man knows himself to be a fool.
Shakespeare, *As You Like It*, Act V, Scene i

P: I've been thinking about that SPECIFIC and NON-SPECIFIC stuff with the INDEFINITE ARTICLE that you were talking about, Marta.

M: And ...?

P: Well, take the noun *cat*. I can say, "A cat walked into the room." That's a SPECIFIC cat, right? I mean, it's kinda weird to think of it as <u>any</u> cat.

M: I'll buy that.

P: And I can say, "A cat would be nice to have." That's <u>not</u> a SPECIFIC cat.

M: Right ... NON-SPECIFIC.

P: Then what about this one: "*A cat* is an animal." *A cat* here feels different somehow. I mean I could be talking about <u>all</u> cats, <u>any</u> cat, <u>the world of</u> cats ...

M: Nice little observation, Patrick ... and what do you make of it?

P: That DEFINITE/INDEFINITE, SPECIFIC/NON-SPECIFIC are irrelevant here.

M: But *A cat is an animal* still uses the INDEFINITE ARTICLE, no?

P: OK, but maybe to express something else, like "cats in general."

M: "In general" is a nice way of putting it ... The use of *a cat* to refer to "any cat" or "all cats" is called GENERIC.

P: GENERIC, huh?

M: Yes, and what about use of the <u>DEFINITE</u> ARTICLE?

P: What do you mean?

M: For GENERIC use, with the "cat" example ...

P: Umm … *The cat is an animal*. Yeah, I see.

M: And the PLURAL <u>IN</u>DEFINITE?

P: Yes … *Cats are animals*. So there are <u>three</u> ways to express the GENERIC!

M: At least with these examples, Patrick. But don't get carried away.

P: Uh oh!

M: Yes, it's never as simple as that. In all three of these GENERIC examples the *cat* item is the SUBJECT of the sentence. What happens if it's not?

P: Marta, I don't have the faintest idea.

M: Well, suppose I imagine that you're a zoologist and that you have a research project involving the study of the feline species and I say to you *What are you studying?* How would you respond?

P: I guess it could be *I'm studying the cat*.

M: OK. What about *I'm studying a cat*?

P: Strange … That has to mean that I'm studying some particular, individual cat, like "Felix" or "Tinkerbell."

M: Then what about *I'm studying cats*?

P: Well, I guess it <u>could</u> be *cats* in the general sense … but it doesn't have to be.

M: How so?

P: It could also mean that I'm studying a certain subset of **cats**, like female **cats**, stray **cats**, or all the **cats** in my neighborhood.

M: So is there any generalization you can come up with after all this?

P: That's asking a lot, Marta!

M: Well, how about something like "Only *the* can keep its GENERIC reference in both subject and object position"?

The heart of <u>a fool</u> is in his mouth, but the mouth of <u>a wise man</u> is in his heart.

Benjamin Franklin, Poor Richard's Almanac

For <u>fools</u> rush in where angels fear to tread.

Alexander Pope, An Essay on Criticism, III, 1.65

PS FIVE addiction to generic terms

Democratic nations are passionately addicted to generic terms or abstract expressions because these modes of speech enlarge thought and assist the operations of the mind by enabling it to include many objects in a small compass ...

Alexis de Tocqueville, *Democracy in America* (1835-40)

In this passage, how many examples of the GENERIC sense can you readily identify?

CHAPTER SIX

SOUND & SPELLING ONE

spelling regularity with vowels and consonants in pairs of related words; "silent" consonants; spelling and pronunciation; "readability" of the language; the "morphophonemic" and "phonological" principles; "irregular" spelling in commonly used words; practical advantages of the English spelling system

Why the g in "sign"?

signs & sines
muscles & mussels

P: English spelling is kind of crazy, don't you think?

M: What makes you say that, Patrick?

P: 'Cause we can say something one way but write it another.

M: Such as …

P: Um … OK, take the word **bomb**. Why the final **b**, since you don't pronounce it?

Why not just **bom** … like **mom**, and **Tom**?

M: Well, what's another word for **bomb**?

P: Can't think of any.

M: What about **bombard**, **bombardment**, **bombardier**?

P: Oh sure … but so what, Marta?

M: So what! … Doesn't the existence of the related word **bombard** give us a clue for why we spell **bomb** with a final **b**?

P: Hadn't thought of that one … probably an isolated example.

M: Oh yeah? Then what about **crumb** and the related **crumble**?

P: Could it be something about words with final **b**?

M: Think some more … How about, say, the word **sign** … Why the **g**? … Why not **sine**?

P: Ah … because there's the related word **signal**, I guess … and also there's already a word **sine** … something to do with geometry.

M: Good point!

P: Are there still more examples like these?

M: You tell me! What about **muscle** … Why the "silent" **c**?

P: OK … 'cause we have **muscular**.

M: …and **condemn**, **hymn**, **damn** … Why the "silent" **n**?

P: Umm … **condemnation**, **hymnal**, **damnation**! And we already have the unrelated words **him** and **dam**.

M: Right on! Any comments so far?

P: Yeah … **sign** may be related to **signal**, but we still <u>pronounce</u> it like **sine**. Seems like we should spell it like we say it.

M: What about when we read it?

P: Hmmm … I guess if **sign** and **sine** <u>mean</u> different things, it maybe helps if they <u>look</u> different in print … when we have to read them, I mean.

M: Any further comments, Patrick?

P: Well, OK … so English spelling is a little less crazy than I thought … but it's still pretty crazy!

M: Think so? We'll take another look … but this should do for now.

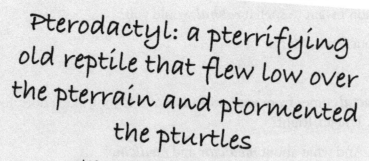

Pterodactyl: a pterrifying old reptile that flew low over the pterrain and ptormented the pturtles

with apologies to Ogden Nash

medicine & medicate
revise & revision
relate & relation

Why not "medisine"?

M: Ready for a further look at English spelling, Patrick?

P: You mean some more stuff about how we write words one way but pronounce them in another?

M: Yes, but you make it sound like some kind of trick.

P: Well, not exactly … but how many pairs like *sign | signal* and *muscle | muscular* are there? Not a lot, I bet.

M: Hang on, we're just getting started. We've looked at pairs where one of the two written consonants is "silent," so to speak. But what about pairs where they're both pronounced?

P: I don't follow you.

M: Well, how about *race* and *racial?* Why the same *c* for two different sounds? Yet you wouldn't want to spell it *rashal,* would you?

P: No … 'course not, Marta.

M: Why?

P: 'Cause *racial* comes from *race*, so you want it to <u>look</u> like it does, for reading purposes, I mean. Right?

M: I'd say so. And what about *medicate* and *medicine*?

P: Same thing … It'd be pretty dumb for them to be written like, say, *medikate* … or *medisine*.

M: Why?

P: Same as before ... They're related ... *medicine*'s the noun and *medicate*'s the verb.

M: Can you think of any more pairs like that? You go to the gym for a workout, don't you, Patrick?

P: Yes, but ...

M: Well, *gym* is the short form for what?

P: Oh, *gymnasium* ... so?

M: So what do people do in a *gymnasium*?

P: They work out, they exercise ... oh, I get it ... *gymnastics*!

M: So you know what the next question is ...

P: Yeah ... Why not spell it *gymnazium*, 'cause it has a z sound, not an s sound? But we already know the answer!

M: Great! There are lots more like this, of course ... *grade | gradual* (not *gradjual*), *resident | residential* (not *residenchal*), *revise | revision* (not *revizhon*) ...

P: ...and *obsess | obsession* (not *obseshon*)!!

M: Couldn't resist, could you! But here's another thing to think about: If *revise* gives us *revision*, why doesn't *divide* give us *dividion* instead of *division*?

P: Hmm ... OK, spelling *division* with a *d* can't give us the pronunciation we want. I mean, nobody says "*dividion* of labor," "long *dividion*," "second armored *dividion*," right?

M: Right, so ...

P: So whatever the spelling, it can't force a pronunciation different from the actual one! ▪

"If from pirate we get piracy, why doesn't chocolate give us chocolacy?"

Why not "edit**e**r"? ... "comp**e**rable"?

compare & comparable
precede & precedent
migrate & immigration
compose & composition
salute & salutation

M: We've looked at written consonants that show up in the pronunciation of one word and disappear in a related word, like in ***thimble | thumb*** ... and looked at consonants that you pronounce differently in a pair of related words, like ***revise | revision*** ... What about vowels?

P: What about them, Marta?

M: Well, to start with, there are tons of word groups that have vowels that sound the same. Here, let me write some of them for you:

*manag**e**r*	*profess**e**r*	*famili**e**r*	*sulf**e**r*
*myst**e**ry*	*hist**e**ry*	*prim**e**ry*	*inj**e**ry*	*inqu**e**ry*

P: **Wait a minute!!** You can't write them like that, Marta! Don't you know how to spell?

M: What do you mean?

P: All the spellings are wrong, except for ***manager*** and ***mystery***.

M: But all of these ***-er*** and ***-ery*** endings <u>sound</u> the same, don't they?

P: Sure, but ...

M: Let me interrupt, Patrick. What do they all have in common ... the endings, I mean?

P: Well, they all have an **r** sound.

M: OK, but what else? Do you put STRESS on these endings? Do you say ***managér***, ***mystéry***?

P: No … just the opposite. Stress the endings and you find yourself almost saying *managérial*, *mystérious*.

M: Try doing the same thing with the others—adding stress to the parts with the *e-r* sound, I mean. See what you come up with.

P: OK … um … *professérial*, oh, sorry … *professórial*, *histórical*, *familiárity*, *primárily*, *sulfúric*, *injúrious*, *inquíre*.

M: Any comments?

P: Familiar words … I guess they're the corresponding ADJECTIVES, except for *inquire*, which is a verb.

M: Anything to conclude from this?

P: Hmm … so we're faced with a choice: Either we let the spelling stay closer to the actual sound—like with *histery* vs. *histórical*—or we let the spelling show the relationship between the two—like *histOry* | *histOrical*. And from "*histery*" we certainly don't want to get "*histerical*." That would be hysterical!

M: So is the choice a difficult one?

P: Not if I want to be able to read the language. That one's a no-brainer!

That <u>homo sapiens</u> is somehow more at ease with a one-letter one-sound system has often been assumed, but no evidence has been produced to substantiate this limitation on man's mental capacities.

R. L. Venezky, The Structure of English Orthography (1970)

Why the i in both "wide" and "width"?

sane & sanity
serene & serenity
divine & divinity
phone & phonic
reduce & reduction

P: I bet I know what comes next.

M: You think so, Patrick?

P: Sure … We've already played with disappearing CONSONANT sounds—no 'b' sound at the end of *bomb*—and displaced VOWEL sounds—no 'o' sound in *history*. And there's the matter of different consonant sounds in a pair of related words—two 'c' sounds in *medicine* and *medicate*.

M: And …

P: So, the same thing for vowels, right? I mean two different sounds for the same written vowel.

M: Like what?

P: Oh … *wide* and *width* … um, *vane* and *vanity* … *extreme* and *extremity* … probably some more like these.

M: Nice observation … It kind of fills out the picture.

P: OK, but if you got the pair *wide* | *width*, with the written vowel *i* in both, how come, say, the pair *long* | *length* is spelled with <u>different</u> vowels?

M: **What**! Think about it … Are you suggesting maybe it should be *leng* | *length*, or *long* | *longth*?

P: Ouch!

M: What's wrong with it?

P: What's wrong? Well … I guess it'd be pretty hard to get the right pronunciation for *long* if you spelled it with an *e* … or for *length* if you spelled it with an *o*.

M: I should think so!

P: But how about this, Marta? I can also think of pairs like *cope* | *cop* … *cane* | *can*

... *kite* | *kit* ... where I don't see <u>any</u> relationships. For example, what does *kite* have to do with *kit*?

M: Nothing ... but why should it?

P: 'Cause if you've got *wide* and *width* ... and, uh, *bite* and *bit* ... *write* and *writ* ...

M: [*silence*]

P: Guess I could have figured that one out myself. The pairs have to be <u>related</u>, like *bite* and *bit* ... but <u>not</u> *kite* and *kit*!

M: So what does all this say about the English spelling system? You've already noted that, aside from the spelling, the PRONUNCIATION has to be the right one.

P: Well, let's see ... One thing that's happening concerns a spelling connection with related words ... like the CONSONANT *g* with different pronunciations in *prodigal* | *prodigious* and the VOWEL *u* with different pronunciations in *reduce* and *reduction* ...

M: But what about, say, the pair *provoke* | *provocation*, where they're related but you've got *k* in one and *c* in the other?

P: Well, you certainly can't write it *provoce* ... 'cause that's not the way we say it!

M: So what happens?

P: I don't know.

M: Oh, come on! You have to spell *provoke* with a *k* to get the <u>right</u> pronunciation.

P: OK, so the principle of having pairs of related words with the same written vowel or the same written consonant sometimes gets overridden in order to save the pronunciation?

M: Yes! Nice way of putting it!

Every word ... has two existences, as a spoken word and a written, and you have no right to sacrifice one of these, or even to subordinate it wholly to the other.
Richard Chenevix Trench, On the Study of Words (1851)

Why can't we spell it like we say it?

I have a spelling checker,
It came with my PC,
It plane lee marks
four my revue
Miss steaks aye
can knot sea.

© *The Journal of Irreproducible Results*

P: I'm still bothered a bit by the spelling thing. I know there's a lot of the kind of regularity we've been looking at, even though it's not the kind that you find in Italian or Spanish. I mean English doesn't have a close one-to-one match-up between sound and letter of the alphabet.

M: Yes … English is not like that.

P: Still, I did come into all this thinking that the English spelling system is chaotic, 'cause I hear that all the time … with people calling even for total reform.

M: But now that we've seen all kinds of regularity with English spelling, Patrick, why do you suppose people keep calling it chaotic?

P: Oh … maybe all the ways you can pronounce the letters *ough*, like in *though*, *through*, *bough*, *ought* … or the letters *o-m-e* in *home* vs. *come* … or the different pronunciation of *o* in *woman* and *women*.

M: Those are good examples of IRREGULARITY! And English does have some of that.

P: <u>Some</u> of that! **They show up all the time!**

M: Because they're among the most commonly used words in the language. But, believe it or not, those words with irregular spelling amount to only about <u>five percent</u> of the hundreds of thousands in the language!

P: Are you saying then that English spelling is <u>ninety</u>-<u>five</u> <u>percent</u> <u>regular</u>!

M: Ninety to ninety-five … yes. That's what the professionals working on it *have come* up with. It's hard *to* believe, I *know*, since most of the <u>ir</u>regularity is limited to the most commonly used words, like *know*, *have*, *come*, *to*, *one*—*ones* that I'm using in these very sentences.

P: But it certainly explains why so many people think the spelling needs to be "regularized," so to speak.

M: Yes, "regularized" to look more like the Spanish system, say, where they don't even have, don't even <u>need</u>, a word for "*spell.*" But look at what you get with the English system …

P: You mean the kinds of stuff we've been talking about, Marta?

M: Yes … Take the three words **notion**, **nation**, and **national**, for example. What do you notice about the three vowels at the beginning, both written and spoken?

P: Um … one of them has **o** and two of them have **a**. But the **a**s in **nation** and **national** are pronounced differently, of course.

M: So two written vowels and three pronunciations … Seems like a prime candidate for spelling reform here, doesn't it … maybe letting the <u>three</u> different spoken vowels be represented by <u>three</u> different written vowels, for example?

P: No, after all these discussions I'm beginning to get the picture. **Nation** and **national** have the same written vowel **a** because they're practically the same word. But the word **notion**, of course, is unrelated, and the different vowel **o** reflects that.

M: Nice! And think about one of the <u>practical</u> advantages of such a spelling system.

P: What do you mean, Marta?

M: I mean the task of learning <u>how</u> to spell. Suppose you're writing a letter and want to use the word **ridiculous** but you're not sure whether it's **r-i** or **r-e**. What simple thing can you do … before taking the time to look it up in the dictionary, I mean?

P: I don't know.

M: Sure you do. What does **ridiculous** come from? What's it made up of?

P: Oh … it's from **ridicule**, the verb, where you know it's **r-i** 'cause now you can hear it. Same "trick" could be used for figuring out, say, that it's **victory** with an **o**, not **victery** with an **e**, since you get **victorious**, and <u>not</u> **victerious**!

M: Any further comments?

P: Three cheers for the English spelling system!

I take it you already know
Of tough and bough and cough and dough?
Others may stumble, but not you
On hiccough, thorough, laugh,
and through?

Anonymous, "Hints on Pronunciation for Foreigners," in The Faber Book of Useful Verse (1981)

PS SIX "like a ghoti out of water"

The author and playwright, George Bernard Shaw, viewed English spelling as quite chaotic and proposed that we adopt a totally new system in which sound and letter of the alphabet show a one-to-one correspondence. As an example of what Shaw thought was wrong with the present system, he offered the made-up spelling *ghoti*, which he stated could logically be pronounced as FISH. His "logic" was that the "f" sound could be as in the word *enough*, the "i" sound as in the first syllable of the word *women*, and the "sh" sound as in the word *nation*. Is there anything illogical about Shaw's "logic"? Bear in mind that in English there are some very common words whose spelling would have to be labeled "irregular," as we've already seen.

CHAPTER SEVEN

ILLOGICAL ~ IRRATIONAL ~ UNREASONABLE

prefixation to verbs and adjectives with *un-* and *in-*; morphophonemic variation with *in-*, *im-*, *il-*, *ir-*; innovation with *un-*; *un-* vs. *non-*; *un-* vs. *dis-*

Day Thirty-one
unlockable

DayThirty-two
unthinkable, inconceivable

Day Thirty-three
illegal, unlawful

Day Thirty-four
**in-
un-
non-**

Day Thirty-five
unqualified vs. disqualified

PS 7
no unnecessary words

unlockable

"I hate you!
And I'll never unhate you or nothing!"

Uttered by a young child very early in the learning experience

P: I was looking through some magazines from years ago and came across an ad for a carbonated soft drink—can't remember the name of it—a soft drink that wanted to set itself apart from familiar "cola" drinks. Guess what it called itself.

M: Beats me.

P: It was *the **uncola***! Isn't that wild, Marta?

M: What's "wild" about it? Lots of words start with the PREFIX ***un-*** … ***untie***, ***unpack***, ***unkind***, ***unconscious*** …

P: I don't know … but for some reason ***uncola*** sounds weird.

M: OK, but how do you go about trying to figure out <u>why</u> it sounds weird?

P: Um … well, I guess since it's just a single word, we could check its grammatical category, like NOUN, VERB, ADJECTIVE …

M: Yes … and you said it appeared in the ad as ***the uncola***; so …

P: Gotta be a NOUN. That's obvious. Now what?

M: Come on! For starters, think of the words consisting of a STEM plus ***un-*** PREFIX that I just mentioned; maybe you can add some more.

P: OK, let's see … ***unpack***, ***unkind***, ***untie*** … maybe ***uninteresting***?

M: I think I'd prefer ***unafraid***. But what do you make of them, in terms of category?

P: Well … ***unpack*** and ***untie***—almost said ***untidy***—are VERBS and … uh, ***unkind***, ***unafraid***, ***uninteresting*** are ADJECTIVES, right?

M: Right … so what can you say about all this?

P: You mean that the prefix ***un-*** attaches to VERBS and ADJECTIVES?

M: Well, what about your "weird" ***uncola*** example?

P: Oh, "cola" is a NOUN and ***un-*** doesn't attach to nouns; <u>that</u>'s why ***uncola*** sounds weird.

M: Well now, what about prepositions, like ***to***? Add ***un-*** and what do you get?

P: ***Unto***, of course, but that's not fair!

M: Why not, Patrick?

P: Because the word **unto** isn't made up of **un + to**!

M: Not the kind of **un-** we're talking about at least, which leads to the question of what the PREFIX **un-** really means. Take the ADJECTIVES we mentioned: **unkind**, **unafraid**, **untidy** … Any ideas?

P: I guess **un-** is like **not**. So **unkind** means "not kind," **unafraid** means "not afraid" … that sort of thing.

M: And what about the meaning of **un-** prefixed to VERBS?

P: Same thing, I guess. No, wait a minute … **unpack**, **untie**: they're like the **reverse** of **pack** and **tie**.

M: …or the **reverse** of the meanings of those verbs. Like the **un-** in **unclear** versus the **un-** in **unclog**?

P: Yes … I mean no! **Clear** is an adjective here; **clog** is a verb. So the **un-** in **unclear** makes it mean "not clear" and the **un-** in **unclog** makes it mean something like "reversing the clogging" … So I guess **uncola** is that weird way of saying "not cola."

M: Yes … which leads me to one last example: **unlockable**. What does it mean and how do you break it down?

P: Let me think for a second … Oh! I get it! The word **unlockable** has <u>two</u> meanings. In one sense it's "able to be <u>un</u>locked," in the other "<u>not</u> able to be locked," or something like that.

M: Very perceptive, Patrick … so breaking it down should be easy!

P: Sure. One reading is **unlock** plus **able** ("able to be unlocked"); the other is **un-** plus **lockable** ("not able to be locked"). **Lock** is a verb in **unlock** and **lockable** is an adjective in **unlockable**.

M: Nice! What's your reaction to all this?

P: There's a lot to know about just that little two-letter prefix **un-**!

The greatest disease in the West today is not TB or leprosy; it is being <u>un</u>wanted, <u>un</u>loved, and <u>un</u>cared for.

Mother Teresa, A Simple Path (1995)

unthinkable, inconceivable

unrhymed, unrhythmical, the chatter goes:
Yet no one hears his own remarks as prose.

W. H. Auden, "At the Party" (c. 1963)

▶ P: Marta, I've been thinking about those words with the **un-** PREFIX that we looked at last time.

M: You mean like **unclog** and **unclear** and so on?

P: Right … So take another **un-** word like **unthinkable**, where I guess it's **un-** plus **thinkable**, not **unthink** plus **-able**.

M: Yes … but what's on your mind?

P: Well, the word **unthinkable** means pretty much the same as **inconceivable**, and also there's the ADJECTIVE **unequal**, which is pretty close to the NOUN **inequality** and also **unbelievable** along with **incredible** … even **unexplainable** plus **inexplicable**. And that's just for starters.

M: Hmm … You've obviously done a bit of digging, Patrick, and those pairs are certainly worth noting. Now what do you make of it?

P: Well, it's the PREFIX **un-** thing, and now **in-** … Why have so many pairs of words with the same meaning?

M: Language is full of more than one way to say the same thing! And much of the time it's not <u>exactly</u> the same thing, or one way is perhaps not as appropriate as another.

P: Can you give me an example?

M: OK … Take **inevitable** and **unavoidable**, for instance. If I say, "*When his brakes failed, hitting that tree was …*" Fill in the word for me.

P: Probably **unavoidable** … **inevitable** sounds a little like—I don't know— "doomsday" maybe. I mean <u>without</u> the PREFIX, **avoidable** sounds fine but **evitable** I never even heard of.

76

M: Not surprising. *Evitable* is borrowed from French and rarely used in English without *in-*.

P: Then it's probably the same thing with another pair that I just mentioned: *unexplainable* and *inexplicable*. I mean, who ever uses *explicable* by itself?

M: Maybe a few people—I don't. But you've succeeded in identifying an important feature of some of the NOUNS and ADJECTIVES carrying the *in-* prefix as opposed to those with *un-*.

P: I have?

M: Yes, and if we have time we should look at that some more in another session.

P: We should?

M: *Indubitably*!

P: *Undoubtedly*?

M: *Incessantly*!

P: *Unceasingly*?

M: *Infallibly*!

P: *Unfailingly*?

M: I'm exhausted, Patrick!

P: So am I!

Life is easier than you'd think;
all that is necessary is
to accept the <u>im</u>possible,
do without the <u>in</u>dispensable.

Kathleen Norris, *Oxymoronica*.
Copyright © 2004 by Mardy Grothe

Survive the <u>un</u>bearable,
put up with the <u>il</u>logical,
and say goodbye to the
<u>ir</u>replaceable!

with apologies to Mardy Grothe

illegal, unlawful

What an <u>un</u>practical person!
What an <u>im</u>practical solution!

▶ M: You look worried, Patrick. What's on your mind?

P: Well, just when I thought we had wrapped things up with all those pairs of *in-* and *un-* prefixes, other things come along that make me wonder.

M: And what are those?

P: I've been noticing that there are lots of other words supposedly in the PREFIX *in-* group that don't come out like those in the *un-* group.

M: I think I know what you're getting at, but tell me what kinds of words you're referring to.

P: Well, there's the ADJECTIVE *unbalanced* and the related NOUN *imbalance* …
Then there are the ADJECTIVES *unreasonable* and *irrational* .

M: You mean no *inbalance*, no *inrational*?

P: Right!

M: But think about it … Is the use of *im-* and *ir-* instead of *in-* arbitrary? Why those two particular variations? And by the way, what's the *in-* pairing with the ADJECTIVE *unlawful*?

P: Oh, of course … *illegal*, not *inlegal*! So there are <u>three</u> variations on this prefix *in-*!

M: Yes, but again is the choice an arbitrary one?

P: Probably not, Marta, or you wouldn't be asking.

M: [*chuckle*] Well, then, is the choice of *in-*, *im-*, *ir-*, or *il-* affected in some way by what sound follows in the rest of the word?

P: Oh, OK, maybe it's somehow easier to say *illegal* than *inlegal*, or *imlegal*, or *irlegal*.

78

M: Let's throw in some more samples …

So *in-* becomes *im-* before -*personal* (*impersonal*)
-*balance* (*imbalance*)
-*mature* (*immature*)

… and *in-* becomes *ir-* before …

P: … before -*responsible* (*irresponsible*)
-*rational* (*irrational*)
- *regular* (*irregular*)

M: … and *in-* becomes *il-*?

P: Obvious: before -*legal* (*illegal*)
-*legible* (*illegible*)
-*legitimate* (*illegitimate*)

M: And these examples are only for starters. There are tons more.

P: … and all of them related to *in-* … which is another way of saying that *in-* ~ *im-* ~ *ir-* ~ *il-* are all variants of <u>one</u> prefix, right, Marta?

M: Right! And what about *un-*?

P: *un-* doesn't vary at all.

M: OK, but what about the coinage of new words?

P: What do you mean?

M: Think back to a couple of sessions ago and the word you saw for the first time that you thought was "weird."

P: Oh, you mean the word *uncola*.

M: Could you imagine them calling it *the incola*?

P: No way!

M: Yes, so *un-* is what you could call the "innovative" prefix. Unlike *in-* you can attach it to almost anything. Wanna try?

P: You mean looking for an *unword*, in an *unsession*, dreamed up by an *unmentor*?

M: Walked right into it, didn't I?

"You have to be <u>un</u>relentless!
You have to do it <u>ir</u>regardless!"

Overheard plea by a certain dean at a certain
prestigious university in the United States

79

in-
un-
non-

- Are you calling their research <u>un</u>scientific?

- No, I'm calling it <u>non</u>-scientific!

▶ P: Marta, I learned something interesting in my science class this week.

M: And what was that?

P: Well, it was in a chapter about bone fragments from ten thousand years ago and whether they were human or not, and this kid raises his hand and says that since the fragments look like tail bones they're probably *inhuman*.

M: So what's the "something interesting"?

P: "*Inhuman*"? Kind of judgmental, don't you think?

M: Well, what do you think the kid <u>should</u> have said?

P: Um … "*not human*," I guess.

M: What about "*non-human*"?

P: Oh, of course … *non-* gives "*human*" a sort of non-committal sense to it, doesn't it?

M: Yes, and speaking of the "judgmental" *in + human*, the same thing can happen with the *un-* prefix.

P: What do you mean, Marta?

M: Well, for example, did your American history lessons ever touch on something called the "McCarthy Era," from roughly the late forties to the early fifties?

P: Yeah, they did, but …

M: Remember the name of that special committee set up by the House of Representatives to investigate so-called "***unpatriotic***" citizens?

P: Oh, sure … What was it … the, um, "House ***Un-American*** Activities Committee"?

M: Right! And "HUAC" was the abbreviation. Any comment, Patrick?

P: Well, it's interesting, I guess, that they <u>didn't</u> name it the "House ***Non-American*** Activities Committee" … and <u>not</u> because "HNAC" you can hardly pronounce!

M: Yes … nothing judgmental about being "***non-American***."

P: The whole rest of the world is ***non-American***!

M: Lots of ***non-entities*** … ***non-alcoholic***, ***non-fattening***, ***non-native***, ***non-verbal*** …

P: So they're mostly ADJECTIVES?

M: Very observant, so far. But what about ***non-smoker***, ***non-fiction***, ***non-violence***, ***non-member*** …?

P: OK … NOUNS too … which reminds me of where we started with all these negative prefixes a couple of sessions ago.

M: Which was …

P: …my wild ***uncola*** example … wild because ***un-*** doesn't usually attach to NOUNS.

M: So what would it be if advertising weren't behind it?

P: ***Non-cola***!

Whoso would be a man must be a <u>non</u>conformist.

Ralph Waldo Emerson, *Self-Reliance*

unqualified vs. disqualified

"We must not confuse dissent with disloyalty."

Edward R. Murrow

P: *un-*, *in-*, *im,- il-*, *ir-*, *non-* ... Just when I thought we'd covered all the English negative PREFIXES, along comes another one!

M: What do you mean?

P: Here's a newspaper item about a prominent married couple who apparently now *dislike* each other, even *distrust* each other. It says that "there's so much *disquiet*, *disorder*, *disharmony*, and *dissatisfaction* in the marriage that they're threatening to *disown* each other, let alone divorce! Each wishes the other would just *disappear*."

M: I'm listening to you somewhat in *disbelief*, Patrick!

P: Well, then, just *disregard* all this if you want.

M: No way! I'm not about to *discourage* you. There are some interesting features of the *dis-* PREFIX that we can try to *disentangle*. Remember the two meanings of *un-* that we looked at a couple of sessions ago?

P: You mean like the "negative" sense of the ADJECTIVE *unclear* and the "reverse" sense of the VERB *unclog*?

M: Yes. So isn't something like that going on in words with the *dis-* prefix as well?

P: You're moving too fast for me, Marta.

M: Well, for example, think of the meaning of *dis-* in *disbelief*, *disloyal*, *dislike* versus the meaning of *dis-* in the verbs *disentangle*, *disarm*, *discredit*.

P: Ah, **_dis-_** in the first three is a real NEGATIVE: "**not** believing," "**not** loyal," "**not** liking," or something to that effect. In the second three, **_dis-_** has the sense of <u>reversing</u> the meaning of the verb. For example, I don't own a gun and therefore I walked into this room **_unarmed_**, but I couldn't be said to be walking in **_disarmed_**, right?

M: Yes, and that's a great example of highlighting the **_un-_ / _dis-_** contrast where the "reversing" meaning is concerned. How about one more?

P: I'm ready!

M: Let's say you're applying for a job as a lifeguard that requires three years of experience, Patrick, but your resumé doesn't even say whether you can swim. For a job like that you'd certainly be … you'd certainly be …

P: …**_unqualified_**.

M: Uh huh, but if your resumé lists prior lifeguard experience, your employer wants to hire you, and then they discover that you were previously fired for drunkenness, you'd …

P: …I'd be **_disqualified_**!

M: And probably a bit **_discouraged_** as well!

Marrying left your maiden name <u>disused</u>.
Philip Larkin, "Maiden Name"

If not actually <u>disgruntled</u>, he was far from being gruntled.
P. G. Wodehouse, *The Code of the Woosters*, Chapter 1

PS SEVEN no unnecessary words

Vigorous writing is concise. A sentence should contain no <u>unnecessary</u> words, a paragraph no <u>unnecessary</u> sentences, for the same reason that a drawing should have no <u>unnecessary</u> lines and a machine no <u>unnecessary</u> parts.

William Strunk, Jr., *The Elements of Style* (1918)

That community is already in the process of <u>dissolution</u> where each man begins to eye his neighbor as a possible enemy, where <u>nonconformity</u> with the accepted creed, political as well as religious, is a mark of <u>disaffection</u> ...

Judge Learned Hand, Speech to the Board of Regents, University of the State of New York (1952)

CHAPTER EIGHT

REALLY BEING POSSESSED

personal pronouns: person and number; loose relations with the possessive suffix "'s"; "alienable" and "inalienable" possession; possessive *–ed* suffix (*talented*, *spirited*, *gifted …*); possessives with *of* (*the mother of the child*, *the title of the book …*)

Day Thirty-six — Mine eyes have seen the glory

Day Thirty-seven — a good night's sleep

Day Thirty-eight — Benji's knee and Benji's key

Day Thirty-nine — quick-witted and open-minded

PS 8 three inflections

Day Forty — the end of the world

Mine eyes have seen the glory

Mother Goose & Grimm (New) © 1991 Grimmy,
Inc. King Features Syndicate

P: In music class the other day we were singing "Battle Hymn of the Republic" and something right in the very first line struck me as kind of odd.

M: How so?

P: Well, it goes "Mine eyes have seen the glory of ..."

M: And what's odd about it?

P: "Mine eyes" ... Why *mine* eyes? Shouldn't it be *my* eyes?

M: Today, yes. But the text of the hymn is reminiscent of the kind of English spoken in Shakespeare's time.

P: So in Shakespeare's time they also went around saying "mine nose," "mine mouth," "mine foot"?

M: No, it was *my nose*, *my mouth*, *my foot*, et cetera ... then as well as now.

P: You mean it used to be *my mouth* but *mine* eyes!

M: Yes! Think about it, Patrick ... *mine* enemy, but *my friend*; *mine* arm, but *my leg* ... So what's going on?

P: Well, I guess it must be the sound of the word that follows ... *eye, enemy, arm* all begin with vowels, *mouth, friend, leg* with consonants.

M: OK, but phrase it in the form of a GENERALIZATION.

P: It's ... rather it <u>was</u> ... *mine* before vowels, *my* before consonants.

M: What about *mine* honor, *my* habit?

P: OK, it's before <u>spoken</u> vowels.

M: Right ... By the way, what do you <u>call</u> the words *my* and *mine*?

P: PRONOUNS? Like *I*, *me*?

M: Yes, but *my* and *mine* are POSSESSIVE PRONOUNS. Are they the only ones?

P: No, 'course not … There's *your*, *their*, *our* … That's all I can think of.

M: Come on! Plot them out the way we did before with the others. Remember? The two dimensions are PERSON and NUMBER …

P: Oh, OK … Let's see, for PERSON you've got FIRST, SECOND, THIRD … and for NUMBER you've got SINGULAR and PLURAL. Here, I'll diagram it for you:

		Person	
	1st	2nd	3rd
Singular	my	your	his/her
Plural	our	your	their

(Number)

M: Beautiful! But what about *mine*, as in *mine eyes* … if we want to be a little historical?

P: Sure. Just make it *my/mine*.

M: Notice anything else worth mentioning in your little diagram?

P: Yeah … the word *your*; it's the only one that's both singular and plural. Why?

M: Well, it didn't use to be that way.

P: Back to Shakespeare again, Marta?

M: Let's say back to earlier times. **You** and **your** used to be plural only; the singular forms were **thou** and the POSSESSIVE **thy**.

P: Oh, like … what was it … "Honor **thy** father and **thy** mother."

M: Yes, and what about "enemy"?

P: Umm … doing or not doing something to "**thine** enemy"; *thy/thine* … just like *my/mine*.

M: **Thy** cleverness is exceeded only by **thine** imagination.

P: **Thou** art really weird!

Why, then the world's mine oyster.
Shakespeare, *The Merry Wives of Windsor*, Act II, scene ii

This above all: to thine own self be true.
Shakespeare, *Hamlet*, Act I, scene iii

Friends, Romans, countrymen, lend me your ears.
Shakespeare, *Julius Caesar*, Act III, scene ii

a good night's sleep

Sally Forth   By Greg Howard

I'VE CALLED NINETEEN SITTERS, AND THEY'RE ALL BUSY SATURDAY. I'M DOWN TO MY LAST NAME.

HELLO. MY NAME IS SALLY FORTH. MY NEIGHBOR'S FRIEND'S UNCLE'S DOCTOR'S NIECE'S BABY-SITTER GAVE ME YOUR NAME...

Sally Forth © King Features Syndicate

▶ M: So what are *my, our, your, his, her, their*?

P: What do you mean, Marta?

M: Well, take *his, her, their* … What, or better, whom do they refer to?

P: Depends … *his money, her money* could be ***Harry's*** money, ***Harriet's*** money …
their money could be ***Harry*** and ***Harriet's*** money.

M: So what's the difference between ***Harry*** and ***Harry's***, ***Harriet*** and ***Harriet's***?

P: Come on! It's the little ***'s***, of course … and you're probably going to tell me it's
the POSSESSIVE.

M: That's the common term, and it certainly seems plausible here to say that *Harry*
(or *Harriet*) in some sense "possesses" the money. So what about ***Harry's*** name?

P: What about it? It's true that *name* isn't something tangible, like *money*, but you <u>can</u>
give it to another person, like a father "giving" his name to a son, for example.

M: All right, but let's see how far we can go with this. What about ***Harry's*** room,
Harry's school, ***Harry's*** teachers, ***Harry's*** grades, ***Harry's*** improvement? These
things don't "belong" to Harry, do they, like *money*?

P: Hmm … No, I see what you're getting at. I understand what they all mean, but it's
very hard to tie them together. There's some kind of loose relation here that I can't
give a name to.

M: Neither can I, Patrick, or anyone else for that matter. Take ***Harry's*** room …
Without any context, it could mean "the room where Harry sleeps (or slept, or
will sleep)," "the (home) room where Harry's class meets (or used to meet),"
"the room where Harry is sitting and waiting to be called," and so on … and on.

P: OK, but at least the **'s** attaches to **Harry**, not to some other item.

M: Yes, but what about something like **the attorney-general's** appointment, or **my new father-in-law's** business trip?

P: I never thought about that kind of thing.

M: Or consider these conversational gems: *I'm trying to remember* **what's-his-name's** *question*, or *What's* **the-guy-in-the-back-of-the-room's** *paper doing on my desk?*

P: Well, I'll be a **monkey's** uncle! OK, so after all this, why call that little **'s** the POSSESSIVE?

M: Think of the term POSSESSIVE as identifying the **'s** not so much as <u>meaning</u> but more as a <u>form</u>, in fact INFLECTION: on the single noun **Harry**, for example, or on the word at the end of a whole hyphenated CONSTITUENT, regardless of what PART OF SPEECH that word represents, like *That's* **the-guy-who-just-came-in's** *mother*.

P: Weird! I understand what it means, and I can even hear myself saying stuff like that, but isn't it a violation of some rule?

M: Well, what kind of violation? Can you think of a better way of saying *That's* **the guy-who-just-came-in's** *mother?*

P: Um, let's see … *That's the mother* **of the guy who just came in**?

M: And what makes it better?

P: I don't know … it just <u>feels</u> better. With the other way there's just too much stuff that the **'s** has to attach to.

M: Nice observation. We'll have more to say about that in another session. But what about PART OF SPEECH? I mean, what's the difference between **the guy's** *mother* and **the guy-who-just-came-in's** *mother?*

P: OK … They're both NOUN PHRASES, and one's just longer than the other. So you could say the **'s** attaches to phrases, not words.

M: That's a very important observation, Patrick! … And if you substitute a pronoun for the POSSESSIVE part?

P: Oh! **his** *mother* … for both of them.

M: Uh huh …

P: Cool, Marta … So are we finished with **today's** stuff? After all this I'll need **a good night's** sleep.

… a day's work, an evening's relaxation, and a good night's sleep

Benji's knee and Benji's key

Dennis The Menace   By Hank Ketcham

"Will you tell Hotdog to get off my lap!?"

Dennis the Menace
© North America Syndicate

▶ M: Last time we played around with a wide range of expressions with 's … more examples could be **Benjamin's** fist, **Beethoven's** Fifth, **the building's** filth …

P: Yeah, that loose "possessive" thing.

M: So, Patrick, how would you paraphrase so-called "possessive" phrases like these? Pretend you're talking to someone who for some reason doesn't understand them. Start with **the building's** filth.

P: "The filthy building"?

M: Uh, no … Try a paraphrase using filth, not filthy.

P: I guess it would be something like "the filth that's in the building," or "found in the building."

M: OK … What about **Beethoven's** Fifth?

P: Oh, that's the short form for **Beethoven's** Fifth Symphony, which I guess means "the fifth symphony that Beethoven wrote, or composed."

M: Sounds reasonable … and **Benji's** fist?

P: Hmmm … "the fist that Benji has? that Benji owns? that belongs to Benji?" … Kind of hard to come up with something that doesn't sound weird.

M: Not surprising … but suppose Benji is a sculptor, and his latest piece is a human fist made out of clay. <u>Now</u> what about **Benji's** fist?

P: Easy … "the fist that Benji made, that Benji sculpted."

90

M: Which means that "Benji made a fist," right?

P: Yes, Marta, but that also has another meaning!

M: Which is …?

P: Like what you get when you close your thumb and fingers.

M: OK, let's stay with that … Can you say *Benji made **Margie's** fist?*

P: Are you kidding! Benji can't make somebody else's fist! Has to be his own!

M: Then what about *Margie got Benji's fist as a present*, and I'm not talking about a "fist" sculpture.

P: Sure … but some present! Benji holding up his fist to poor Margie!

M: No, not that, Patrick. I mean that Benji's fist "changed hands," so to speak.

P: This is crazy … Benji can't give away his own fist, any more than he can literally give away his own finger or his own nose, unless you want to make it something pretty gruesome.

M: Can he "lose" or "misplace" his fist, finger, nose, ear …

P: No! Same thing!

M: So what's the real difference then between, say, **Benji's** *knee* and **Benji's** *key*, where POSSESSIVE **'s** is concerned?

P: *Key* he can lose, misplace, give away; *knee* he can't … Uh, like **there's two** <u>kinds</u> **of possession**?

M: Why not? █

(Two women in conversation)
A: My first husband was a brute. We had some terrible fights. In our last fight I sprained an ankle, wrenched a wrist, and fractured a leg.
B: Oh, how awful!
A: No, they were all his.

quick-witted and open-minded

What's "a gifted child"?
— A kid who gets a Ferrari from his
grandparents for learning to tie his shoe.

From the "B.C." comic strip by Johnny Hart. © Field Enterprises,
Inc. 1983. Reprinted by permission of John L. Hart FLP and Creators
Syndicate, Inc.

M: Patrick, let's take another look, so to speak, at **Benji's fist** … OK?

P: What's so fascinating about Benji's fist, whoever this guy Benji is anyway?

M: Well, let's suppose he's a boxer, and a good one, where his two fists have won him a few fights. You could say he's what kind of fighter?

P: A good one; you just said so, Marta.

M: No, I mean another way of saying a "fighter who uses his two fists."

P: Let's see … a **two-fisted fighter**?

M: Yes. Can you break the word **fisted** down a bit, the way we did a few sessions ago with, say, the noun *waiter*?

P: Sure … You got *fist* plus **-e-d**.

M: What's the *-ed* doing? Is it past tense **-ed**?

P: No way! … *Fist* is a noun, not a verb, and *fisted* is sort of an adjective.

M: And what's it mean?

P: Umm … kind of like "having a fist."

M: And if Benji "has poise," what is he?

P: He's *poised*!

M: And if he's wearing a helmet?

P: *Helmeted*!

M: So could you say he's "possessed" of his two fists, a helmet, poise …?

P: In a sense, yes … I see what you're getting at, Marta.

M: Which is?

P: The *-ed* attaches to nouns and is kind of like another POSSESSIVE, along with *'s*.

M: You're getting to be pretty *sure-footed* with this stuff.

P: And you're pretty *strong-willed*!

M: Bravo, Patrick! Can you think of some more? How about listing some qualities of people that you happen to like …

P: Oh, that's easy … They're *mild-mannered*, they're *kind-hearted*, *quick-witted*, *open-minded* …

M: And those you <u>don't</u> like …

P: Well, they're *thick-skinned*, *simple-minded*, *short-sighted*, *dim-witted* …

M: Nice collection! I'd say you're pretty *talented*!

- Joey's a tattletale. He told Mom that I took a piece of candy.
- But weren't you <u>entitled</u> to that candy?
- No.
- Oh … so you were <u>entattled</u>!

the end of the world

The Discovery <u>of</u> the Americas
The fall <u>of</u> the Roman Empire
The Battle <u>of</u> Hastings
The end <u>of</u> the world

Beethoven'<u>s</u> Fifth
Sophie'<u>s</u> Choice
The Devil'<u>s</u> Dictionary
The Queen'<u>s</u> English

M: OK, Patrick … so we have so-called POSSESSIVES expressed in several ways … Considering, for instance, that books have titles, take an example like *The book's title is* Silent Spring, *by Rachel Carson.* How else can we express it?

P: I don't know …

M: Yes, you do. We just finished talking about things like *gummed labels, helmeted police, two-headed monsters, long-stemmed roses,* and so on …

P: Ummm … Oh yeah, it would be *The book is titled* Silent Spring.

M: Fine! And I …

P: …But there's even another way to say it, Marta … an obvious one.

M: What's that?

P: It's *The title of the book is* Silent Spring.

M: Yes … I was just getting to that … You're way ahead of me this time!

P: <u>That</u>'s a switch … So I guess there are <u>three</u> ways of expressing POSSESSIVE …

M: OK, but be careful! It's never as simple as that.

P: What do you mean, Marta?

M: Well, take something easy like *Iraq was invaded* … Can you say *Iraq's invasion?*

P: Sure!

M: Can you talk about the *invasion of Iraq?*

P: Absolutely!

M: Then what about *Iraq is invasioned?*

P: Yikes!

M: Let's start again … How about *the mother of his child.* Is that OK?

P: Sure.

M: … and *his child's mother*?

P: Again, OK.

M: What about *His child is mothered*?

P: Not the same … different meaning! *Mother* is a verb here … the *-ed*'s not the possessive.

M: Good! Possessive *-ed* seems to be restricted. How about "the mother **of** all battles"?

P: OK, Marta, but that one's got a special meaning.

M: Yes … it's a METAPHOR. So *all battles' mother*?

P: Out!

M: Well, how about *the mother **of** great fame*?

P: Fine! … Means "the famous mother."

M: Yes, so what ab—

P: Stop! I know what you're going to ask and it's terrible!

M: What?

P: I can hardly bring myself to even say it … *great fame's mother* … ugh!

M: You're really catching on. So what can you say now about POSSESSION using the PREPOSITION *of*?

P: *Of* is certainly doing a lot of different things. Seems like it's freer than POSSESSIVE *'s* … and *'s* is freer than POSSESSIVE *-ed*, no?

M: Seems like it, Patrick. But think of this as a tentative guess; you'd need to look at a lot more examples before you could call it a real generalization. ▪

POSSESSIVE QUEST

We've spent some amount of time in this chapter looking at ways in which English speakers express the concept of POSSESSION, albeit loosely defined. Listed below are some familiar examples, those using apostrophe s on the left, those using a PREPOSITIONAL PHRASE headed by *of* on the right. See how far you can extend these lists by adding other common examples with which you're familiar. How many of them could go either way? For example, *England's Queen* and *The Queen of England*.

Mother's Day	"The Charge of the Light Brigade"
the cat's meow	The Rock of Gibraltar
Schindler's List	a day of reckoning
California's gold	The Statue of Liberty
a day's journey	The Picture of Dorian Gray
a good night's sleep	the point of no return

The headline below appeared in 2004 in the *Los Angeles Times*, followed by this bit of text: "Georgia's superintendent of schools said Thursday that she would restore the word 'evolution' to the public schools' proposed science curriculum."

Schools Chief's Viewpoint Evolves

Appearing in these four words are three different INFLECTIONS, though phonologically speaking they are identical. Identify them and state what kind of inflection each represents.

CHAPTER NINE

SOUND & SPELLING TWO

consonant clusters, their positions, their constraints, and the loose
relation to spelling; syllabic consonants; British and American spelling;
tense/lax vowels, strong/weak stress, and consonant doubling

consonant clusters

"brick" sounds fine.
"blick"? Never heard of it.
"bnick"?? Impossible!

▶ P: You know, Marta, I often read news stories from around the world that contain some pretty strange place names.

M: "Strange" in what way?

P: Well, they're spelled in a way that you can't pronounce.

M: Can't pronounce? Like what, for example?

P: Like that long river in eastern Europe that runs through parts of Russia and the Ukraine ... I'll have to <u>write</u> the name of it for you, 'cause I can't say it: *Dnieper*

M: C'mon ... At least <u>try</u> to say it!

P: Um ... *duh <u>neeper</u>*? But I'm sure that's not very close to how it comes out in Russian.

M: So what's the problem? I mean, you don't have any trouble with *Kiev* or *Moscow* or *Vladivostok*, do you?

P: 'Course not. But those **d-n** consonants together! How can anyone say them?

M: Well, what about English proper names like *Edna* and *Rodney*, for example? You don't have a problem with the **d-n** sequence in <u>them</u>, do you?

P: Umm ... no, but they're in the <u>middle</u> of a word, not at the beginning!

M: Patrick, can you rephrase that with perhaps a little more precision ... say, in terms of SYLLABLES?

P: OK ... It's *Ed-na* and *Rod-ney*, <u>not</u> *E-dna* and *Ro-dney*. So in English the **d-n** consonant sequence can't occur at the <u>beginning</u> of a SYLLABLE.

M: Seems so, doesn't it? And what about at the <u>end</u> of a syllable?

P: What about it? There's **end**, **send**, **bend** ... No, wait a minute! Those are **n-d**; you're asking about whether English can have words like maybe ... I don't know ... **mudn**, or **bedn**, or **lidn**, or **padn**, or **sodn**?

M: Right … So what about words like **sudden**, **hidden**, **deaden**, **gladden** … I'm sure you can add a bunch more.

P: I don't get it, Marta … Those are all **en**, not the **n** sound.

M: Well, that's the spelling, of course; but is that the way you say them: **sud-en**, **hid-en**, and so on?

P: No! Now that I think of it, we say them more like "sudn," "hidn," but of course we don't write them like that … there'd be a vowel missing.

M: Yes, and we'll come back to that. So where were we?

P: We were talking about no words in English beginning with the sounds **d-n**, like "**Dnieper**."

M: Yes … We call two or more consonants occurring together in one syllable a CONSONANT CLUSTER. Are there any more place names with unusual initial CONSONANT CLUSTERS? What about **Phnom Penh**, the capital of Cambodia … or **Brno**, a large city in the Czech Republic … or **Tbilisi**, the capital of the Republic of Georgia, and lots of others?

P: Some more impossible sounds … er, impossible CONSONANT CLUSTERS!

M: Impossible? For the Cambodians? For the Czechs? For the Georgians?

P: No, but certainly for the English language.

M: Let's just say that English is a language in which such CONSONANT CLUSTERS at the beginning of a syllable do not occur as part of the sound system.

Joseph Haydn:
an eighteenth-century Austrian composer

Joseph Hayden:
a twentieth-century American poet

tongue twisters

"How can you <u>pronounce</u> a word like 'strengths'. . . eight 'consonants' and only one vowel!"

▶ P: OK … so there are CONSONANT CLUSTERS in English like **d-n** and **t-b** that don't belong at the beginning of a SYLLABLE. But what about at the end of a syllable?

M: Are you thinking of anything in particular?

P: Well, yeah … how about the word *strength*, or even more its plural: *strengths*. Talk about CONSONANT CLUSTERS!

M: And how many consonants are in your clusters here?

P: Five, obviously: n, g, t, h, s.

M: Oh, come on, Patrick! <u>Think</u>! Are we talking about sounds or letters of the alphabet?

P: Well, I guess I should know better by now. "<u>Think</u>" … yes. The **t-h** in *strength* stands for only <u>one</u> sound, like in … *think*.

M: And the **n-g** … is that a cluster? Say the words spelled **s-u-m**, **s-u-n**, **s-u-n-g**.

P: OK … *sum, sun, sung* … and I guess the **n-g** in *sung* is only one sound, like the **m** and the **n**.

M: So how many real consonants do you <u>hear</u> now in the CONSONANT CLUSTER at the end of your *strengths* example?

P: Um … only three, I guess: represented in the alphabet by **n-g**, **t-h**, and **s**.

M: Right … and here's another one for you, Patrick. How would you pronounce the plural of the fraction written 5/6, say, in "five-_____" of an inch?

P: Uh … *s-i-k-s* … *s-i-k-s-th* … *s-i-k-s-th-s* … can hardly get my mouth around it!

M: …and how many consonants do you hear <u>this</u> time in the final cluster?

P: Oh … three again: **x, th,** and **s**.

M: Think again … How do you sound out what's written as the letter **x**?

P: I see … It's **k-s**, of course … two consonants … should have known that. So the final cluster that you hear in *sixths* is <u>four</u> consonants: **k, s, th,** and **s**.

M: OK … and as long as we're on the topic of sounds versus letters of the alphabet, is *th* the only example of two letters representing one sound?

P: Well, let's see … oh, no, there's *ph*, as in *phone* … and *sh*, as in *shone* …

M: …and *ch*, as in *chat* … and what about *wh* as in *what*?

P: What? Oh, *what* … and maybe also *where*, *when*, *which*, *why* … But I've heard some people pronouncing these words *hwere*, *hwen*, *hwich* …

M: Yes, I have too … very observant! And what about *zh* … remember *Dr. Zhivago*?

P: Oh! … but how common is that one, Marta?

M: I thought you'd say that! Maybe I'm being a little unfair. *Zhivago* is a TRANSLITERATION from Russian, and the sound *zh* doesn't occur at all in English at the beginning of a word, though occasionally it appears at the end: *garage*, for example.

P: What about in the middle?

M: Ah, the middle … How do you pronounce these? Here, I'll write them for you:

fusion   Asian   cohesion

P: OK … FYU zhon … EY zhon … ko HEE zhon.

M: Yes … tons of those with final *-sion*. And what's a word meaning, roughly, "spare time"?

P: Uh … *leisure*?

M: OK … and what's another name for "blue" … *az—*

P: Um … *azure*? So lots of *zh* sounds, but mostly in the middle of a word.

M: Yes!

P: But why doesn't English spelling use new symbols with just one letter to replace all those with *th*, *ph*, *sh*, *ch*?

M: A lot of it is rooted in the history of the language and would be very resistant to change. But it's an interesting question, Patrick.

The sixth sick sheik's sixth sheep's sick.

... believed to be the hardest tongue twister in English

syllabic consonants

me*ter* or met*re*

cen*ter* or cent*re*

thea*ter* or theat*re*

▶ P: Can I pick up a bit on the SYLLABLE thing, Marta?

M: Shoot.

P: Well, take a word like *center*, spelled c-e-n-t-**e-r** in American English but c-e-n-t-**r-e** in British English, right?

M: Right.

P: OK, and it's a word with two SYLLABLES, but there's something funny about this.

M: Funny?

P: Yeah, because there's the adjective form, *central*, and <u>that</u>'s got two syllables too.

M: Go on.

P: But the adjective is formed by adding the SUFFIX -*al*, isn't it?

M: Yes … so …

P: Well, how can you have a noun like *center/centre* with two syllables, add the one-syllable SUFFIX -*al*, and get *central*, with still only two syllables?

M: OK, now think, Patrick … Where's your syllable break in the word *central*? What are the two halves?

P: Umm … I was gonna say it breaks into *cen* + *tral*, but that doesn't make sense because neither half is either a word or an AFFIX.

M: Right … so then where's the break?

P: I guess it has to be *center* + *al*. But there's still the problem of what happened to the missing syllable. I mean, the word is *central*, not *centeral*.

M: But suppose now that there <u>is</u> no "missing syllable." What assumption of yours would you have to go back and revise?

P: OK. Then I guess *center/centre* would have to be analyzed as one syllable … but what about the *e-r* or *r-e*?

M: What about it? What sound do they represent?

P: Uh … *rrr*? But **r** is a consonant, and a syllable has to contain something like a vowel, doesn't it? Didn't we notice something like that a couple of sessions ago with the **n** sound in *sudden* and *hidden*?

M: Good reasoning, Patrick. Think of **r** and **n** in these examples as consonants with vowel qualities. You can call them SYLLABIC CONSONANTS.

P: But if that's the case, then why don't we spell it **c-e-n-t-r**, leaving off the **e**?

M: Well, it's maybe worth noting that no word in English with final syllabic written **r** is spelled without the final **e**.

P: Then the Brits come closer, don't they, Marta? …'Cause the final -re spelling makes a little more sense, and there are probably lots of words like that.

M: I don't know about "lots," but maybe *metre*?

P: Yeah, with *metric,* or *metrical*.

M: *Theatre*?

P: *Theatrical*!

M: Ready for some more syllabic consonants?

P: Didn't know there <u>were</u> any more.

M: What about *example*? What about *prism*?

P: OK … *prism's* gotta be one syllable, 'cause if you add *-atic*, which is two syllables, you get *prismatic*, which is three. Right?

M: Right! And what's the evidence for the other one? What's a word derived from *example*?

P: I don't know, but it's probably two syllables and *l* is the SYLLABIC CONSONANT. That much I can figure out now.

M: How about *exemplar*?

P: Ah! Yes, I do know that word. So how many SYLLABIC CONSONANTS <u>are</u> there?

M: Well, we have the words *centre*, *circle*, *prism*, and *prison*. That's about it.

P: Four SYLLABIC CONSONANTS … wow!

cycle > cyclic
calibre > calibrate
prism > prismatic
Poetry is opposed to science,
and prose to metre.
Samuel Taylor Coleridge, "Definitions of Poetry" (1811)

weak/strong & tense/lax I

cancelled or canceled focussed or focused

▶ P: It's only a few hundred years since Americans were British subjects. So why can't we all keep spelling words the same way?

M: Even though we're separated by a big ocean?

P: But it's not like we don't travel to each other's countries … plus, they read our books and newspapers and we read theirs …

M: Well, you should know that historically the biggest influence on American spelling is the early nineteenth-century scholar, Noah Webster, who wrote a famous dictionary.

P: Oh … Webster's *Dictionary* … that's what I have!

M: Yes, Patrick, but the original came out two hundred years ago and there've been a lot of revisions since then.

P: Well, it looks like Mr. Webster should have left some English spellings alone, Marta, 'cause you just showed me how British *centre* makes more spelling sense than American *center*, for example.

M: Ah, but "spelling sense" can go the other way too. For example, how would you complete a sentence like "Tom prefers [VERB]-*ing* by train," using the verb *travel*? Can you write it for me?

P: Um … *Tom prefers travelling by train.*

M: Why the double L?

P: No special reason, I guess … could just as well have written it *traveling*.

M: How many syllables in *travel* and where's the main stress?

P: Uh … easy … two syllables and the first one has the stress: *tra- vel*.

M: All right, now try another: Take the verb *compel*, which has an adjective form in -*ing*. How would you complete a sentence like "Tom's argument for taking the train is very _____ing." Write this one too.

P: OK … *Tom's argument for taking the train is very compelling.*

M: Again, why the double L?

P: Has to be double L … That's how it's spelled.

M: Double L in *compelling* and single L in *traveling* … Why the difference?

P: Beats me.

M: Well, how many syllables in **compel** and where's the main stress this time?

P: Oh ... two syllables and the <u>second</u> one has the stress: *com* **-pel**.

M: Anything to conclude so far, at least with these examples?

P: Sure, Marta ... If the final syllable is stressed, the L is doubled before a suffix.

M: Looks like it ... but take a pair with a different consonant and add *-ing* again: **shop** and **develop**. How are they written?

P: Uh ... *shopping* and *developing*.

M: Any comment?

P: Sure ... *shop* is stressed and the final syllable of *develop* is not. So with *-ing* added, the *p* is doubled for *shopping* but not for *developing*.

M: Great! Now what about the verb *elope*, adding *-ing* ... What do you get and how is it written?

P: Um ... *eloping*?

M: So *-lope* and **shop** are both stressed but *eloping* has one *p* and *shopping* has two. Why? What's happening this time, Patrick?

P: I don't know, Marta.

M: Well, what about the sound of the <u>vowels</u> in *elope* and *shop*?

P: Uh, the *o* in *elope* sounds like "oh" and the *o* in *shop* sounds like "ah."

M: Uh huh ... and the descriptive term for the *o* vowel in *elope* is TENSE; the *o* in *shop* is LAX. And what about that *o* in the verb *develop*?

P: You can hardly hear it!

M: Yes, the STRESS on that syllable is WEAK. Think of these in terms of a three-way contrast. First, is the vowel WEAK or STRONG? Second, is the STRONG vowel TENSE or LAX? But we'll come back to this next time.

P: I hope so!

The wayward, unhappy house cleaner: mópping, móping, and trólloping

weak/strong & tense/lax II

combíning
beginníng
determiníng

M: Let's go back to where we left off last time.

P: You mean the stuff about STRESS, and different kinds of vowels?

M: Right … and <u>what</u> kinds of vowels?

P: Uh … TENSE and LAX?

M: Give me an example, Patrick.

P: The ones I remember are *elope* and *shop* … oh, and *develop*.

M: And which is which?

P: OK … the *o* in *elope* is TENSE, and in *shop* LAX … and the *o* in *develop* is WEAK.

M: Yes, but remember that the STRESS LEVELS of STRONG and WEAK apply to the whole syllable. Let's lay these out in some lists of verbs, which might make it a little clearer.

P: OK.

M: Well, here's the layout I've drawn up for you … Strong tense vowels are **in bold** in the first column; strong lax vowels in the second column; and weak vowels in the third.

Strong vowel stress		Weak vowel stress
Tense	Lax	
inháling	*enthrálling*	*équăling*
prepáring	*wárring*	*cóllăring*
compléting	*forgétting*	*trúmpĕting*
revéring	*reférring*	*óffĕring*
recíting	*befítting*	*édĭting*
combíning	*begínning*	*detérmĭning*
elóping	*shópping*	*devélŏping*
dóting	*dótting*	*pilŏting*
confúsing	*bússing*	*fócŭsing*
secúring	*occúrring*	*múrmŭring*

Any comments?

106

P: Yeah ... All the verbs in the first column are spelled with a final *e*: *inhale, complete, secure,* and so on, but none of the verbs in the second column: *enthrall, forget, occur ...*

M: Nice observation! But what about where the consonant doubles, and where it doesn't?

P: Hmm ... TENSE and LAX, STRONG and WEAK ... but only the tense and lax are strong, and the doubling is only after lax vowels. Can't we say this in some simpler way, Marta?

M: OK ... Let's turn it into a little exercise about where you double the consonant and where you don't. Think of it this way:

> *(1) If the vowel preceding suffixation is lax* →_____
>
> *(2) Otherwise (tense vowel, or weak stress)* → _____

How would you fill in the blanks?

P: At the end of (1) I'd write *double*. At the end of (2) I'd write *do not double*. So I guess the double-L "misspellings" of *travelling, travelled, labelling, labelled,* and so on, all represent a violation of rule (2).

M: You got it! And with this you can predict, for example, the correct spelling of an often misspelled word such as *accómmodate*. Compare it with *accúmulate*.

P: I <u>have</u> made that mistake ... but not anymore!

He that travelleth into a country
before he hath some entrance into
the language, goeth to school
and not to travel.
Francis Bacon, "Of Travel" (1625)

PS NINE syllabics and the indefinite article

One of the so-called "standard" rules of English grammar concerning the indefinite article is that *a* is used before words beginning with a consonant (e.g. *a question*) and *an* is used before words beginning with a vowel (e.g. *an easy question*). That's fine as far as it goes, but what about *useful*, as in *a useful tool*; *Ouija*, as in *a Ouija board*; *herb*, as in *an herb garden*? A simple CONSONANT/VOWEL distinction doesn't really work here, so we need something else. Recall what we learned in the previous sessions about the spelling contrasts in American and British English for words like *center* (*centre*), *theater* (*theatre*), etc. and the attention paid to the SYLLABIC CONSONANTS [ɹ̩] as in *metre*, [l̩] as in *circle*, [n̩] as in *prison*, [m̩] as in *prism*. Since all vowels are by definition syllabic, adding in the syllabic consonants, how would you now improve on the standard rule for the use of the INDEFINITE ARTICLE variants *a* and *an*?

The English indefinite article
is <u>an</u> rather than <u>a</u> ...

CHAPTER TEN

WORDS & CATEGORIES

changes in grammatical category: part of speech and +/– stress shift; auto-antonyms; the suffix -ify vs. –ize; use of adjectives as verbs

Day Forty-six
inválid vs. ínvalid

Day Forty-seven
I brake for animals

Day Forty-eight
"dusting" and "seeding"

Day Forty-nine
classifying, categorizing

Day Fifty **productive suffixes**

PS 10
desertification vs. desertization

inválid vs. ínvalid

The Sanitation Department had to <u>refúse</u> more <u>réfuse</u>.
Why can't agriculture <u>prodúce</u> more <u>próduce</u>?
We should <u>presént</u> everybody with a <u>présent</u>.

P: Marta, can we talk a little about some odd stuff with English words?

M: What do you mean "odd"?

P: I mean "odd" like a word that has one spelling but two pronunciations.

M: You mean [bo] as in *bow and arrow* and [baw] as in *bow and scrape*, for example.

P: No. It's where they also have the same meaning.

M: OK, then: the word spelled **v-a-s-e** … It's pronounced [vez] in the States but [vaz] in Britain.

P: No. Maybe it's not <u>quite</u> the same meaning.

M: I feel like I'm in a game of some kind, Patrick. What <u>is</u> this "odd stuff" you're talking about?

P: It's like the word spelled **p-e-r-m-i-t**; if they *permít* you to drive, they give you a *pérmit*.

M: It may be "odd stuff" but it's interesting. Besides the contrast in STRESS—in other words, pronunciation—do they differ in other ways … in PART OF SPEECH, I mean?

P: Oh, yeah … *permít* is a VERB and *pérmit* is a NOUN.

M: Right. Can you think of any other pairs like that?

P: Let's see … OK, maybe *convíct* vs. *cónvict*? Or *impórt* vs. *ímport*, *suspéct* vs. *súspect*? One's a verb, the other's a noun. Probably more where those came from.

M: Yes. So now think for a minute, Patrick. Is this the first time we've encountered pairs of related words that differ by PART OF SPEECH or grammatical category?

P: I think so.

M: What? It was only a short while ago that we were playing around with related pairs like *compute* / *computer*, *fury* / *furious*, and so on.

P: Sure, Marta, but I don't get the connection. In all those examples like *fury* / *furious* you change the grammatical category by <u>adding</u> something—the SUFFIX *-ous*. No suffixes figure in *permít* vs. *pérmit*.

M: You're missing the point—which is the matter of category change. How does it happen?

P: Well, adding a SUFFIX is certainly one way.

M: Yes, and the "odd stuff" you were referring to is another. Take the verb *prodúce*, for example. Can you think of a noun that derives from it?

P: Sure … *production*.

M: What about *próduce*?

P: OK. I get it. But *production* and *próduce* don't mean the same thing.

M: Not exactly, no … though in some core sense, yes. But stay with the notion of category change, Patrick. Earlier we saw how with certain verbs you can do it through suffixation. And now …

P: Now I see with certain verbs you can do it through a change of STRESS. And with a verb like *prodúce* you can do it with both.

M: Congratulations!

"Always suspect everybody."
Charles Dickens, *The Old Curiosity Shop* (1841)
"Round up the usual suspects."
Casablanca (1942 screenplay), spoken by Claude Rains

I brake for animals

▶ M: Remember the examples we saw last time with the verb *produce*, of how you can form new words from it with a different grammatical category?

P: You mean the noun *production*?

M: Yes, and also ... by shifting the STRESS to the first syllable ...

P: Oh yeah, *próduce*.

M: Well, we can also change the grammatical category by doing nothing at all—no suffix, no shift of stress. For example, a familiar bumper sticker reads like this:

I BRAKE FOR ANIMALS

What's the VERB?

P: *Brake*, of course.

M: And what does it mean?

P: In this context it means "apply the brakes"—in other words, "slow down."

M: Any comments to offer on the word *brake* in these two examples: *brake for animals* and *apply the brakes*?

P: Sure. The first one's a verb and the second's a noun.

M: Any idea which comes from which?

P: Well, it would be kind of weird to talk about the <u>use</u> of a tool—like *to brake*—before you have the tool itself—the noun *brake*. So the noun came first, no?

M: Good reasoning. Sometimes you amaze me, Patrick!

P: Give me a break!

M: Calm down! By the way, did you do that on purpose?

P: What do you mean?

M: *Break* and *brake* ... wonderful! They're actually HOMOPHONES—remember?—and even related if you go back a few centuries, but more on that later. What's the grammatical category of *break*?

P: Well, I forget what I just said that got you going ... but in, say, *break a leg* I guess it's a verb.

M: What about the IDIOM *break for coffee* and *take a (coffee) break*?

P: Oh, it's a little like *brake* ... *break* in *break for coffee* is a verb and in *take a break* it's a noun.

M: So again, Patrick, which comes from which?

P: It's got to be the VERB *break* … feels like it can have a more literal meaning, like *breaking* something … maybe *a cup, a pencil, a leg*.

M: That's pretty good for a start. So notice that to get the noun *break* from the verb *break*, or the verb *brake* from the noun *brake*, we didn't have to do anything … no suffix, for example. What's your take on this process? How common do you think it is?

P: Probably very, or you wouldn't be asking, right?

M: OK, but don't take my word for it. I've been making notes on this whole conversation, so let's back up a bit. Here are some of the sentences we've just used; see if you can spot the words like *break* and *brake* that can be used in a different grammatical category … Ready?

P: Fire away, Marta!

M: All right. Here's the first example: *we can also change the grammatical category*.

P: *Change*! Here it's a verb, but it could be a noun, like in *category change*.

M: Great! Here's the next: *that's pretty good for a start*.

P: *Start*! Noun here, but it's got to be from the verb *start*.

M: Next: *what's your take on this process*?

P: *Take*! Got to be the noun from the verb *take*.

M: And the next: *see if you can spot the words*.

P: Easy, *spot*! Probably the verb from the noun.

M: One more: *calm down*.

P: Wow! The ADJECTIVE *calm* is used here as a verb.

M: You're on a *roll*—another one, by the way. But never mind, here's the last one: *no suffix, no shift of stress*.

P: Ha! Two of them! One's *shift* … the noun from the verb, I guess; the other's *stress* … probably also a noun from a verb.

M: So …

P: So I suppose this sort of thing's very common.

M: Go to the head of the class!

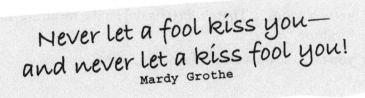

Never let a fool kiss you—
and never let a kiss fool you!
Mardy Grothe

"dusting" and "seeding"

"Like Webster's Dictionary, we're Morocco <u>bound</u>."

From the title song of the movie *Road to Morocco*

P: I wish we didn't have so many ways of changing a word's GRAMMATICAL CATEGORY.

M: What do you mean, Patrick?

P: Well, there's adding a SUFFIX, like changing the verb *convict* into the NOUN *conviction*. But you can change *convict* into another NOUN with a different meaning, *cónvict*, by simply moving the STRESS from the end to the beginning.

M: And don't forget where you don't do anything at all, like *taste, laugh, catch, cover, walk, turn*, etc.—all VERBS that you can also use as NOUNS. And how about NOUNS you can use as VERBS? Remember?

P: Yeah, like, um, *brake, spot* …

M: And *corner, coat, skin, water, hand, pilot, milk, dust, ship* … and so on. There are tons of them. Just for fun, how <u>do</u> you use these as VERBS?

P: OK … **corner** the market, **water** the plants, **hand** me that wrench, **milk** the cow, **ship** it airmail … Is that enough?

M: Sure, but let's take a closer look. What actually happens in **water** *the plants*?

P: The plants get watered; that's obvious, Marta.

M: No. I mean literally. Without using *water* as a verb, what happens?

P: You put *water* <u>on</u> the *plants*.

M: And in **milk** *the cow*, do you put *milk* <u>on</u> the *cow*?

P: [*laughter*] 'Course not. But I see what you're getting at. **Water** *the plants* is like, say, **butter** *the bread*, **oil** *the hinge*, where you put something <u>on</u> something else. **Milk** *the cow* is like maybe **juice** *the orange*.

M: Nice examples! Now what about **dust**? That's an interesting one.

P: How so? Pretty obvious … There's **dust** (NOUN) on the furniture; so you **dust** (VERB) the furniture.

M: Meaning "you take the **dust** off the furniture," right?

P: Of course.

M: All right, so much for "**dusting** the furniture"; what about "**dusting** the crops"?

P: Same thing … No, wait a minute … In *dusting the* <u>*furniture*</u> you take the *dust off*; in *dusting the* <u>*crops*</u> you put the *dust* <u>*on*</u>! It's like *water the plants* and *milk the cow* rolled into one—except that with *dust* it's only one VERB!

M: Yes, and there are some other examples of this kind of thing. What do you find inside of oranges, lemons, grapes?

P: *Seeds*, I guess.

M: And when the seeds are removed, the oranges are what?

P: *Seeded*!

M: Now, what do you sprinkle on the ground if you want to grow some grass?

P: Fertilizer?

M: No! Come on, Patrick …

P: *Seeds* again, grass seeds.

M: So when you sprinkle the seeds, your lawn is what?

P: *Seeded*! Again! I get it now, Marta. It's like *dust*. *Seeded* oranges versus *seeded lawns*—seeds taken out versus seeds put on.

M: Bravo! You've just glimpsed a few of the rare examples of **a word whose meaning contains its own opposite.**

The noun <u>oversight</u> means both "looking closely at something" (from <u>oversee</u>) and "ignoring or forgetting something."
- A misspelling? That's an oversight.
- More misspellings? What's needed is some oversight!

The verb <u>overlook</u> means both "offering a commanding view" of something and "failing to see or notice something."
- The house we want should <u>overlook</u> the ocean!
- Well, don't <u>overlook</u> the price for such a house!

classifying, categorizing

To Scheck, to Schectify, to Cochranize are verbs in all our vocabularies from now on.

Los Angeles Times, October 8, 1995
(at the close of the O. J. Simpson trial)

▶ M: On the subject of how words change grammatical category, I'd like to pick up again on a few things from a while back.

P: I have a short memory, Marta.

M: I can refresh it, Patrick. We talked about similarities and differences like the endings of the adjectives *curious* and *serious*. And also that "the state or condition of being" *curious* is **curiosity**, but "the state or condition of being" *serious* is not **seriosity** … rather, **seriousness**. Ring a bell?

P: Um … OK.

M: But with nothing else to go on, it's hard to predict the suffix, at least with these examples. Yet sometimes, with other examples, you probably can predict. How would you go about arranging different kinds of food in terms of some particular **category** like "vegetable," "fruit," "meat," "bread," etc.? What verb would you use?

P: I'd **categorize** them?

M: Fine! So what did you do? How did you form the verb?

P: Simple … Take the noun **category** and add **-ize**.

M: OK. Now suppose you took foods like apples, broccoli, pork, bread, potatoes, etc., and arranged them in terms of the **class** identified by quantity of calories—say, "high," "low," "none"? What verb would you use in this case?

P: Easy. I'd **classify** them.

M: And how did you form the verb this time, Patrick?

P: Another softball … Take the noun **class** and add **-ify**.

M: Notice the semantic similarity here with **categorize** and **classify**—"causing things to be put in categories or classes." Is the attachment of **-ize** or **-ify** an arbitrary one? Could the attachments have been reversed?

P: What? Let's see … You mean … **categorify**? **classize**? That's awful, Marta!

M: Well, is there anything at all that can be said about choice of SUFFIX here?

P: Maybe the choice has to do with the length of the word … *-ize* for long words, *-ify* for short ones.

M: So how do you go about finding out for sure?

P: We look for other examples, right?

M: Good! Here's a bunch of them for starters:

person-ify	*pressur(e)-ize*
humid-ify	*character-ize*
cod(e)-ify	*alphabet-ize*
solid-ify	*human-ize*
fals(e)-ify	*general-ize*
just-ify	*equal-ize*
pur(e)-ify	*memor(y)-ize*
intens(e)-ify	*popular-ize*
object-ify	*institutional-ize*

Anything to make of this?

P: Well, it can't be just "longer" versus "shorter," since … OK, **institutionalize** is longer than **justify**; but **intensify** is longer than **equalize**.

M: Good. So if length alone doesn't do it, what else can you consider? How are words divided up?

P: Oh, syllables! OK … Looks like words with *-ify* have fewer syllables than words with *-ize*.

M: Look again, Patrick. What about **humid** and **human**, for example—both two syllables? One becomes **humidify**, the other **humanize** … no *humanify*, for example!

P: Oh, right. But at least the one-syllable ones—*code*, *just*, *pure*—take *-ify*, no?

M: Looks like it; and what about the rest?

P: Hmm … Well, I don't see anything but *-ize* on words of more than two syllables, so **it looks like the two-syllable ones can go either way**. 'Cause on the one hand you have **person**, **humid**, **solid**, **intense**, **object**—all two syllables and all taking *-ify*; and on the other hand you have **pressure**, **human**, **equal**—all two syllables and all taking *-ize*.

M: Nice little generalization.

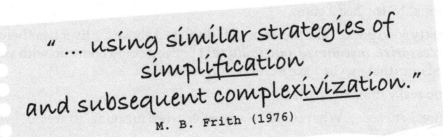

" … using similar strategies of simplification and subsequent complexivization."

M. B. Frith (1976)

productive suffixes
ACCESSORIZE YOUR SYSTEM!

from an advertisement for audio accessories
(cables, antennas, speaker stands, etc.)

This emergency gives us the opportunity to energize, incentivize and free our employees to find innovative ways to serve the company.

Los Angeles Times, with reference to the earthquake of
January 17, 1994

BROWN SUGGESTS THAT PARTY TANGIBILITIZE

Los Angeles Times headline, reporting former Governor Edmund G.
Brown's coinage of a term meaning "to make tangible,"
in reference to the California Democratic Party

M: Quite a few sessions back, we talked about how some suffixes seemed to be more common than others, and ...

P: I remember one, Marta. It was the SUFFIX *-ness*. I think your example was *seriousness*. But you can stick it on almost anything ... Let's see ... uh, *mad-ness*, *together-ness*, *ridiculous-ness*, *halfhearted-ness* ... tons of them!

M: Good, but *-ness* doesn't attach to just anything ... no *book-ness*, *jump-ness*, *under-ness*, for example.

P: Gross!

M: And think again, Patrick, about what we came up with in the last session ... I mean concerning the *-ify* and *-ize* suffixes. One of the two, like *-ness*, is much more likely to be used in forming new words—in other words, much more PRODUCTIVE.

P: Probably *-ize*. Just a guess.

M: Pretty good guess. Take the examples displayed above ... Ever hear before of *accessorize*, *incentivize*, *tangibilitize*? I bet you could come up with your own, and ones that maybe have never occurred before.

P: You really think so, Marta?

M: Sure. Let's see ... What could be a possible word meaning "to create consonants"?

P: Umm ... *consonantize*?

M: Sure! And suppose you wanted a word meaning "to make someone into a Czechoslovak," assuming that could be done, of course?

P: Well, there is no Czechoslovakia any more … but **Czechoslovakize**?

M: Why not? And how about a word meaning "to create an improbability" … probably not a very probable creation, I'll have to admit.

P: Wow! **Improbabilitize**?

M: Hey, Patrick, you've turned into a real **virtuositizer**! One more thing … these are category-changing innovations using familiar suffixes like **-ness** and **-ize**. But you can also do it with lots of words minus <u>any</u> suffixation. Remember, a couple of sessions back, the common examples like **brake** (the verb from the noun), **shift** (the noun from the verb), **calm** (the verb from the adjective)?

P: Sure do.

M: Well, get a load of this … Some years ago a well-known company that manufactures electric razors ran the following advertisement headline:

> ANNOUNCING A NEW DISCOVERY THAT **OBSOLETES** THE WET SHAVE!

Any comment?

P: Yeah. **Obsolete** is an adjective. Never saw it used before as a *verb*!

M: Well, just so you don't think this is one of a kind, here's another ad from the manufacturer of a golf ball that the golfer can supposedly hit a great distance:

> SMALL COMPANY'S NEW GOLF BALL FLIES <u>TOO</u> FAR;
>
> COULD **OBSOLETE** MANY GOLF COURSES

P: Really jumps out at you, doesn't it?

M: Yes … bit of a shock, I'd say. And a clever device for an advertiser to grab your attention!

P: Talk about "category-changing innovations"!

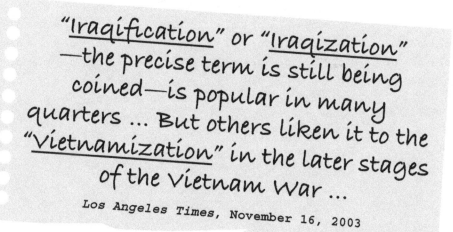

"Iraqification" or "Iraqization"—the precise term is still being coined—is popular in many quarters … But others liken it to the "Vietnamization" in the later stages of the Vietnam War …

Los Angeles Times, November 16, 2003

PS TEN desertification vs. desertization

In Day 49 we took a close look at the CAUSATIVE SUFFIXES *-ify* and *-ize*, as exemplified in pairs like *humid-ify/human-ize*. These verbs can undergo further (quite common) suffixation that turns them into nouns denoting "state" or "condition": *humidifi(c) -ation* and *humaniz-ation*.

Two *-ification/-ization* scientific terms appear in news dispatches that have occasionally surfaced over the past decade: ***desertification*** and ***desertization***. Both are used in reference to the steady expansion of desert areas in various parts of the world. However, one of them refers to change induced by climate-driven factors such as drought, the other to change attributable to human activity such as deforestation and development. Try presenting this information to others at random and then asking them to guess which term refers to which. Tally the responses as you proceed and discover whether the guesses are purely random or whether they are influenced in one way or the other. If they <u>aren't</u> random, do you think there is anything inherent in the <u>structure</u> or <u>form</u> of the words ***desertification*** and ***desertization*** that might offer a clue?

CHAPTER ELEVEN

"who" and "whom" in embedded sentences; queclaratives; question tags and tag
questions; multiple wh- questions; bridge verbs; wh- constructions & discourse function

Day
Fifty-one

talk to who(*m)ever comes by ...

Day
Fifty-
two

What difference does it make?

Day Fifty-three

Let's look at it, shàll wé?

Day Fifty-four

Who hit who?

PS 11

Who do you think you are!

Day Fifty-five

What big teeth you have!

talk to who(*m)ever comes by ...

A certain young man never knew
Just when to say <u>whom</u> and when <u>who</u>;
"The question of choosing,"
He said, "is confusing;
I wonder if <u>which</u> wouldn't do?"

Christopher Morley, "The Unforgivable Syntax," in *Mince Pie* (1919)

▶ P: You know, Marta, we've been using all kinds of questions in these conversations of ours, but we haven't said much about them, especially those where you have to decide whether it's *who* or *whom*.

M: Ah yes ... WH-QUESTIONS, along with *what, when, where, why, whose* ... even *how*. But *who* is alone, of course, in having the alternative *whom*.

P: What do you mean, "alternative"? *Who* and *whom* aren't interchangeable, are they?

M: You tell <u>me</u>, Patrick.

P: Well, suppose you remark that `Whys & Therefores` is a good source for stuff about the English language and someone else replies, *Who says so?* ... or even a bit sarcastically, *Says who*! But <u>***Whom*** says so</u>, or *Says <u>whom</u>*, never!

M: Why not?

P: Well, let's see ... I guess in *Who says so?* *who* is questioning the SUBJECT of the verb *says*.

M: So what's an example of where you would use <u>***whom***</u> in a question?

P: Umm ... OK ... How about *Whom do you know*?

M: But can you imagine yourself ever actually saying <u>***Whom*** do you know</u>?

P: Hmm ... Sounds kind of stilted. I'd use *who*, I guess.

M: Sure. In conversation you tend to be informal. But in <u>formal</u> writing it's a little different, as in perhaps a newspaper report that *They wonder **whom** the people will elect*.

P: ...and *Who will they elect?* is fine, of course.

M: Well, are the two *who*'s functioning in the same way in *Who says so?* and *Who will they elect?*

122

P: No … they can't be; one's SUBJECT (*Who says* …), the other OBJECT (*Who … elect? … elect who?*). And I can also say *Who elects who?* Again two different *whos*.

M: How about *Who votes for who?* … or *for whom?* What are *who* and *whom* doing here?

P: Uh … *whom* and the second *who* are both OBJECT of *for*, which is a PREPOSITION. So I guess *whom* can only serve as OBJECT (of both VERBS and PREPOSITIONS), whereas *who* is SUBJECT but can also occur, informally, as OBJECT.

M: Sounds pretty reasonable to me, but let's keep going. Suppose you ask the question *Who(m) should I vote for?* and I reply *Vote for whomever appeals to you.* Any reaction?

P: Doesn't sound quite right, Marta, but I don't know why.

M: Well, what's *whomever* doing here?

P: Umm … I guess it's OBJECT of the PREPOSITION *for*.

M: Really? Then what about the VERB *appeal*?

P: Oh! … *whomever appeals* … no, that's not right. What's going on?

M: Think of it this way, Patrick: What's the internal structure of *wh … appeals to you?*

P: Well, for one thing, I guess the *wh-* thing is SUBJECT … so it should be *whoever appeals* … but the whole phrase *whoever appeals to you* is OBJECT of the PREPOSITION *for*, so why isn't it *whomever?*

M: Look again … What kind of sentence have you got here?

P: Hmm … Well, it's really a sentence inside of a sentence, 'cause the person you *vote for* is expressed in the form of another sentence: *whoever appeals to you.*

M: Bravo! You could sort of lay it out as *Vote for [Whoever appeals to you].*

P: I get it! So what determines the *who-* or *whom-* form here is what's in the inside sentence!

Don't ask what are questions, ask what do questions, don't ask why questions, ask how questions.

Karl Popper, quoted by Bernard Levin in the *Sunday Times*, April 16, 1989

What difference does it make?

Where is it written in the sky that we have to learn grammar by memorizing rules?

M: By the way, in that stuff about *who* and *whom* that we discussed in the last session, did anything strike you as kind of odd?

P: Not off hand … Why?

M: Well, what about words like *who* and *whom*, and *what* and *where* … WH-WORDS? What do we use them for?

P: To ask questions, of course!

M: OK, so then what about your example? You said something like "A guy named Bill remarks that `Whys & Therefores` is a good source of information about English, and his friend, Lynne, replies, *Who says so*?" Is Lynne asking a simple question here?

P: Well, she could be, I suppose … but more likely she's challenging the accuracy of Bill's statement. She'd make it even stronger by coming back with *Says who!*

M: Can *Says who!* be taken as a question at all?

P: Not very likely, I guess. So are we talking now about just some little obscure thing in the language? Otherwise, who cares, Marta?

M: Ha! Say that again!

P: What … *who cares?* … Oh! In other words, I'm really saying *Nobody cares*. Still seems like no big deal, though. *What difference does it make*?

M: I don't believe what I'm hearing! Do you keep doing this on purpose, Patrick?

P: Doing what? … oh! …again! In other words, *It doesn't make any difference* … but I guess it really does.

M: So what's really happening in all these questions?

P: Well, they all <u>look</u> like questions, but they're really not. They're more like

124

statements … negative statements. So is it like using question <u>form</u> to say something with the <u>meaning</u> of a negative?

M: Yes. Can't argue with that … or maybe: ***Can anybody argue with that?***

P: Hmm … This is starting to get interesting. So we can do the same thing with YES-NO QUESTIONS … I mean, using question form to make a negative statement? But ***why have so many uses for question form?***

M: Say that again!

P: ***Why have … Why (do we) have*** … Wow! Another negative statement … with just ***why*** and a VERB!

M: ***Why not?*** And ***why <u>not</u> have different uses?*** Language is rich in this sort of thing, Patrick.

P: …and a <u>positive</u> statement with ***why <u>not</u>*** and a VERB … or just ***why not?*** But it still seems like a bit of overkill. As I said before, ***since when does language need so many different uses for question form?***

M: Wonderful! It doesn't stop! Think of what you just said … Are you asking a real question?

P: Um … I suppose not; it'd be funny to answer with something like ***since 1600***. I guess I'm really questioning ***whether language needs those different uses***, implying that it doesn't—the negative.

M: Uh huh … but suppose instead of ***since when does language need*** … you said ***since when has language needed so many different uses***?

P: Well, now it's ambiguous … One meaning is a straight question calling for the ***since 1600*** kind of answer, but the other is the negative statement. These examples with ***since*** are really odd, Marta.

M: What do you mean?

P: Look what happens with just a change in verb form: ***has needed*** versus ***does need***. One sentence is ambiguous; the other isn't.

M: Very perceptive! ▪

> What is left when honor is lost?
>
> Publilius Syrus (1st century BC), Maxim 265

Let's look at it, shàll wé?

I'm late, <u>aren't I?</u>
You're angry, <u>aren't you?</u>
S/he's here, <u>isn't s/he?</u>
We're early, <u>aren't we?</u>
They're gone, <u>aren't they?</u>
It works, <u>doesn't it?</u>
They sing, <u>don't they?</u>

n'est-ce pas?
¿verdad?
non è vero?
nicht wahr?

P: Marta, I've been thinking that English grammar has a bit of complicated stuff that it really doesn't need.

M: Oh, **you think** so, **dò yóu?**

P: Yes, but I guess **I sound** a little presumptuous, **dón't Ì?**

M: No, but tell me what "complicated stuff" you have in mind, **wòuld yóu?**

P: OK, **let's look** at it, **shàll wé?** … I mean English compared with a few other familiar languages like French, Spanish, Italian, German … ones that I happen to know a few words in.

M: Sure … but **we're** starting to play a little game here, **áren't wè?** It's leading up to something, I can tell.

P: Well … think about familiar little expressions, **wìll yóu**, like **n'est-ce pas?** in French or **non è vero?** in Italian or **¿verdad?** in Spanish or **nicht wahr?** in German. **You don't** happen to know what those foreign expressions really <u>mean</u>, **dò yóu?**

M: What do they <u>mean</u>, **you're asking?** What do <u>you</u> think they mean, Patrick?

P: I'm asking <u>you</u> … **It's** tricky, **isn't ìt?** … since you can have umpteen different kinds of little endings to an English sentence that all get translated as **n'est-ce pas?** in French, for example.

M: Apparently, **you think**, **dón't yòu**, that <u>every</u> "little ending" to an English sentence has a **n'est-ce pas?** translation in French or a **¿verdad?** in Spanish, or …

P: OK, not <u>every</u> ending … just the ones with little tags like **you are, áren't yóu? it is, ìsn't ít? he does, dòesn't hé?, they can, càn't théy?** … and so on.

M: Those "little tags" are QUESTION TAGS, **by the way**, and the whole sentence is a TAG QUESTION. But you're saying all four with the same TONE LEVEL patterns. (**You are, áren't yòu?**) Have you noticed? I mean, think of the two **aren't you?**s that we just used.

P: You mean *you are, àren't yóu?* What about them, Marta? I don't understand.

M: Then let me write them for you, maybe with something more added, **OK**?

> *You're an athlete, àren't yóu?* (I'm not sure)
>
> *You're an athlete, áren't yòu?* (I'm pretty sure)

P: …and what about if you're sure or not sure that I'm <u>not</u> an athlete?

M: Oh! Right! Here … *You're not an athlete, àre yóu?* (I'm not sure)

> *You're not an athlete, áre yòu?* (I'm pretty sure)

P: OK, I see what you're getting at … but a Spanish speaker would end these sentence pairs with just a simple *verdad?* … *¿verdad?*

M: Not quite, Patrick … It would be more like this: *Tú no eres atleta, ¿verdad?* *(I'm not sure)* *¿Verdad que tú no eres atleta?* (I'm pretty sure)

P: Yes … interesting … but *you have to admit*, *dòn't yóu*, that English QUESTION TAGS are a lot more complicated than a simple *¿verdad?* … no matter <u>where</u> you stick it!

M: I suppose so. But when any language seems "complicated" in one area it always seems "simple" in another. Since you brought up the Spanish example, remember that Spanish verbs have much more INFLECTION to be learned. Here … I've written them out for you using the verb *work*, or *trabajar*:

> (yo) trabajo   I work
> (tú) trabajas   you work
> (él/ella) trabaja   he/she works
> (Usted) trabaja   you (formal) work
> (nosotros) trabajamos we work
> (vosotros) trabajáis   you work
> (ellos/ellas) trabajan they work

Any comments?

P: Well, I guess it's maybe a trade-off … lots of, um, INFLECTION in Spanish, French, Italian, German, etcetera, but lots of *don't we?*, *shouldn't I?*, *have you?*, *will she?*, etcetera, in English.

M: "Trade-off" is a nice way of putting it! ▪

> Cold outside, <u>isn't it?</u>
> Lots of snow on the ground,
> <u>isn't there?</u>

Who hit who?

*which did <u>who</u> attach
when,
<u>where</u>,
<u>why</u>,
<u>how</u>,
and with <u>what</u>?

P: I was thinking again about the **who/whom** words we were talking about a few sessions ago.

M: Yes, I remember, Patrick. What about them?

P: Well, not just **who/whom**, but other **wh-** words too.

M: And …

P: OK … I was driving in town yesterday with a friend of mine when another car ran a 'STOP' sign and we had a little accident.

M: **Who** hit **who where?**

P: Excuse me, Marta, but don't you mean "**Who hit <u>whom</u>**?"

M: Not unless I want it to sound a bit formal. We talked about this. Remember? Anyway … **Who hit who where?** … **when?** … **how?** We already know the **why**.

P: That's exactly what the insurance people asked. But how can you put so many **wh-** words into one sentence?

M: Not so fast, Patrick! The only "real" sentence was **Who hit who where? When** and **how** stood by themselves.

P: Well, suppose you asked **Where did who hit who?** To me that sounds terrible.

M: Me too! So now what's happening?

P: Don't have a clue … anything to do with what's being questioned? … and the verb?

M: Good thinking! What do the two *who*s question in *Who hit who?* ... I mean in relation to *hit*?

P: You mean like SUBJECT and OBJECT?

M: Right. Those are pretty basic functions ... and if they're <u>already</u> being filled with a *wh-* form, then superimposing an additional <u>non</u>-basic *where* (or *when* or *how* or *why*) seems not to feel right ...

P: ...and even though I can still get some kind of meaning out of ... um ... say, *Why did who hit who?*

M: Uh huh ... nothing surprising about that. But let's go back a bit. With regard to the insurance people, *when did you say you had the accident?*

P: Well, as soon as I got them on the phone, of course.

M: No ... I mean the accident itself!

P: Oh, yesterday about 4 pm ... That's interesting, Marta.

M: What?

P: Your *when* question ... two different answers possible.

M: Depending on what's being questioned.

P: Yes ... the time of the saying or the time of the accident! Is it the verb *say* that allows this?

M: ...and *tell*, *report*, other verbs of "saying." Nice observation!

P: Start looking at *wh-* questions and you open up a Pandora's Box!

M: We've hardly scratched the surface.

He: Did you, by chance, call me this morning around eleven?
She: No ... <u>why</u>?

What big teeth you have!

SALLY FORTH By Greg Howard

Sally Forth © King Features Syndicate

P: On the subject of *wh-* QUESTIONS, I hear people say things all the time like ***What nice shoes you're wearing!*** But that can't be a question, can it, Marta?

M: You tell me.

P: Well, as a question, it would have to be *What nice shoes **are you** wearing?* not ***you're*** *(you are)* …

M: Good thinking, Patrick! What do you make of it?

P: Umm, I suppose in saying ***What nice shoes you're wearing!*** he or she was offering a compliment.

M: Right, but what about the <u>form</u> of the sentence? You've already noticed that it's not QUESTION form, and it's certainly not in the form of a STATEMENT; nor is it a DIRECTIVE, as in *Wear your nice shoes.*

P: The <u>form</u>, huh … beats me.

M: Well, what's the punctuation if you put it in writing?

P: Oh, you mean like an EXCLAMATION POINT? OK … the <u>form</u> of ***What nice shoes you're wearing!*** is EXCLAMATION. So it's a matter of both the form and what it's used for … in this case, I guess, to express a compliment.

M: Yes … and here's another: suppose I say to you ***I wonder what time it is***. What's the form? Is it a QUESTION?

P: Yes … uh, no. It's a STATEMENT. But it's really the <u>same</u> as a question … like asking ***What time is it?***

M: And if you say to a friend of yours *Do you know what time it is?* would an appropriate response be "yes"?

P: Not unless that friend wants a kick in the shins! The *Do you know* … question is <u>another</u> way of asking *What time is it?*

M: How about if I say, *Would you mind handing me that newspaper?* What am I really doing?

P: Well, the <u>form</u> looks like a YES/NO QUESTION, but what you're really saying is something like *Please hand me that newspaper*.

M: Which is …

P: Um … a REQUEST?

M: Sure. And remember the so-called "questions" from a couple of sessions ago like *What difference does it make? Can anybody argue with that? Who says we have to?* and so on. QUESTION <u>form</u> again, but …

P: Uh … wait … oh, negative STATEMENTS: like "It doesn't make any difference." "Nobody can argue with that." "We don't have to."

M: So what do you make of all this, Patrick?

P: Well, for one thing you can appear to be saying one thing but mean something else.

M: You mean *we're often being a little cagey when we use language?*

P: No, I don't mean that. It's more like the language provides a wide range of devices for various kinds of expression. You can ask a QUESTION, for example, with a STATEMENT like *I wonder if we need help* … and you can make a STATEMENT by asking a QUESTION: *Who says we need help?*

M: …and I can offer a COMPLIMENT with an EXCLAMATION: *How interesting!*

When did Columbus discover the
New World?
Who can answer that?
<u>What time</u> did Columbus discover
the New World?
<u>Who in blazes can answer that!</u>

We've already seen in some of the recent sessions how a single sentence can be interpreted in more than one way, depending on the context. For example, the STATEMENT "You're sitting in Sue's chair" can be taken as a straightforward observation or, more likely, a REQUEST to get up and let Sue have it. Although all of the following sentences are in the form of a DIRECTIVE, their interpretations are different, the possibilities to be chosen from the following:

(a) INVITATION, (b) WARNING, (c) OFFER, (d) SUGGESTION, (e) PROHIBITION, (f) ORDER, (g) RECOMMENDATION, (h) INSTRUCTION, (i) WISH, (j) PLEA.

Match each of the directives with a plausible interpretation and supply what you think could be an appropriate punctuation.

1. (*b*) Look out !

2. ( ) Have some of this cake

3. ( ) Let's go for a walk

4. ( ) Help

5. ( ) Make yourself at home

6. ( ) Go straight ahead and turn right

7. ( ) Cease fire

8. ( ) Don't touch

9. ( ) Have a nice day

10. ( ) Try to get some exercise

11. ( ) What do you think you're doing

CHAPTER TWELVE

WHAT NEXT, YOU IDIOM?

cliché; verb particle and verb preposition; metaphor; "come" and "go"; freeze

Day Fifty-six **a thorny issue**

Day Fifty-seven **Look it up; then look at it**

Day Fifty-eight **Love is fire, love is magic**

Day Fifty-nine **go into a coma, come out of a coma**

PS 12 **this, that, and the other**

Day Sixty **here and there, plus or minus**

a thorny issue

If the shoe fits, take the bull by the horns of the dilemma and open that can of worms while the iron is hot!

with apologies to the modern Irish poet, Paul Muldoon

P: You know, this language of ours sometimes lets us say crazy things.

M: "Crazy things," huh, Patrick?

P: Yeah … like there's the expression "***Look before you leap***," which I guess means you should be a little careful, but ….

M: What's crazy about that?

P: No, let me finish … I've also heard people say "***He who hesitates is lost***." Don't the two sound a little contradictory?

M: Yes, I see what you're getting at. An expression like these, by the way, is often called a CLICHÉ.

P: Never heard <u>that</u> term before. What does it mean?

M: Well, it's not very easy to define … bit of ***a thorny issue*** … Actually, it's the past participle of the French verb *clicher*, which means "to stereotype."

P: Oh, that's sooo helpful, Marta!

M: Sorry about that … Think of a CLICHÉ as an overused or hackneyed expression, like, say, "***pie in the sky***," "***flavor of the month***," "***spill the beans***," "***food for thought***," "***manna from heaven***," "***eat like a horse***" …

P: Are they all about food and eating?

M: Ha! No, just a coincidence. But ***take it from me***: we use them all the time, hackneyed or not. So do you, though you don't realize it. That's ***straight from the shoulder***.

P: ***You're putting me on***, Marta! Are you sure it's not just ***a figment of your imagination***?

M: Oh, no. Of course, my little brother thinks I'm *getting on in years*, but *far be it from me* to *give you a bum steer*, if you *get my drift*.

P: I guess *there's method in your madness*. But about those contradictory CLICHÉS … Is there *more to them than meets the eye*?

M: Oh yes … Hold on now … *Let me put on my thinking cap*. OK, how about *lay your cards on the table* versus *hold them close to your vest*?

P: *No comment*.

M: Then what about *paddle your own canoe* but *two heads are better than one*?

P: A bit *hit or miss*, don't you think?

M: Oh … *you drive a hard bargain*. All right, here's another … *an eye for an eye* but *turn the other cheek*.

P: Body parts! *Just for the record*, can you come up with any more like that?

M: Well, *fasten your seat-belt*. And here we go … *Keep your ear to the ground, your nose to the grindstone, your eye on the prize, your hand on the throttle, a finger in every pie, a foot in the door*, and *your head and shoulders above the rest* … with *a leg up* all the while!

P: [*clapping*] Bravo, Marta!!! But maybe *enough is enough*?

I have laboured to refine our language to grammatical purity, and to clear it from colloquial barbarisms, licentious <u>idioms</u>, and irregular combinations.

Samuel Johnson, *The Rambler*, no.208, 14 March 1752

Look it up; then look at it

You <u>turn</u> us <u>on</u>.
We'll <u>turn</u> you <u>on</u>.

Newspaper ad for a television station

You **<u>take off</u>**
at night.
We <u>take off</u> 20%.

Airline advertisement

▶ M: Can we pick up on a couple of expressions from the last session?

P: You're the boss, Marta!

M: Come on now! This is supposed to be a collaborative effort. Anyway, at one point you said, "*You're **putting me on**"*; then I said, "*Let me **put on my thinking cap**.*" Remember?

P: Yeah, I think so.

M: Well, what's the verb here, Patrick? Use the **put on my thinking cap** example.

P: It's **put**, I guess.

M: Really? Then what's **on my thinking cap**? Is that a reference to where the "putting" took place? In other words, is it a unit, or—recalling the term we've been using since the first week—a CONSTITUENT?

P: No. 'Course not, 'cause **on** feels like it "goes with" **put**, not with **my thinking cap**.

M: OK, but can you say what you just said using real terminology instead of "goes with"?

P: Sure … **put** and **on** here are a unit, a … a … a <u>CONSTITUENT</u>!

M: Yes. The verb consists of both **put** and **on** … an example of what's often called a PHRASAL VERB.

P: I'll try to remember that. But something still bothers me. Let's just talk now about "**putting on a cap**." Suppose you say to me, "**Put on your cap**" and I hesitate; then you say, "Go on … **put it on**."

M: And?

P: Well, if **put on** here is a so-called CONSTITUENT, then how come you can split it up? I mean, shouldn't I be saying "Go on … **put on it**"?

M: Good thinking, Patrick! But often constituents <u>can</u> be split apart, and without really losing their "togetherness," so to speak. I can also say "**Put your cap on**," for example. So do you see what's going on here?

P: Not really.

M: Yes, you do. Look … *Put your cap on* is OK, *Put it on* is OK,
   Put on your cap is OK, but *Put on it* is <u>not</u>. So …

P: Oh, OK. Both noun stuff and a pronoun can split the phrasal verb but only the noun stuff can come after. But why, Marta?

M: Why what?

P: Why is it like this? Why <u>don't</u> we say *Put on it*?

M: I was afraid you'd ask me that. It's a very tough question to answer … that is, if there really <u>is</u> an answer.

P: And, of course, *put on*'s not the only PHRASAL VERB in the language, right, Marta?

M: How'd you guess? There are lots … try *look up* (*a number*), *take off* (*a hat*), *try on* (*a shoe*), *clean out* (*a drawer*), *bring in* (*a paper*), *turn down* (*an offer*), and so on. And they all work the same way as *put on*, as you might guess.

P: Uh … you mean like *look it up*, *take it off*, *try it on*, *clean it out*, *bring it in*, *turn it down* …

M: Right. But don't get carried away quite yet. What about these examples: **stay off** *the grass*, **believe in** *science*, **look at** *the sunset*, **care for** *the sick*, **call on** *my neighbor*, **come by** *the house*, **approve of** *a deal* …

P: So these are different? *Look* <u>up</u> *the title*, say, is different from **Look** <u>at</u> *the title*, except for the meaning? In what way?

M: How soon we forget … Put them to the test!

P: Oh, sure … Umm … *Look the title up* is OK … but *Look the title at* … Terrible!

M: And try inserting a MODIFIER, like *quickly* into the phrasal verb … What do you get?

P: Uuuh … **Look** *quickly* **at** *the title*, and … umm … *Look* *quickly* up *the title*. No!

M: So, in terms of CONSTITUENCY …

P: It's *look up* | *the title* … but **look** | **at** *the title*.

M: Anything more to say?

P: Yeah … it looks like there's more than one kind of PHRASAL VERB.

M: Yeah!

When your <u>output</u> is more than your <u>income</u>, your <u>upkeep</u> may be your <u>downfall</u>.

Love is fire, love is magic

... a work that neither the wrath of love, nor fire, nor the sword, nor devouring age shall be able to destroy

Ovid, *Metamorphoses*, XV, 1.871

▶ P: Since all that PHRASAL VERB stuff in the last session, I'm now beginning to hear phrasal verbs every time somebody opens his mouth!

M: For example?

P: OK, just a short while ago I overheard a woman arguing that she was so ***burned up*** about some political thing that she was ready to ***spark off*** a rebellion. But right away somebody else said he'd be ready to ***snuff*** it ***out***.

M: Seems like you've really become attuned to this kind of thing, Patrick. Interesting occurrence: ***burn up***, ***spark off***, ***snuff out***. The woman was probably ***smoldering*** with anger. I can imagine her ***spitting fire***, and ***smoke coming out of*** her ears.

P: I can tell you're leading up to something, Marta.

M: Guess!

P: OK, it's pretty obvious ... The ***sparks***, ***smoke***, ***burning***, ***smoldering***, and so on, do have something in common ...

M: Which is ...

P: **Fire**, of course.

M: And what was the feeling of the woman?

P: **Anger**!

M: Yes. All of those fire-related expressions are called METAPHORS, and in this case metaphors for "anger." So in this sense you could say that ... that ...

P: **Anger is fire**?

M: Right on! But "fire" metaphors aren't limited to just "anger." What do you make of expressions like *That **old flame in their marriage** has died out*, or *She **carries*** *the torch* for him, or *Their meeting* **kindled strong feelings** *in them both?*

P: Pretty obvious … In these cases **fire** provides a METAPHOR for **love** … **Love is fire** here.

M: Yes, it's very common. Even Shakespeare, in *As You Like It*: "*and then* **the lover, sighing like a furnace** …"

P: So, **anger** and **love** … Is that the extent of the **fire** METAPHOR?

M: Well, when you started this conversation with the PHRASAL VERB stuff, you sounded pretty **fired up**, like your enthusiasm had been **ignited**, so I was looking for ways to **fan the flames**. The last thing I wanted to be was a **wet blanket**.

P: I'm impressed! Wow! You answered my question, Marta. So now it's, what … **Enthusiasm is fire**?

M: Why not?

P: So is **fire** the only concept that figures in METAPHORS? Can **love**, say, be something besides **fire**? I mean, what about when a guy says, **I'm crazy about Mary**?

M: Good thinking. Let's say your "guy" **raves about Mary** … He's **wild about her** … He **went out of his mind** over her … So what's **love** now?

P: Well, it's not **fire** … How about **insanity**?

M: Or **madness**! And if Mary **casts a spell** over him … **He's entranced** … He's **charmed** by her … **She's bewitching** … **Love** here is what?

P: **Magic**! Where does it stop?

M: It doesn't, Patrick. METAPHOR is everywhere … we've hardly begun. And don't forget the MIXED METAPHORS like **window into the future** from many sessions ago. But maybe this is enough for now. ■

Love in your hearts as idly burns
As fire in antique Roman urns.
Samuel Butler (1600-80), Hudibras

Love is indestructible,
Its holy flame forever burneth;
Robert Southey, The Curse of Kehama (1810)

go into a coma, come out of a coma

For men may come and men may go, But I go on forever.

Alfred, Lord Tennyson (1809-92), "The Brook"

▶ P: Marta, I've been intrigued by something that's come up more than once in these sessions.

M: And what's that?

P: Um … Last time you conjured up the METAPHOR of a guy "*going out of his mind*" over some girl and before that you referred several times to something "*coming to mind*," so to speak.

M: Yes, I remember. Go on …

P: Well, it's this *coming* and *going* stuff. And I've heard other people say things like *They came to an understanding*, *Kim went into a coma*, *An idea came to me*, *Something went wrong*, and so on.

M: Yes, IDIOMS using the verbs *come* and *go*. So what's the "intrigue" about?

P: Well, it certainly seems like there's something systematic about it … I mean, about which one we use in which expression, or IDIOM, as you call it.

M: Seems so, doesn't it? "Systematic" is a good way of putting it, Patrick. Take your example of *Kim went into a coma* … What's the opposite? Kim did what?

P: *Kim came out of a coma* … of course.

M: Keep going … What's another way of saying "The motor died"?

P: Uh … *The motor went dead*, I guess.

M: Fine, so all someone did was plug the motor back in and it … it …

P: …*it came back to life*! Hmmm. Certainly nobody would ever say, "The motor *came* dead" or "The motor *went* back to life." Can't be just an accident. So what's going on, Marta?

M: You can figure that one out. Think of IDIOMS like *The bread went stale*, *The butter went rancid*, *The cat went astray*, *The business went bankrupt*, *The family went nuts* …

P: Oh, those poor people!

M: I'm not finished! … Now consider *Marie's dreams came true*, *Herb's facial color came back*, *Linda came into a lot of money*, *Larry came to his senses*, *The family came to realize their mistakes*, and then *They all came to an understanding*.

P: So *come* is positive and *go* is negative?

M: Really? Then what about *They went to sleep*? What's negative about that …

under ordinary circumstances, I mean? Or *She went into a trance*. Trances don't have to be negative.

P: Now I'm really baffled!

M: Let me try something different, Patrick. What's normal body temperature, in Fahrenheit terms?

P: It's 98.6°, but what's that got …

M: Hold on! Suppose someone took your temperature an hour ago and found it to be 100°. What did it do?

P: Oh … *It went up*.

M: Now suppose instead that your temperature <u>was</u> 100°, somebody just took it, and now it's 98.6°. What did it do this time?

P: Ha! *It came down*. I get it. And if my temperature was 98.6° but now it's 98°, *it went down* … Likewise, if it was 98° but now it's 98.6°, *it came up*.

M: So what's going on here? Anything "systematic"?

P: Well, 98.6° is <u>normal</u> body temperature, so the use of *come* and *go* here refers to movement toward or away from the norm, right?

M: Sounds pretty good to me … And what about all those IDIOMS … like *She went into a trance and soon came out of it*?

P: Same thing … A trance is not a normal state. Food being stale, sour, bad, rancid is not normal, and so on. But what about *She came into a lot of money*? I don't think you could call <u>that</u> "normal."

M: Good thinking. "Normalcy" certainly doesn't apply to that one … something else going on here. So what's your take on these: *Bill Clinton came through a lot*.
   Bill Clinton went through a lot.

P: <u>That</u>'s interesting … The idiom with *came* is maybe a little more likely to come from a Democrat, the one with *went* from a Republican.

M: Yes … feels like that, doesn't it? So it's like you're making an "evaluation" of some kind: a positive one with *came*, negative—or maybe neutral—with *went*. Probably something similar with *The event came/went off as expected* … even *Clinton had to over<u>come</u>/under<u>go</u> a lot*.

P: Normal states, evaluations … *come/go* idioms are a little more complex than simple positive and negative.

M: Right. And here are two more for the grand finale: A couple of planes flying around developed a little engine trouble. *One plane came down* but *The other plane went down*.

P: "One plane landed" but "The other plane crashed"! Wow!

"Will you come here, or shall I go there?"

here and there, plus or minus

The Pepper and Salt Association wants to turn the English language outside in. The cheek-in-tongue movement, based in Alabama, Birmingham, wants phrases changed caboodle and kit. People will listen to roll 'n' rock, eat butter and bread, and travel fro and to.

Quoted in *Grit*

P: Marta, can I bring up something about the ***come/go*** IDIOMS from the last session?

M: Shoot …

P: OK, every time the two verbs occur together it seems like it's always ***come and go***, ***coming and going***, ***came and went***, and so on.

M: Well … yes.

P: But why? By the law of averages you might expect to hear at least an occasional ***go and come***, ***going and coming*** … no?

M: That wouldn't be surprising. We probably do have some familiar expressions where ***come*** and ***go*** could occur in either order. But what about *easy* ***come***, *easy* ***go***, or *March* ***came in*** *like a lion and* ***went out*** *like a lamb*?

P: Hmmm … *easy* ***go***, *easy* ***come*** … ***went out*** *like a lamb and* ***came in*** *like a lion* … Nope!

M: Or let's shift gears for a second, Patrick … Take idioms like ***here and there***, ***this*** *and* ***that***, ***near*** *and* ***far***, ***hither*** *and* ***thither*** … Any comments?

P: Well, it would sure sound funny to say ***that*** *and* ***this***, ***there*** *and* ***here*** … I guess it has something to do with the person who's speaking.

M: Sounds good so far … So <u>now</u> what about ***come and go***, ***coming and going***?

P: Oh, I get it, Marta … toward the speaker and away from the speaker. So ***come*** is movement toward "***here***" and ***go*** is toward "***there***." And I guess ***this*** is "***here***," in some sense, and ***that*** is "***there***" … and also ***near*** is close to "***here***" and ***far*** is "***there***" … Is that what you're driving at?

M: If it makes sense. So can you form some kind of generalization at this point for the word order that we're seeing here?

P: Yeah … simple … the "***here***" related stuff precedes the "***there***" related stuff.

M: Yes, or maybe better, **close to speaker precedes farther from speaker**.

P: And I've been obeying this principle without even knowing about it!

M: So has everybody else, Patrick! Idioms of this kind with a fixed order are often called FREEZES. But bear in mind that we're talking here about <u>tendencies</u> … You do hear an occasional *far and near*, *going and coming* …

P: That's good … I'd hate to think of myself as a robot.

M: So would I. Anyway, all these FREEZES are related to SPACE or LOCATION. There's more to say on that subject, but for now let's look at word order in some other FREEZES. Think about these: *now and then*, *sooner or later*, *today and tomorrow*, *yesterday and the day before*, *tomorrow and the day after* … Any thoughts?

P: Well, the previous ones had to do with SPACE … These are about TIME.

M: Care to go on?

P: OK … I guess **closer to "now" precedes farther from "now."**

M: I'll buy that … So far we've talked about FREEZES concerning space and time. Offhand, can you think of any referring to something else? They're very common, you know.

P: Let me think … umm … *plus or minus*? *win or lose*?

M: …and *for or against* … *pro and con* … *now or never* … What are these about?

P: Uuhh … I guess maybe **positive before negative**?

M: Not bad … How about *one or two*, *once or twice*, *singular and plural*, *Snow White and the Seven Dwarfs*?

P: Easy … **singular before plural!**

M: You're getting pretty good at this, Patrick … Next, *father and son*, *mother and daughter*, *parent and child*, *cat and kitten* …

P: OK … **adult first?**

M: Why not? One more set … *sun and moon*, *bow and arrow*, *car and driver*, *horse and carriage* …

P: That's a tough one … hmm … I don't know … What do *sun*, *bow*, *car*, and *horse* have in common?

M: You might think of them as a kind of "power source." Also maybe even *gin* in *gin and tonic*.

P: Power source, huh? Oh … OK … so **the power source comes first**.

M: Good enough.

this, that, and the other
hook, line, and sinker
lock, stock, and barrel

PS

TWELVE this, that, and the other

Here's an extended list of the three-place "freezes" that appeared at the end of Day 60:

this, that, and the other

hook, line, and sinker

hop, skip, and a jump

stop, look, and listen

lock, stock, and barrel

fair, fat, and forty

ifs, ands, or buts

tall, dark, and handsome

signed, sealed, and delivered

beg, borrow, or steal

eat, drink, and be merry

calm, cool, and collected

men, women, and children

land, sea, and air

Try saying these with their three items in a different order: for example,

sinker, line, and hook

dark, handsome, and tall

be merry, drink, and eat

cool, collected, and calm

If they now don't sound "right," can you think of a possible reason (unfamiliarity aside), and also a reason that would apply to the whole list? If you come up with something concerning the third item in that list, is there anything else that could apply to the ordering of the first two items?

CHAPTER THIRTEEN

NEGATIVES ... NEGATIVES ...

Idiomatic expressions using negatives; multiple negatives; subject-verb inversion and negation; lexical negation; negative scope; multiple uses of "any"

Day Sixty-one
We've **hardly** scratched the surface

Day Sixty-two
Little did you realize ...

Day Sixty-three
Never will it ... **Soon** it will ...

Day Sixty-four
any

PS 13
Better late than **never.**

Day Sixty-five
the Zen of any

We've **hardly** scratched the surface

"No the sun shining"
"No I see truck"

Uttered by a young child very early in the English learning experience

▶ M: Remember all those negative prefixes that we talked about a while back?

P: You mean like in, maybe, *unable*, *inability*, *disable* … stuff like that?

M: Yes, and I think now it's about time we took a look at other kinds of NEGATION.

P: But what about those TAG QUESTIONS we looked at … There's plenty of NEGATION with <u>them</u>, **isn't there**?

M: You're right, Patrick! Almost forgot about that. So what else in English do you think of when the word "negative" or "negation" is mentioned?

P: Uh … well, let's see … maybe *don't*, *doesn't*, *didn't*, *shouldn't*, *won't* … and tons more like that?

M: Does it always have to be with the word **not** or the **n't** contraction?

P: I **hardly** think so. Otherwise, you would**n't** be asking me, Marta.

M: Did you do that on purpose … the word *hardly*, I mean?

P: **No** … why?

M: Well, think! Leave it out, and what's left?

P: Um … Oh, I get it … What's left is *I think so* … no more negative. So *I **hardly** think so* and *I **don't** think so* must mean the same thing … and **hardly** here is another NEGATIVE!

M: Let's just say that it has NEGATIVE force. There are other ways to confirm that … I seem to remember you saying when we came in that you **didn't** sleep well last night.

P: Yes, I **hardly slept a wink** … hmm … That's weird, Marta.

M: What's weird?

146

P: *Sleep a wink* ... *I didn't sleep a wink*, *I hardly slept a wink*, but it would sound funny, if I <u>didn't</u> have a sleep problem, to say *I slept a wink*.

M: So what do you make of it?

P: Umm ... that *sleep a wink* is a kind of idiom that occurs only with a NEGATIVE?

M: Or NEGATIVE force. And there are others ... Here, Patrick, feed me these questions that I've written up for you.

P: OK, here goes. Think we'll all be rich some day?

M: *Not a ghost of a chance!*

P: What do you think of that loudmouth in the other room?

M: *Wouldn't give him the time of day!*

P: Are you worried about the price of coffee?

M: *Wouldn't give it a second thought!*

P: Hear about that new stock option?

M: *Wouldn't touch it with a ten-foot pole!*

P: Negatives ... negatives ... they're all around us!

M: We've *hardly scratched the surface!*

- I hear that a few of the protesters do<u>n't</u> pay taxes.
- Yes, but they have a reason for <u>not</u> paying them.
- Oh, you mean they <u>don't</u> <u>not</u> pay taxes for <u>nothing</u>.
- Yes, in other words, it's <u>not</u> for <u>nothing</u> that they <u>don't</u> pay taxes.

Little did you realize ...

Never in the field of human conflict was so much owed by so many to so few.

Winston Churchill, Tribute to the Royal Air Force,
in the House of Commons (1940)

▶ P: This NEGATION stuff is kind of tricky, Marta, don't you think?

M: How so?

P: Well, sometimes a negative in one part of a sentence seems to have an effect on another part of that sentence.

M: NEGATIVE FORCE, yes. But what are you referring to?

P: OK, I happened to notice a sentence in something I was reading, about an aspiring comedian. It went like this: ***Not even*** *when he told a* <u>*very*</u> *funny joke* ***did the audience laugh***. I mean, it didn't say *the audience laughed* … it said ***did the audience laugh***, as if it were a question, which it wasn't!

M: Yes … Nice observation! Do you think it's just a one-of-a-kind little language quirk?

P: I bet it's not, but I can't think right away of another example.

M: Oh, come on; we can make them up. Let's see … ***Not even*** *if you beg* <u>***am I going***</u> ***to*** *give in*, or ***Never*** <u>***have I***</u> *been so full of hope*, or ***At no time*** <u>***did we***</u> *feel put upon*, or ***On few occasions*** <u>***was there***</u> *cause for worry* …

P: OK … I get it. But what about your *few* example? … I tend to think of NEGATIVE words as beginning with the letter **n**: like ***not***, ***never***, ***no***, ***none***, ***neither***, ***nothing*** …

M: Then it's time for a little update, Patrick. What's the opposite of *often, frequently* …?

P: Umm … ***seldom***? ***rarely***?

M: OK … and let's have a sentence <u>starting</u> with those words!

P: Sure … *Seldom some guys* … sorry, **Seldom do** *some guys shave* … and, **Rarely does** *the bank open on Saturday*.

M: Yes, and how about **Hardly ever do** (*some guys shave*)? And also the word *little* … **Little did you realize** (*how widespread negation is*) … But you just brought up the word *few*, so how would you use that?

P: Oh … like in maybe the expressions "*win a few, lose a few*," "*a few good men*," "*be back in a few minutes*" …

M: No, not **a** *few* … just *few*. How about starting a sentence with **few times**?

P: OK … **Few times have I seen** *so many negative words*! And they don't always have to begin with the letter **n**!

M: Touché! So what's the difference between *few* and *a few*? Put them in short sentences: *She has _____ friends.* And what do they mean?

P: Uh … *She has a few friends* (like "five or six") and *She has* **few friends** (like "not many") … so it would be **Few friends** <u>does she</u> **have**.

M: You're moving right along! So now can you do the same thing with *little* and *a little*? Let's say in short sentences again: *He has _____ ambition.*

P: Sure … It would be *He has a little ambition* (like "some") and *He has* **little ambition** (like "not much") … so it would be **Little ambition** <u>does he have</u>. But I don't think I'd usually be <u>starting</u> sentences with **few** and **little** very often!

M: Probably not. But we do have *few* and *a few*, *little* and *a little* in the language. Anything more to say about them, with and without the INDEFINITE ARTICLE *a*, I mean?

P: Yes. **Few** (*friends*) and **little** (*ambition*) have a NEGATIVE connotation; *a few* and <u>a</u> *little* don't.

M: Bravo!

A little knowledge is a
dangerous thing.
old saying

Little knowledge is a <u>very</u>
dangerous thing!
"New saying"

Never will it ... Soon it will ...

Optimist: I think <u>in</u> <u>no</u> time <u>we</u> <u>will</u> see a four-day work week.

Pessimist: I think <u>at</u> <u>no</u> time <u>will</u> <u>we</u> see a four-day work week!

P: Can't help thinking what a huge difference there is, Marta, between *few* and *a few*.

M: Yes ... also *little* and *a little*. What do you make of it?

P: Well, without the INDEFINITE ARTICLE, it's like *few* and *little* take on that kind of NEGATIVE force that reaches deep into the sentence.

M: Nice way of putting it! Call it "scope." In a sentence like **Few** *members of that committee have* **any** *imagination*, the negative SCOPE of the word **few** in the SUBJECT of the sentence reaches all the way to **any** in the OBJECT.

P: ...and it would sound peculiar if it were <u>a</u> *few* ... like *A few members ...have* **any** *imagination*!

M: Yes ... more likely *A few members ...have imagination ...* or **some** *imagination*, but not **any**! But there's more to say about the SCOPE issue, Patrick.

P: I'm ready!

M: We've been talking about sentences like **At no** *time* **will it** *snow in this part of the country*. But change **at** to **in** and what happens?

P: You get, um, **In no** *time* **will it** ... no ... **In no** *time* **it will** *snow*, and so on ...

M: So what happened, in terms of SCOPE, I mean?

P: Oh, the scope of *at no time* is wider than *in no time*, because it triggers the switch to **will it** *snow* from **it will** *snow*.

M: Yes! In fact, you can substitute an ADVERB for each of the two phrases and still keep the same word order and the same meaning. Want to try?

P: Sure ... *in no time* is like, uh, *soon* ... and **at no time**, maybe **never**? So ... **Never will** *it snow in this part of the country*, but (somebody else says) **soon it will** ...

M: That's great, Patrick!

P: I think I'm getting the hang of it.

M: Then you're ready for this. One of the most striking examples of NEGATIVE SCOPE appeared in a well-known study of English NEGATION some years ago. The example consists of two contrasting sentences. I'll write them for you here and ask what you make of them:

In not many years Christmas will fall on Sunday.

In not many years <u>will</u> <u>Christmas</u> fall on Sunday.

First of all, are they both grammatical?

P: Sure.

M: OK. Do they mean the same thing?

P: No, definitely not!

M: …even though you've got <u>exactly the same words</u> in both sentences?

P: Nope.

M: Then what <u>do</u> they mean … for you?

P: Well, I guess the difference lies in the initial phrase, *in not many years*, which I think has to be AMBIGUOUS.

M: Go on.

P: In the first example, *in not many years* has the meaning of, maybe, "soon." But in the second example it would mean something like "seldom." And the word *seldom* is like a NEGATIVE (maybe "not often"), so its negative SCOPE is what triggers the inversion of *Christmas will* to **will Christmas**.

M: I couldn't have said it better myself!

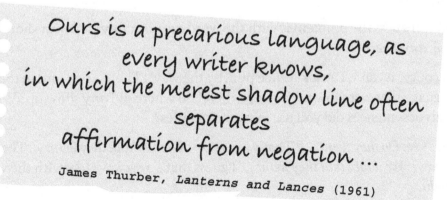

Ours is a precarious language, as every writer knows, in which the merest shadow line often separates affirmation from negation …

James Thurber, *Lanterns and Lances* (1961)

any

We <u>doubt</u> that they have <u>any</u> interest.
We <u>refuse</u> to give them <u>any</u> help.
We <u>forbid</u> you <u>ever</u> to say <u>anything</u> critical.
We <u>deny</u> that we <u>ever</u> broke <u>any</u> laws.

▶ P: Marta, can we go back to an example that you came up with in the last session?

M: Sure … go ahead.

P: It was "*Few members of that committee have **any** imagination*" and the relation between *few* and *any*. But *any* seems to show up all over the place.

M: Where, for example?

P: Oh, in sentences like, uh, *Do they want **any** help? I don't think they want **any** help. We doubt that they want **any** help.*

M: What about sentences like *They want **any** help, I do think they want **any** help, We know that they want **any** help?*

P: They sound awful!

M: All I did was change your question into a statement and your NEGATIVE into AFFIRMATIVE.

P: OK … I guess the problem is with the word *any*. But *any* can't just show up, well, *anywhere* …

M: <u>Of course</u> it can't, Patrick! (Nice pun, by the way!) There's no word in the language that can show up just <u>anywhere</u>! So where <u>did</u> *any* show up? What kinds of sentences did you use in your examples?

P: Let's see: *Do they want …?* That's a QUESTION. *I don't think they want …* That's a NEGATIVE. *We doubt that they want …* I guess that's a NEGATIVE too, with the verb *doubt*.

M: Right … so what's the GENERALIZATION here?

P: GENERALIZATION?

M: Yes … or "rule" if you prefer.

P: Well, I guess it's that the word *any* appears only in QUESTIONS and NEGATIVES.

M: There's more to it than that, Patrick, but it's pretty good for starters.

P: But isn't it kind of weird to have a rule that applies just to questions, negatives, and the verb *doubt*?

M: Nice observation … Yes, it <u>would</u> be weird. So what would improve the generalization here?

P: Um … like there must be other verbs with a kind of NEGATIVE "flavor" that have the same effect as *doubt* … other verbs that can appear with *any*?

M: Yes … perhaps *refuse*, for example … or *deny* … Can you think of possible sentences with these, maybe others?

P: OK … *They refused us any help … so we denied them any mention* … and maybe a sign that says IT IS FORBIDDEN TO SET FOOT <u>ANYWHERE</u> ON THIS PROPERTY.

M: Nice! … and how about, say, *I was too tired to do any more work*?

P: …the word *too* too! … er, also?

M: What do <u>you</u> think? … *It's too dark to see anything … It's too noisy to talk to anybody … It's too expensive to fly anywhere.*

P: I guess you've made your point, Marta! ■

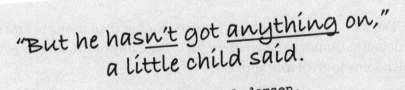

"But he hasn't got <u>anything</u> on," a little child said.

Hans Christian Andersen, "The Emperor's New Clothes"

the Zen of any

There is <u>no</u> right to strike against the public safety by <u>anybody,</u> <u>anywhere,</u> <u>any time.</u>

Calvin (later President) Coolidge on the Boston police strike of 1919

P: There's a question that begs to be asked in all these recent sessions, Marta, and I think it's time I asked it.

M: Question? It's probably obvious, but tell me.

P: It's that word *any*. I know we've used it quite a few times, but I'm not sure I know what it means. And it's not just *any* … There's also *anybody*, *anything*, *anywhere*, *anyway* … Probably tons more.

M: Probably.

P: It's easy to talk about where *any* shows up: It's in NEGATIVES like *They don't have any time* and QUESTIONS like *Do they have any time?* … and lots more, I guess …

M: Yes, it's certainly easier to say where *any* <u>occurs</u> than what it <u>means</u>.

P: And I do*n't* have *any* idea where to start … could just as well be *I have <u>no</u> idea where to start*.

M: Right, Patrick … a quite <u>emphatic</u> NEGATIVE. Rather than trying to find *anything* like a definition, it might be more useful to note *any* of the various environments in which some form of *any* appears.

P: Would that get us *anywhere*?

M: Well, can you think of *any* better way to do it … *anything* at all? And isn't this what we've been doing so far?

P: You mean the various uses of *any* are all going to show up about *any* old time in this conversation if we keep it going *any* longer?

M: Hold on! I probably should*n't* have been implying *anything* like that. I've laid out here a list of quotations in which some form of *any* appears. Take a close look at the <u>context</u> in which each one occurs. Think of it, maybe, as *the Zen of "any."*

Thou canst <u>not</u> then be false to <u>any</u> man.

Shakespeare, *Hamlet*, Act I, scene iii

They know so <u>little</u> of <u>any</u> life
but their own.

C. Day-Lewis

I love <u>any</u> discourse of rivers,
and fish and fishing.

Izaak Walton

"<u>Anybody</u> can be pope; the proof of this
is that I have become one."

Pope John XXIII, *Wit and Wisdom of Good Pope John* (1963)

"<u>Anything</u> You Can Do, I Can Do Better"

Title of song from *Annie Get Your Gun*

<u>Any</u> fool can tell the truth, but it requires
a man of some sense to know
how to tell a lie well.

Samuel Butler, *The Note-Books of Samuel Butler* (1912)

PS THIRTEEN Better late than never.

Better late than <u>never</u>.

(Potius sero quam numquam)

Livy (59BC–AD17), *Histories*, Book IV

<u>Nobody</u> has ever expected me to be president.

Abraham Lincoln, campaign speech (1858)

<u>Nothing</u> succeeds like success.

(Rien ne réussit comme le succès)

Alexandre Dumas the Elder, *Ange Pitou* (1854)

Liberty is ... the possibility ... of saying "<u>No</u>" to any authority ...

Ignazio Silone, *The God That Failed* (1950)

To do two things at once is to do <u>neither</u>.

Publilius Syrus (first century BC), Maxim 7

"I think <u>No comment</u> is a splendid expression."

Winston Churchill

CHAPTER FOURTEEN

COMPARISON & CONTRAST

as … as comparatives and compounding; the importance of *that* and *than*; *too* ADJ *to* VERB; standard of comparison; ambiguity; comparative variety; spurious comparatives

---

Day Sixty-six
razor sharp/as sharp as a razor

Day Sixty-seven
smaller than … more small than …

Day Sixty-eight
better than tennis, or Dennis

Day Sixty-nine
more attractive women

PS 14
comparatives and superlatives

Day Seventy
that, than, to, of, as

razor sharp/as sharp as a razor

Beauty's but <u>skin deep</u>.

John Davies of Hereford, *A Select Second Husband for Sir Thomas Overburie's Wife* (1616)

▶ M: Remember those expressions with *too* that we talked about last time, expressions like *I was **too** tired to do any more work*?

P: Sure do, Marta.

M: Well, imagine it's you, Patrick. ***Tired*** to what extent, for example? Maybe something like *very* …

P: …hmm, ***very tired*** … you mean, let's see … **<u>*dog tired*</u>**, **<u>*dead*</u>** *tired*?

M: OK, and it doesn't help that there's a lot of noise coming from the next apartment and the walls are thin, ***very thin*** …

P: …they're **<u>*paper*</u>** *thin*?

M: Yes, but suppose the weather's hot and, before turning in, you decide you want something to drink, something ***really cold***, something …

P: …something **<u>*ice*</u>** *cold*?

M: Ah, but you didn't stock the fridge with your favorite beer this time because you're on a tight budget and the price has gone up; it's high now, ***very high*** …

P: …The price is **<u>*sky high*</u>**?

M: We're on a roll! But think some more about these little expressions. Is there another way to say ***ice cold***, for example, I mean using those same words?

P: Well … sure: ***as cold as ice*** … and probably ***as thin as paper***, even ***as high as the sky***.

M: …and *as tired as a dog*?

P: Hmm … not so good, for me at least … and *as tired as dead* sounds awful!

M: Yes … some of these meanings <u>can</u> be expressed in two ways: for example, the **as … as** PHRASE: **as sharp as a razor** and the COMPOUND: **razor sharp**. We'll have more to say about COMPOUNDS in another session.

P: What about more than one expression with the same adjective? I mean, you got me to say **sky high** and **as high as the sky**, right, Marta?

M: Right.

P: Well, in my dialect there's also **as high as a kite**, but *kite high*? No!

M: Very nice observation. What's the "pivotal" word in all these expressions, by the way?

P: What do you mean?

M: I mean PART OF SPEECH … VERB, NOUN, ADJECTIVE, ADVERB, and so on …

P: Oh … *high, sharp, cold, thin* … ADJECTIVE!

M: Yes, and what meaning do the expressions seem to have in common?

P: You mean "very"?

M: Seems like it, doesn't it? But have you ever heard the expression **skin deep**?

P: Sure, Marta … as a matter of fact, my tattoo is *only* **skin deep**.

M: Tattoo? Hmmm … Well, is *skin deep* very *deep*?

P: No, 'course not … and I guess that's why the word "only" fits in there. I mean it would be strange to say *Prices are only sky high* or *The drinks are only ice cold*.

M: …and of course we don't say that your tattoo is *as deep as skin*! **Skin deep**, by the way, is the only example I know of that has that "only" meaning. ■

> It can hardly be a coincidence that no language on earth has ever produced the expression "as pretty as an airport."
>
> Douglas Adams, *The Long Dark Tea-time of the Soul* (1988)

smaller than ...
more small than ...

Shall I compare thee to a summer's day? Thou art <u>more lovely</u> and <u>more temperate</u> ...

Shakespeare, Sonnet 18

M: What do you think of those expressions, Patrick, like *rock hard* and *as hard as a rock* that we looked at last time?

P: What do I think of them?

M: Yes, suppose *rock hard* and *hard as a rock* refer to what you're sitting on right now. In other words, your "seat and a rock are both hard."

P: Well, I suppose there's a kind of equality here between "rock" and "seat." I mean, we're <u>not</u> saying that my seat is **harder than** a rock.

M: Right, but that's what we want to turn to now ... the <u>in</u>equality issue. What kind of car do you drive, by the way?

P: A Honda Civic.

M: Really? ... And how does it compare to, say, a Ford?

P: The Honda's **smaller**; it's **easier** to drive; it weighs **less**; and it gets **better** mileage **than** a Ford.

M: What about size compared to, say, comfort?

P: Umm ... well, Hondas are really **smaller** ... I mean **more small ... than comfortable**.

M: Why did you switch from **smaller** to **more small**? You didn't say, wouldn't say, *Hondas are more small than Fords*, would you?

P: No ... 'course not, but I guess I was comparing size with degree of comfort and it just sounds better to say *Hondas are **more small than** comfortable* here, not *smaller*. I don't know why, Marta.

M: Yes, you do … It's the kind of difference in what's being compared; you just said so.

P: Oh … so in one case it's comparing <u>two</u> cars (Ford versus Honda) in terms of comfort and in the other it's comparing size versus comfort with reference to <u>one</u> car (Honda).

M: Yes, two different STANDARDS OF COMPARISON: "comfort" in one case and the Honda in the other. Ever hear the expression **deader than** *a doornail*?

P: Sure.

M: …and how about *The poor cat was fished out of the water* **more dead than** *alive*?

P: OK … **deader** in one and **more dead** in the other … different STANDARDS OF COMPARISON again.

M: Great! By the way, Patrick, how did you get here today?

P: I drove. My apartment's **more than** *a mile* from here.

M: You mean you'd **rather drive than** *walk* or *ride* your bike?

P: **On the contrary**! I ride my bike **more often than not**. But today it's a little **too rainy for bike-riding**. Normally, I **prefer the bike to the car**.

M: You probably ride your bike **more often than** I drive <u>my</u> car.

P: Hmmm … Are you doing all this on purpose, Marta?

M: Doing what?

P: Steering this conversation to prompt the use of **as many different** COMPARATIVE **phrases as** possible..

M: [*laughter*] I was going to say nothing could be **farther from the truth**, but then I **thought better of it**!

There was an old owl lived in an oak.
The <u>more</u> he heard, the <u>less</u> he spoke.
The <u>less</u> he spoke, the <u>more</u> he heard.
Now wasn't he a wise old bird!

Punch (1875), vol.68

better than tennis, or Dennis

The reason why we have two ears
and only one mouth
is that we may listen <u>the more</u>
and talk <u>the less.</u>

Diogenes Laertius (3rd century), *Lives and Opinions
of Eminent Philosophers*

P: This COMPARISON thing can make you think, can't it, Marta?

M: Yes … it certainly can. Did you have something in mind?

P: Well, I happened to overhear a bit of conversation between a guy and his girlfriend about a trip they're taking out of Boston and one of them said, "The first day we should try to drive ***further than*** Elizabeth."

M: Go on.

P: So I'm thinking maybe they're in a race with some woman called "Elizabeth." Then I discover that the "Elizabeth" they're talking about is a city in New Jersey.

M: Interesting bit of AMBIGUITY … which, of course, there wouldn't be if they had said "We should try to drive ***farther than*** Elizabeth *does*." ***Farther*** and ***further*** derive from the same root in Old English, by the way.

P: And I remember you said in the last session at one point, what was it? … *Nothing could be **farther** from the truth.* So then ***farther*** must be the COMPARATIVE form of ***far*** … right?

M: Right.

P: Well, does that mean that *mother* would have to be a COMPARATIVE form of *moth* and *brother* a COMPARATIVE of *broth* … maybe *bother* from *both*, *wither* from *with* …?

M: [*silence*] You're doing this on purpose, Patrick!

P: My apologies … I couldn't resist! … *mother* is not *moth* + *er* … *brother* isn't *broth* + *er* … In fact, *moth, broth, both,* and *with* are not even adjectives!

M: I know you were joking, but does this mean that a single-word COMPARATIVE <u>must</u> be analyzable as ROOT plus **-er**?

P: I guess so.

M: Then what about the wicked line:

> Oth<u>er</u> **than** that, Mrs. Lincoln, how did you enjoy the play? or
> She'd read a book **rath<u>er</u> than** watch television or that line from Kipling:
> You're a **bett<u>er</u>** man **than** I am, Gunga Din!

P: OK ... obviously no *oth*-, no *rath*-, no *bett*-! So I guess the word **than** here is what completes the COMPARATIVE reading.

M: Or CONTRAST ... COMPARISON and CONTRAST are very close. Think of the difference between these two sentences, where there are only two <u>words</u> that differ:

> *Denise plays ping-pong* **better than tennis.**
> *Denise plays ping-pong* **better than Dennis.**

What's being compared, or contrasted?

P: Umm ... In the first one, I guess it's Denise's different abilities in ping-pong versus tennis, and in the second, let's see ... the ping-pong abilities of Dennis versus those of Denise?

M: Pretty good, Patrick! ... And if you chose to "fill them out," so to speak, adding parts that are "understood," you would get what?

P: OK ...

Denise plays ping-pong **better than she plays tennis.**

And, let's see ...

Denise plays ping-pong **better than Dennis does.**

M: ...and I can't imagine working with *a better student*!

> *If thou thinkest twice before thou speakest once, thou wilt speak <u>twice</u> <u>the better</u> for it.*
> William Penn, *Some Fruits of Solitude* (1693)

more attractive women

"The zoo has <u>more</u> exotic animals
<u>than the pound</u>."
Oh ... I thought you said ...
"The zoo has <u>more exotic</u> animals
<u>than the</u> HOUND."

▶ M: Let's go back to COMPARATIVE constructions with the word **more**. A couple of sessions ago we had the example *Hondas are **more small than comfortable***. Remember, Patrick?

P: Sure do ... **more small**, not **smaller than** ... at least not in this example.

M: Then let's look **some more** at the **more/than** constructions. (Sorry about that!)

P: Almost like a pun!

M: Well, we can work our way **further** into these rather tight "**more**" COMPARATIVES with some useful examples. So let's create two characters—call them "Rex" and "Regina"—and COMPARE them in terms of knowledge of other women and of their degree of "attraction."

P: I'm not sure what you're getting at, Marta.

M: I don't blame you ... Let me try this: With regard to the two characters I just created, how would you interpret a sentence like the following?

> *Rex knows **more** attractive women **than** Regina.*

P: Um ... *Rex knows **more** women who are attractive **than** Regina.*

M: ... **than** Regina what?

P: ... **than** Regina knows?

M: OK, but can't "Regina" be interpreted as "attractive" too?

P: Yeah … right. So another reading could be *Rex knows **more** women who are attractive **than** just Regina.*

M: Fine, if you're talking about "quantity of women"; now what about comparison in terms of "degree of attraction"?

P: [*sigh*] Uh, let's see … *Rex knows **more attractive** women **than** Regina … is!*

M: Not bad! And what about where Regina knows attractive women as well? In other words, *Rex knows **more attractive** women …*

P: …***than** Regina … knows*!

M: Bravo! Bravo! Your intuitions are right on! So, Patrick, what can you say now about an utterance like *Rex knows **more** attractive women **than** Regina*?

P: Um … you mean it's AMBIGUOUS?

M: Right … just AMBIGUOUS or <u>very</u> AMBIGUOUS?

P: Very!

M: <u>How</u> <u>many</u> different meanings?

P: I counted … let's see … four!

M: So did I. And here they are again. I've written them out for us:

Rex knows more attractive women than Regina:

> *more women who are attractive than Regina (knows)*
> *more women who are attractive than (just) Regina*
> *women who are more attractive than Regina (knows)*
> *women who are more attractive than Regina (is)*

> Shall I compare thee to a summer's day?
> Thou art more lovely and more temperate:
> Rough winds do shake the darling buds of May,
> And summer's lease hath all too short a date.
> Shakespeare, Sonnet 18

that, than, to, of, as

The test was <u>harder than</u> I could imagine. It was even the <u>hardest that</u> I could imagine.

P: You know, Marta, I've been thinking … Lots of words in English begin with a **th-** sound … *think, thought, through, thank, theory*, and so on. And these are all pronounced with the θ sound.

M: Yes. And?

P: Well, there's a bunch more like *the, this, that, these, those, though, them, there, than* … words that we've been working with in these sessions, where the **th-** sound is pronounced ð. Have you ever noticed?

M: Sure have … Any basic difference between the two groups? I mean, why *thank* with a θ and *than* with ð?

P: Hmm … I guess words in the *thank* group tend to be CONTENT words and words in the *than* group are all FUNCTION words.

M: Very nice observation! And all those in the *than* group, by the way, go back quite far in the history of the language. But what did you want to make of it?

P: Seems like we could maybe pare down a little those few in the *than* group.

M: Pare them down? What do you mean, Patrick?

P: Well, take the words *that* and *than* … We can say things like *The shelf's **so high** <u>that</u> I can't reach it*, but we can also say *The shelf's **higher** <u>than</u> I can reach*.

M: Yes, and …

P: Well, why have <u>both</u> *that* and *than*? They're practically the same word, Marta!

M: Interesting that you should notice that, if you'll pardon the pun. Go back far enough in history and you'll discover that *that* and *than* <u>did</u> use to be one word.

P: Well, I hope there's nothing more beyond that in this COMPARATIVE stuff (pardon <u>my</u> pun)!

M: Hold on, Patrick! What <u>kind</u> of construction do you see following *than* and *that* in your example?

P: Um … let me think … *that I can't reach* … *than I can reach* … Well, there's a SUBJECT (*I*) and a VERB (*reach*)!

M: And what about utterances like *The shelf's too high for us to reach?* or *such a high shelf that we can't reach it?* What kind of construction do you see following *too (high)* and *such a high shelf?*

P: You're probably fishing for SUBJECT and VERB again, but *us? to reach?*

M: Yes, but look at it in terms of relationships: between *we reach* and *for us to reach* … between *we* and *us*, and between *reach* and *to reach*.

P: Never thought of it that way.

M: There's more, Patrick … How about *The shelf's so high that we can't reach it?*

P: Ah, but it fits right in! *The shelf's so high that* … It's *such a high shelf that* …

M: Anything like a pattern in all of this?

P: Hmmm … Well, we've got something that's … what? … maybe a kind of <u>focus</u> or <u>core</u> in the comparison … nouns mostly (*work, time, fun, problem*), but adjectives too (*big, young*) …

M: Keep going.

P: …and then there's something that modifies the core, like *too, too much, as, more*, an adjective with the *-er, -est* ending … things like that. Ah, then there's the tricky part with *that* and *than*.

M: …and *to, of, as* … followed by something limiting the scope of comparison, right?

P: Oh sure, Marta … like not just *too young* but *too young to vote, to drive, to drink*.

M: We've covered *more territory than you would have guessed*, don't you think?

<u>too</u> young <u>to</u> vote
<u>too much</u> work <u>to</u> do
<u>so little</u> time <u>to</u> relax
<u>such</u> fun <u>that</u> we stayed longer
a bigg<u>er</u> problem <u>than</u> we imagined
the bigg<u>est</u> problem <u>of</u> all
<u>as</u> much fun <u>as</u> ever

the more the merrier
the sooner the better
the lesser of two evils
better safe than sorry
easier said than done
Two heads are better than one.
Half a loaf is better than none.

cool as a cucumber
neat as a pin
dead as a doornail
good as gold
old as the hills
quick as a flash
quiet as a mouse
sick as a dog
deaf as a post

for better or worse
a fate worse than death
thousands worse off than you
His bark is worse than his bite.
his own worst enemy

Put your best foot forward.
Make the best of a bad job.
unkindest cut of all
survival of the fittest
It's always darkest before dawn.
Have you heard the latest?
at your earliest convenience

The bigger they are, the harder they fall.
Absence makes the heart grow fonder.
The grass is always greener on the other side of the fence.
Actions speak louder than words.
different as chalk and cheese
as well as can be expected
crazy like a fox
eat like a horse
in less than no time
more haste, less speed
old enough to know better
too numerous to mention
too good to be true

CHAPTER FIFTEEN

SOUND & SPELLING THREE

stress in words of Greek origin; stress shift with affixation; stress levels in English; vowel pairs and syllabification; "psychological reality" in English spelling; intonation in speech; spoken vs. written language

Day Seventy-one
movable stress

Day Seventy-two
prótest protést módest

Day Seventy-three
lair & liar, vail & vial

Day Seventy-four
face/facial, medicine/medicate

Day Seventy-five
Icanunderstandyouperfectlywell

PS 15
anthropophony and psychometer

movable stress

Démocrats in a democracy are democrátic

▶ P: Marta, remember those sessions where we talked a lot about how English spelling works?

M: Sure do.

P: Well, it got me to thinking …

M: Nothing wrong with that, Patrick!

P: …that we have pairs of words like *convíct ~ cónvict* and *suspéct ~ súspect*, where the first word of the pair is a verb and the second's a noun, but the spelling doesn't change … In fact, nothing changes except where the STRESS falls.

M: Right. But we also saw that there are other pairs like *húmid / humídify*, *pérson / persónify*, and so on, where …

P: Let me finish! … Yes, where you add *-ify* and move the stress to the next syllable.

M: Sorry I interrupted.

P: That's OK. But how about stuff like *phótograph / photógraphy / photográphic*?

M: Go on …

P: Well, look at where the stress is … three different places! …with two different SUFFIXES.

M: Yes, those are related English words of Greek origin and …

P: You mean the ancient Greeks had cameras, took pictures, and …

M: Wait! What kind of reasoning is that? You might as well say that since the English word *car* came via Latin, the early Romans must have been driving around in Fiats!

P: Very funny, Marta.

M: I'm serious. Take the word ***photograph*** … What part of speech is it?

P: Noun, of course.

M: What's it made up of?

P: Uh … *photo* plus *graph*, I guess.

M: And when you say them as individual words in isolation, as you did, you give one syllable in both of them MAIN STRESS … You said *phóto* and *gráph*. But put them together and you get what?

P: *phótograph* … Oh, and the MAIN STRESS here is only on *phóto*. I mean, nobody says *phótográph*.

M: OK … but you also mentioned *photography* and *photographic*. What's happening here with the stress … and maybe why?

P: Ah … *photógraphy* … It moves to the next syllable … 'cause we added *-y*.

M: Which does what?

P: I don't know what you mean … both are nouns … Oh, OK, they're not the same, of course … A *phótograph* is a "thing" and *photógraphy* is … what … a "concept," an "occupation"?

M: I'm listening.

P: So another stress shift with *photográphic* … 'cause I added *-ic* instead of *-y*, which changes the grammatical category to ADJECTIVE here.

M: Anything to note about MAIN STRESS after all this, Patrick?

P: Well, it can move when you add suffixes like *-y* and *-ic*, I guess. Oh, and each of the words we've been looking at has only one MAIN STRESS. True for all words?

M: Sure looks like it!

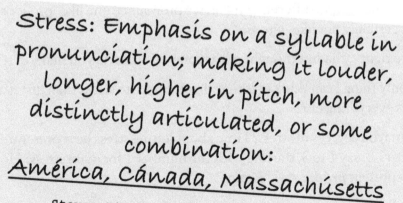

Stress: Emphasis on a syllable in pronunciation; making it louder, longer, higher in pitch, more distinctly articulated, or some combination:
América, Cánada, Massachúsetts

Steven Pinker, *Words and Rules* (2000)

prótest protést módest

He's not the sort to <u>digress</u>,
But he thinks he saw a <u>tigress.</u>

with apologies to Ogden Nash

▶ P: Marta, about that stuff on WORD STRESS that we saw last time and even earlier …

M: You mean like *permít* and *pérmit* … *protést* and *prótest* … that sort of thing?

P: Yes, and take another pair … like *prodúce* and *próduce*. You got, uh … speaking of vegetables, *Mexico and Chile* **prodúce** *a lot* and *A lot of* **próduce** *comes from Mexico and Chile.*

M: Yes … those are good examples too.

P: OK, but what about a word like **lettuce**, which is pronounced the same as "let us" in, say, *Let us pray*. Could just as well be *Lettuce pray*.

M: [*chuckle*] True, but what are you getting at, Patrick?

P: Well, **próduce** and **léttuce** both have two syllables and both have main stress on the first syllable. But the second syllables are different.

M: They don't <u>look</u> different …

P: No, but they <u>sound</u> different. I mean we pronounce one like "<u>pró</u>doose" but the other certainly not like "<u>lé</u>toose."

M: You're right … hadn't thought of that one. So what do you make of it?

P: The only thing I can think of is that there's more to stress than just MAIN STRESS versus everything else.

M: Like maybe <u>degrees</u> of stress? How about letting stress be represented by numbers … say 1 to 3, starting with the number 1 for main stress? How would you represent **próduce** and **léttuce**?

P: OK, I'll try to write it: *produce   lettuce*
                                        1 2   1 3

Oh, and the verb **prodúce**:   produce
                                       3   1

M: Great! So number 1 for MAIN STRESS. What do you want to call 2 and 3?

P: Well, 1 is strong … so I guess 3 is WEAK. And 2 … hmm … maybe just SECONDARY.

M: Nice! Any <u>other</u> contrasting pairs like **próduce** and **léttuce**?
                                                   1 2   1 3

P: Can't think of any.

M: How about **prótest** and **módest** … and add the verb **protést**? What are the stress patterns? Can you write them out, starting with the verb?

P: Let's see …   protest   protest   modest
                   3 1   1 2   1 3

M: Want some more?

P: I just thought of one! It has to do with what you're doing to me, Marta.

M: Uh oh!

P: Sure … the verb torment …   the noun torment
                      3   1   1   2

M: …and the third?

P: It's what you throw at me … a **torrent**!
                                  1   3

M: *Touché.*

Probably he was a man of
philological crotchets;
he said, for instance, 'pro-<u>spect</u>'.

George Gissing, Demos (1886)

lair & liar, vail & vial

i before e, except after c,
save where sounding like 'ay'
as in 'neighbor' and 'weigh'.

Old saying

P: Can we look at something else concerning English spelling?

M: Sure, Patrick … What's on your mind?

P: OK, the other day I came across an ad for "*trial membership*" in an outdoors club that sponsors "*walks on trails in our local forests.*"

M: Go on …

P: Well, for some reason—I don't know what—I picked up on two of the words in their quotes … *trial* and *trail*.

M: Very common words … what's to notice about them?

P: Uh … for one thing, they both use the same letters of the alphabet, plus the only difference in the way they <u>look</u> is that the two VOWELS are *i a* in one and *a i* in the other.

M: Nothing unusual about that.

P: Then what about the fact that *tri-al* is <u>two</u> SYLLABLES and *trail* is only <u>one</u>?

M: I can make a guess, but it would help to have some more examples.

P: Well, I started looking and came up with a whole bunch. Here, I've written them down: one-syllable *ai*:   *pail fair wait main raid (com)plaint*

two-syllable *ia*:   *dial liar giant bias pliant* …

… and even another whole pair: *vail vial*

M: Maybe you're on to something. What about other combinations of two vowels?

P: I was just going to tell you … once I got started it was hard to stop. So I began to look for some more. Some combinations are only one way: *ea* (*beach, year*), but no *ae* … or *ou* (*your, tour*), but no *uo*.

M: Go on …

P: OK … take *oi* and *io*: *loin, coin, hoist* are one syllable; *lion, prior, trio* are two. Or take *au* and *ua*: *haul* is one; *dual* is two. Or *oa* and *ao*: *coast* is one; *chaos* is two.

174

M: Well, the only possible "explanation" I can think of covers some of your examples but not all of them, by any means.

P: That's OK … even just a clue would help at this point!

M: Then think about some of your two-syllable *ia* examples … *liar* (someone who lies) is *lie* + *ar*; *trial* is *try* + *al*; *pliant* (flexible) is *ply* (bend) + *ant* … and I suspect many of your other two-syllable examples are "complex" in this way too, but I'd have to look them up in a good dictionary.

P: That's interesting, Marta. So I guess we should be talking about tendencies here, not hard-and-fast rules.

M: That's a good way to look at it, Patrick, especially with language.

P: But there's no problem in **knowing how to spell** most of these two-vowel combinations, 'cause usually you can actually <u>hear</u> whether it's one or two syllables … that is, with one big exception.

M: I knew you were leading up to something.

P: Ever have a problem remembering whether a word like [sɪv] is spelled *s-i-e-v-e* or *s-e-i-v-e*? Or whether [sɪj] is *s-i-e-g-e* or *s-e-i-g-e*? Or whether [receive] is *r-e-c-e-i-v-e* or *r-e-c-i-e-v-e*? I know <u>I</u> certainly have.

M: Aha! So that's the reason for the reminder "*i* before *e*, except after *c* …" and so on … an "old saying" that we apparently need only for the *e-i/i-e* pair …

P: …because whether it's *e-i* or *i-e*, it's always one syllable, so you can't decide just by hearing it.

M: Hey, Patrick! Never thought of it that way … nice bit of research on your part!

A spelling reformer indicted
For fudge was before the court cicted.
The judge said: "Enough—
His candle we'll snough,
And his sepulcher shall not be whicted."

Ambrose Bierce, *The Devil's Dictionary* (1999), p. 138.
Reprinted by permission of Oxford University Press.

face/facial, medicine/medicate

Is a thing *created* by a "*creachure*" a "*creashon*"?

> P: A while back we talked about pairs of related words like *race* and *racial*, *medicine* and *medicate*.

M: I remember, Patrick.

P: You just "feel like" there's a *c* in all these, even though it's pronounced [s] in *race*, [š] in *racial*, and [k] in *medicate*.

M: Yes … no problem for anybody who already knows the language, but often vexing to somebody who's trying to learn it, like maybe a native speaker of Spanish or Arabic.

P: OK, Marta, but I just came across two more—*space* and *spatial*—that would seem to complicate the situation a bit. I mean, shouldn't it be written *spacial*, if it's related to *space*? We'd still get the right pronunciation out of it, wouldn't we?

M: Good reasoning, Patrick! Actually both words, I think, derive ultimately from Latin (*spatium*), but *space* has come down to us by way of French. You <u>would</u> pick just about the only pair of that kind! I think the other is *palace* and *palatial* (Latin *palatium*), not *palacial*.

P: [*laughter*]

M: It's interesting that you said you can just "feel" there's a *c* in pairs like *race*/*racial* and *medicine*/*medicate*. "Feel" the same way about the *s* in *revise*/*revision* … the *t* in *relate*/*relation*?

P: I think so.

M: You're not alone.

P: OK, but what about *divide*/*division*?

M: What about it? That's a bit different.

P: But the two words are related, aren't they?

M: Yes, but one is spelled with **d** and the other **s**, as you can see.

P: Well, suppose, for the sake of consistency, we spelled it **dividion**?

M: We talked about this before. Spelling it with **d** won't give us the right pronunciation.

P: Well, if the **t + i** in **relation** gives us the "sh" sound, why wouldn't a **d + i** in **dividion** give us a "zh" sound?

M: Oh … I see what you're getting at … perfectly good reasoning … again! It's just that the two words have come down to us from Latin (**divido**) through French with **d** and **s** … and no **dividion**! Otherwise, you might be "feeling" a **d** in both.

P: Should I stop "feeling," Marta?

M: Absolutely not! Your "feeling" the **c** in **race** and **racial**, by the way, is what's sometimes referred to as PSYCHOLOGICAL REALITY.

P: Really?

M: Yes, and it can extend pretty far. Take the words **create**, **creature**, and **creation**, for example, maybe even the dialectal form **critter** … any comment?

P: Sure … four **t**s … <u>four</u> different pronunciations … and the **t** in all of them is, um, PSYCHOLOGICALLY REAL! I hear it in my head.

Don't put your spelling where your mouth is; put it where your head is.

Wayne O'Neil, English Orthography (1980)

Icanunderstandyouperfectlywell

Why do we separate words when we write them butrunthemtogetherwhenwespeakthem?

▶ P: I got to thinking the other day, Marta, about this device we call PUNCTUATION.

M: Oh? And what prompted it?

P: Well, I overheard a woman say, "**It's hard to understand him when he speaks … he doesn't punctuate.**"

M: And what do you think she meant, Patrick?

P: That the guy doesn't separate his words when he speaks.

M: You mean wishing **that … the … guy … wouldn't … run … his … words … together**?

P: Well, yes, but …

M: …or wishing he would <u>identify</u> his punctuation?

P: What do you mean?

M: OK, think about it … So, do we ever <u>talk</u> about punctuation of language: spoken language? I mean, imagine somebody repeating what we're saying here as "*So* **comma** *do we ever talk* **underlined** *about punctuation of language* **colon** *spoken language* **question mark**."

P: That'd be pretty silly, I guess.

M: So <u>why</u> don't we talk like this?

P: Um … first of all 'cause it would be confusing and impossibly cumbersome … trying to separate the language words from the punctuation words. But second, 'cause we don't have to.

M: Why?

P: Why? Because spoken language has other ways of doing what punctuation does in written language.

M: Like what … maybe <u>shouting</u> "exclamation point" instead of just saying it?

178

P: Very funny, Marta! Actually, I think you can do more with your voice, in speaking, than you can with punctuation in writing.

M: Yes! Want to elaborate?

P: Sure ... Take something in writing like the song title

$$(1) \textit{What Is This Thing Called Love?}$$

In speaking it could be

    What

              is this thing   **ve**

                    called lo

or   **What is this thing called**

                    love (or dear, Bob, Ann, etc.)

       at ...   **love**

or   **Wh**

          is this thing called

M: Nice! What you're representing is the different INTONATION of three different versions, which you can only underline{approximate} in writing. Want to try?

P: Sure. The first one we already have. The second would be maybe ...

$$(2) \textit{What is this thing called, love?}$$

... and the third something like ...

$$(3) \textit{What! Is this thing called \underline{love}?!}$$

M: And what about the questions themselves ... I mean what kinds?

P: Oh, yeah ... I think I remember the terms ... (1) and (2) are WH-QUESTIONS ... (3) is a YES-NO QUESTION.

M: But what about the "what" in (3)?

P: "What" here isn't asking a question ... It's sort of an EXCLAMATION. The actual question is what follows.

M: So what about the different intonations among the three?

P: Well, the YES-NO QUESTION **"Is this thing called love?"** has rising intonation ... the WH-QUESTIONS—(1) and (2)—have level or falling intonation. OK? Oh, and the comma in (2) reflects the pause in the spoken version.

M: Sounds pretty good, Patrick!

P: I read somewhere about writing being simply speech that's transcribed. After all this, I think that's a bit misleading.

M: In what way?

P: Well, for one thing, speech is like continuous sound. I mean, we don't even think about separating words when we speak …

M: …Yes, we wouldn't even <u>want</u> to … might even make it <u>more</u> difficult to understand! If you look at a spectrograph of a conversation, for example, it shows very little break in the stream of speech … but I interrupted.

P: Uh … well, how about if I say that no amount of punctuation in written language can fully capture the tremendous variety and subtlety of spoken language. It's almost like two <u>kinds</u> of language.

M: Mind if I quote you?

SINGLE SLICES By Peter Kohlsaat

Sara, we HAVE to talk…
Sara, WE have to talk…
Sara, we have to TALK…
SARA, we have to talk…

Robert Fenton realizes that tonight he has to do more than just choose his words carefully.

PS FIFTEEN anthropophony and psychometer

We saw in Day 71 how PRIMARY STRESS is assigned in words of Greek origin like *phótograph*, *photógraphy*, and *photográphic*. English has <u>many</u> words in the realm of science and technology whose parts derive ultimately from Greek. For example, *tele-* in Greek means roughly "far off" or "afar" and *-graph* means roughly "writing." Put them together in English and you get *télegraph*, where the MAIN STRESS (to which we can assign the number 1) falls on the <u>first</u> syllable. Derive the concept of "telegraphing" from *telegraph* by adding *-y* and you get *telégraphy*, where the main stress now falls on the <u>second</u> syllable. Derive an ADJECTIVE from *telegraph* by adding *-ic* and you get *telegráphic*, where the main stress now falls on the next-to-last or PENULTIMATE syllable. We therefore have the following pattern

	NOUN (THING)		NOUN (CONCEPT)		ADJECTIVE
	télegraph	>	*telégraphy*		*telegráphic*
	1		1		1
Similarly:	*démocrat*	>	*demócracy*	>	*democrátic*
	1		1		1

and from the list on the next page, such examples as …

télescope >	[*teléscopy*] >	*telescópic*
1	1	1
[*bíolog*] >	*bíology* >	*biológic(al)*
1	1	1

where the words in [square brackets] are <u>possible</u> but rarely used, if at all.

181

PS 15

Taking one element from each of the two lists below of a sampling of Greek ʀᴏᴏᴛꜱ (A and B), make up words, pronounce them (noting where the main stress falls), and assign a meaning to them. Although the words need not be familiar ones (e.g., *anthropóphony*, *psychómeter*), they still obey the rules of stress placement and can still be interpreted (as, perhaps, "sound of man," "device for measuring the mind").

		A	B		
1	human	*anthropo-*			
2	pressure	*baro-*			
3	book	*biblio-*			
4	life	*bio-*			
5	time	*chrono-*	*-gram*	message	a
6	earth	*geo-*	*-graph(y)*	writing	b
7	small	*micro-*	*-log(y)*	knowledge	c
8	love	*philo-*	*-metr(y)*	measure	d
9	light	*photo-*	*-phon(y)*	sound	e
10	mind	*psycho-*	*-scop(y)*	aim	f
11	society	*socio-*	*-sophy*	truth	g
12	far off	*tele-*			
13	god	*theo-*			
14	heat	*thermo-*			

Finally, drawing again from the above list, compose and pronounce a word that matches each of the following definitions, again being careful to note where the stress falls:

- **measurement of humans**
- **measure of human** (adjective)
- **a device for measuring small things**
- **a message book**
- **knowledge of god** (adjective)
- **the sound of heat**
- **aiming at the mind**

Continue on your own, taking one element from each list, and create more words that you've never heard or seen before, giving the resulting combination a meaning, and pronouncing it! For example: *mícrograph* ("piece of small writing"), *philómetry* ("measuring or measurement of love"), even *philómeter* (an instrument for such measurement!), etc.

Have fun!

CHAPTER SIXTEEN

COMPOUND INTEREST

compound as neologism; stress patterns of compound vs. nominal phrase; compound within a compound; right-hand head rule; compound in other languages

---

Day Seventy-six
horseshoes & alligator shoes

Day Seventy-seven
híghchaìrs vs. hîgh chaírs

Day Seventy-eight
small car mileage claims

Day Seventy-nine
"Go right, young compound!"

PS 16
"the cabin key of the captain . . ."

Day Eighty
left bank & rive gauche

horseshoes & alligator shoes

"How would you define a 'dream room,' you guys?"
"Uh ... a room where you had a certain dream?"
"Or a room you've been dreaming about having?"
"Maybe a room where a person goes to dream?"

M: Patrick, I'd like to pick up on something we talked about a couple of weeks ago concerning expressions like **skin deep**, **paper thin**, **ice cold**, **sky high** ...

P: Fine, Marta ... I think that stuff's still pretty much in my head.

M: Good! These items have meanings that are fairly obvious; I mean most of them have possible paraphrases in the **as ... as** construction: **as cold as ice**, for example. And of course they're all the same PART OF SPEECH, right?

P: Umm ... yeah ... ADJECTIVES.

M: ...and the construction itself we identified as a COMPOUND. Let's take a look at another kind. How would you define the COMPOUND **skin cancer**?

P: Uh ... "cancer of the skin," I guess.

M: ...and what about **cancer cure**?

P: Simple ... it's a "cure for cancer"!

M: Then how about **rest cure**? ... **work cure**?

P: Never heard of these, Marta! ... Oh, all right ... **rest cure** ... well, maybe "resting as a cure for some ailment"? ... and **work cure**? Let's see ... "a cure that lets you avoid going to work"? Hmm ... I really like that one!

M: You do, do you! But you never heard of them and yet you came up right away with possible interpretations. What do you make of that?

P: Well, I guess I'm pretty creative!

M: Don't get carried away, Patrick. A while back we talked about other words that lots of people never heard before but could still assign a meaning to, like *infotainment*, *veggieburger*, *cyberspace*. Remember the term we used for them?

P: OK. Let me think … NEOLOGISM!

M: Yes! So let's see how adept <u>you</u> are at "neologizing," if you'll pardon the expression. How would you interpret, say, *horseshoes*?

P: Easy! "Those metal things that go on a horse's hooves … shoes that a horse wears."

M: How about *alligator shoes*?

P: Ah! Very clever, Marta! <u>Not</u> "shoes that an alligator wears"! It's "shoes made of alligator skin."

M: Then what about, say, *bicycle shoes*?

P: Well, I guess that could mean "shoes that you wear when you ride a bicycle"?

M: And *kitchen table shoes*?

P: *Kitchen table shoes*? That's crazy! Can't mean <u>anything</u>!

M: Oh, come on, Patrick! Conjure up something. Use your imagination!

P: Hmm … OK … "multiple pairs of shoes scattered around the house in different places and one of the pairs is on the kitchen table"!

M: See? You're a real "neologizer" … just like the rest of us!

"How humiliating …
to be 'in the doghouse'!"
"You're too big to fit in
the doghouse!"

híghchaìrs vs. hîgh chaírs

I didn't say "Whîte Hoùse"...
I said they líve in "a whîte hoúse"!

▶ M: You know, Patrick, we talked a bit about the STRESS PATTERNS within words a few sessions ago, but we haven't said anything yet about the pronunciation of COMPOUNDS and what gets stressed, or not.

P: Well, is there anything special about them? I mean ... *hórseshòes*, *dréam ròom*, *cáncer cùre*, *véggiebùrger*, *dóghòuse* ... they're all pretty heavy on the first word.

M: True, but what about, say, *îce cóld*, *sprîng féver*, *clâm chówder*, *fûr cóat*, and tons more like that?

P: OK ... I guess there's more to it.

M: Yes. So what do you notice about the STRESS PATTERNS of these two items: *cîvil sérvant* and *lôyal sérvant*?

P: What do I notice? Looks like the patterns are the same.

M: But are they the same kind of construction ... COMPOUND, for example?

P: I guess so, Marta.

M: You've got a case of "compound-itis," Patrick! What does *lôyal sérvant* mean?

P: Uh ... "a servant who's loyal," I guess.

M: ...and *cîvil sérvant*?

P: "A servant who's civ ..."? No, that can't be. A *cîvil sérvant* is a member of the **Cîvil Sérvice**. So *cîvil sérvant* and *lôyal sérvant* are probably different kinds of constructions.

M: ... even though they have the same STRESS pattern. That's the kind of deduction I was hoping for. So what makes them different?

186

P: Well, I guess *lôyal sérvant* is the common ADJECTIVE + NOUN pattern … like *bîg hóuse*, *yêllow flówer*, *fûnny pérson*. But **cîvil sérvant** … I don't know.

M: But you've already identified the connection between **cîvil sérvant** and **Cîvil Sérvice**!

P: Ah … of course! The first is <u>derived</u> from the second, and they're both COMPOUNDS, not ADJECTIVE + NOUN.

M: Yes, but often you find that ADJECTIVE + NOUN have <u>evolved</u> into a COMPOUND. Take the example of "a chair that's high," which we would of course refer to as a *hîgh cháir* … ADJECTIVE + NOUN, or NOMINAL PHRASE, to be precise. Some might call a bar stool a *hîgh cháir*.

P: …and I think I know what you're leading up to, Marta.

M: Which is?

P: …that over time the NOMINAL PHRASE *hîgh cháir*—the kind of chair that an infant sits in at the dinner table—has evolved into the one-word COMPOUND **híghchàir**.

M: Yes! … and similar, for example, to the NOMINAL PHRASE *blûe bírd*, or "a bird that's blue," eventually becoming, I'm guessing, the species **blúebìrd**, which is a COMPOUND.

P: Is that anything like the contrast between the US *Depârtment of Státe* and the COMPOUND **Státe Depàrtment**?

M: Sure is! And consider this, Patrick: We tend to think of the words "street" and "avenue" having close to the same meaning, but give them a name—say, "Seventh"—and what happens?

P: What happens? OK … **Séventh Strèet** … **Sêventh Ávenue** … ah! Both of them COMPOUNDS but with different stress patterns?

M: Very likely … but the "linguistic jury" might still be out on that! █

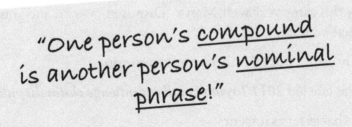

"One person's <u>compound</u> is another person's <u>nominal phrase</u>!"

small car mileage claims

WEIGHT LOSS SURGERY RISE WORRIES INSURERS

Headline, *Los Angeles Times*, June 7, 2005

▶ P: This COMPOUND thing is beginning to look a bit wild, Marta.

M: "Wild," huh?

P: Yeah … It seems like I see compounds now wherever I look. Most of them are short, usually two words, like the ones we've been talking about.

M: …and there are lots of those.

P: But they can also get a bit long. I noticed I've been doing this myself without even thinking!

M: Doing what, Patrick?

P: Well, a friend of mine recently bought a *2011 Toyota*; it's a small car that's supposed to get pretty good mileage.

M: Yes, *small car mileage* is usually quite high.

P: Ah, but the *2011 Toyota small car mileage* is claimed to be the highest.

M: Not surprising.

P: And I think it's probably obvious who's making the *2011 Toyota small car mileage claim*.

M: But hasn't that claim recently been widely disputed?

P: You play this game very well, Marta. "Disputed," yes, … and you can probably guess what's coming next.

M: I certainly can … but I'd rather hear it from you.

P: OK, it was labeled *2011 Toyota small car mileage claim dispute*.

M: …and is that as far as it went?

P: Not quite. Apparently, they settled the dispute, according to the headline in today's paper.

M: Go ahead … This should be a real *record-breaker*.

P: Well, here it is, Marta. I've clipped it out for you:

2011 TOYOTA SMALL CAR MILEAGE CLAIM DISPUTE SETTLEMENT

Quite a COMPOUND, no?

M: …and such a lot of information packed into a relatively small space. If we didn't have the COMPOUND option, how might all this be expressed in a single SENTENCE?

P: Well, first of all, you'd have to supply a SUBJECT, because it doesn't appear in the COMPOUND.

M: Good thinking! So let's just use "they" for our purposes. How about writing it on the board, and I'll do a little underlining.

P: OK …

They settled the dispute <u>over</u> the claim <u>of</u> mileage <u>on</u> the small car manufactured <u>by</u> Toyota <u>in</u> 2011.

M: What's the PART OF SPEECH that I underlined?

P: Uh … PREPOSITIONS?

M: Right! So *mileage **on** the small car* is ***small car mileage***
                 *claim **of** mileage* is ***mileage claim***
                 *dispute **over** the claim* is ***claim dispute***
                 settled the dispute is ***dispute settlement***.

P: COMPOUND within a COMPOUND within a COMPOUND … and I've been doing this a lot myself, just like everybody else!

Two Indicted in Phony
Oil Well Investment
Fraud Scheme
Los Angeles Times, August 12, 1987

"Go right, young compound!"

read + -er vs. re- + read

▶ P: Marta, I keep thinking more and more about this COMPOUND stuff … about NOMINAL PHRASES, about PARTS OF SPEECH like NOUN, VERB, ADJECTIVE, and so on.

M: Thinking? That's the whole idea, Patrick! So what's on your mind?

P: Well, take a COMPOUND like *réntal càr* … that's a kind of car … one that you rent or hire.

M: Go on.

P: …and a COMPOUND like *cár rèntal* … that's a kind of rental, like *trúck rèntal*, or *bíke rèntal*.

M: OK …

P: Well, a *réntal càr* is still a car, and a *cár rèntal* is still a rental.

M: …and a *hórror mòvie* is still a movie and a *móvie hòrror* is still a horror …

P: Please let me finish, Marta! These are all with NOUNS. But take *pâper thín*, which means "very thin" … "thin" is an ADJECTIVE. Reverse it and you get *thín páper*, where now you're talking about "paper," which is a NOUN. Seems like what comes last is what tells you what PART OF SPEECH the compound is.

M: That's very perceptive, Patrick, and it touches on something beyond just the structure of compounds. Take the word "driver," for example. How would you break it down? We talked about this quite a few weeks ago.

P: Easy … the verb *drive* plus the SUFFIX *-er*.

M: Remember what <u>kind</u> of suffix it is?

P: Ummm … INFLECTIONAL? … No! DERIVATIONAL.

M: …and <u>why</u> do we call it DERIVATIONAL?

P: Uh … 'cause there's a DERIVATION involved. (Sorry, Marta. I didn't mean to be flippant!) It's DERIVATIONAL because you add *-er* to the VERB *drive*.

190

M: …and go from *drive* the VERB to *driver* the NOUN.

P: …which makes the suffix *-er* the "deriver" in a sense!

M: [*laughing*] Yes, so now take words like **re-shuffle, re-read, re-examine** … lots of words like that. Does the PREFIX **re-** do the same thing in these words as the SUFFIX *-er* does in the word **driver**?

P: Same thing? … Hmm … No! 'Course not! **Shuffle** is a VERB and **reshuffle** is still a VERB … **re-** doesn't change anything, except the meaning.

M: So consider again what we've just been talking about: COMPOUNDS, the *-er* SUFFIX, the **re-** PREFIX … I'll line up some examples for us here on the board and use the subscripts $_N$ and $_V$ and $_A$ for NOUN, VERB, and ADJECTIVE:

$$ice_n\ [cold_a]_a$$
$$ice_n\ [cream_n]_n$$
$$read_v\ [er_n]_n$$
$$re\ [read_v]_v$$

Any comments?

P: I'm not sure what you're looking for, Marta, and … wait a minute … OK, it looks like the A, N, or V at the end of the whole construction is always the same as the A, N, or V of the last word or SUFFIX.

M: Most of the time, yes. In other words, the rightmost element of COMPOUNDS and DERIVATIONS—call it the HEAD—reveals for us the category of the whole construction. So where there's an A, N, or V inside that bracket there's an A, N, or V outside labeling the whole thing. You've hit upon a very important structural property of the English language, Patrick! ▪

I am at a loss in what
class to place
compound verbs.

Anselm Bayly, A Plain and Complete Grammar
with the English Accidence (1772)

left bank & rive gauche

<u>N</u>orth <u>A</u>tlantic <u>T</u>reaty <u>O</u>rganization (<u>NATO</u>)
<u>O</u>rganisation du <u>T</u>raité
de l'<u>A</u>tlantique du <u>N</u>ord (<u>OTAN</u>)

P: COMPOUNDS, Marta ... can't stop noticing new things about them.

M: Love to hear that from you, Patrick. So what's the "new thing" this time?

P: Um ... some friends of mine just returned from a trip to France and were talking about the various places they visited in Paris ... museums, monuments, buildings located on streets with names like, uh, *Rue de Rivoli, Boulevard de Sébastopol, Avenue Franklin Roosevelt* ...

M: Sounds like fun! What <u>about</u> those names?

P: Well, for one thing, if <u>we</u> had streets, avenues, and boulevards named after those people and places, we'd be saying "**Rivoli Street**," not "Street of Rivoli," and so on.

M: And if we had streets named after that famous Aztec emperor, it wouldn't be Mexico City's *Avenida Cuauhtémoc* but rather "**Cuauhtémoc Avenue**" ... and from Rome we'd have "**Veneto Street**"—ouch!—instead of *Via Veneto*. I think I know what you're getting at, Patrick, but you tell <u>me</u>.

P: OK ... it looks like in English we use a COMPOUND where the same expression in French would be with a ... let me think ... NOUN plus PREPOSITIONAL PHRASE. So the order of the main words gets switched across the two languages.

M: "Main words" ... Hmm ... What's *rive gauche* in English? What's *langue facile*?

P: Um ... "left bank" ... "easy language" ... not "bank left," not "language easy."

M: So what can you say about the tendencies of MODIFICATION within the NOUN PHRASE in French and English?

P: Well, I guess in English the MODIFIER, probably the ADJECTIVE, is before the NOUN and in French it's usually after.

M: A little oversimplified but not bad for starters.

P: Do other languages have COMPOUNDS too?

M: They certainly do, and often a different <u>kind</u> of COMPOUND as well. Consider what they can do in Japanese and Chinese. The Japanese have a COMPOUND *yoshiashi*, made up of *yoshi* "good" and *ashi* "bad." But together as *yoshiashi* ("good" plus "bad") you get a COMPOUND meaning "quality."

P: That's amazing! That's like having a compound meaning "temperature" made up of "hot" plus "cold."

M: Yes, and Chinese has something similar with the COMPOUND *dàxiǎo* meaning "size," which is made up of the words "large" plus "small."

P: Wish we could do that in English, Marta!

M: Well, we do have expressions like ***win-lose*** proposition, ***love-hate*** relationship, ***open-and-shut*** case. But of course they're of a somewhat different <u>kind</u> than the Chinese and Japanese examples. Can you tell me why?

P: Umm … I think so. ***Win-lose*** would have to be interpreted as maybe "competition"; ***love-hate*** could be "emotion"; and ***open-and-shut***? Hmm … "completion"? And I just thought of another one: ***sink-or-swim*** situation. That one could be … I don't know … "outcome"?

M: Not bad, Patrick!

Organization of American States (OAS)
Organisation de l'Armée Secrète (OAS)
Secret Army Organization (SAO)

PS SIXTEEN "the cabin key of the captain . . ."

der Donaudampfschifffahrtgesellschaftskapitänskajütenschlüssel

"the cabin key of the captain of the Danube steam ship journey company"
From J. Russ, *Teach Yourself German Grammar* (2003)

der Donau	*Danube*
der Dampf	*steam*
das Schiff	*ship*
die Fahrt	*journey*
die Gesellschaft	*company*
der Kapitän	*captain*
die Kajüte	*cabin*
der Schlüssel	*key*

How much of this very long German compound can be rendered as a compound in an English translation?

CHAPTER SEVENTEEN

CONTRACTIONS, CONTRACTIONS!

contraction, inflection, and the apostrophe; contraction with "have"; the meanings of "have" and dialectal variation; "wanna," "hafta," "gonna," "gotta"; cliticization

Day Eighty-one
the dog's back

Day Eighty-two
usage with have

Day Eighty-three
want to & have to

Day Eighty-four
gonna & gotta

Day Eighty-five
Mary, I think, 's happy.

PS 17
The solution to the problem is not working.

the dog's back

It's blowin' up a storm out there!
Its blowin's knockin' down trees!

P: You know, Marta, one thing that confuses me is the spelling of what you pronounce as [Its]. [Its] is either *i-t-s* or *i-t*-apostrophe-*s*, but which is which drives me nuts. I mean, if I write *The dog hurt it's paw* it seems OK, since we write *Rover's paw*, *Ginger's paw*, and so on ... but I bet [Its] not.

M: [Its] not, but your logic is right on. So what's the problem? Let's take a slightly longer version of what you wrote. Here:

> *[Its] the dog (not the cat) that hurt* [ITS] *paw.*

Suppose I want to argue that [Its] <u>not</u> *the dog (but the cat)* and you strongly disagree; what do you say now?

P: I guess I could say *It **is** the dog.*

M: Well, Patrick, is ***It's the dog*** any different from ***It is** the dog*, except for the STRESS on *is*, of course?

P: I guess not. Hmmm ...

M: ***It's*** is the CONTRACTION of *it is*. So what does this tell you about the little **'**, which we call an APOSTROPHE? Is it doing the same thing in ***It's the dog*** and ***the dog's paw***?

P: Oh ... no ... In ***It's the dog*** the apostrophe stands for the missing *i* in ***is***.

M: But in ***the dog's paw***? Nothing missing there ... What's it doing now?

P: No-brainer ... The paw <u>belongs</u> to the dog; all dogs have paws.

M: So what's the term? We talked about it many sessions ago.

P: Oh, the ending **'s** on ***dog*** is INFLECTION, like plural inflection (***dogs***), even verb and adjective INFLECTION (***dogged***), and so on.

M: Right, but what <u>kind</u> of INFLECTION?

P: Umm … POSSESSIVE!

M: Yes. And I don't mean to suggest that the ***its*** / ***it's*** issue is a simple one. After all, we do refer to "*Betty's*" as **hers**, not "*her's*," or "*Betty's* and *Jimmy's*" as **theirs**, not "*their's*," and so on.

P: One of those little historical quirks, I suppose.

M: You could think of it that way. Here's another example to think about: ***The dog's back***. Anything unusual here?

P: [*pause*] … Ha! Two meanings, because of the definition of the word ***back***: One means "***The dog is back***" (or "The dog has returned") and the other means "***the back of the dog***."

M: Bravo!

> In the sixteenth century there was great confusion among compositors over the use of the apostrophe. At first they used it only as a marker of an omitted letter; its use as a marker of possession came much later, in the eighteenth century.
>
> David Crystal, *The Fight for English* (2006)

usage with have

- Who do you call when your husband's a pain in the neck?
- Nobody ... I just tell him off!
- No, I mean who do you call when he has a pain in the neck?

M: Remember the discussion we had last time about CONTRACTIONS and *it's* and *its*?

P: How could I forget, Marta?

M: Well, you should know that there's more to be said about the contraction bit. We were looking before at the contraction of *is*, a form of *be*. Like *He's angry*, from *he is* ... Give me another example using, say, *annoyed*.

P: You mean like *He's annoyed*?

M: Yes, and what's been contracted?

P: Well ... *is*, I guess.

M: Fine. Now what about *He's annoyed everybody*? Same thing, Patrick?

P: Whoa! You're trying to trick me. Has to be *has*: *He has annoyed everybody*. Hmm ... Looks like <u>both</u> the verbs *be* and *have* can contract.

M: Maybe. But what about this: *He's a pain in the neck*?

P: What about it?

M: Well, in some dialects it's AMBIGUOUS: *He has* or *He is a pain in the neck* ... literal in one sense (a neck pain), METAPHORICAL in the other (he's annoying).

P: *He's a pain in the neck* can mean "He <u>has</u> a pain ..."? That's weird.

M: Weird? All languages have dialectal differences. But back to your speculation ... <u>Can</u> both *be* and *have* contract?

P: Oh, *be*, yeah. *Have*, I guess not always. But I bet it's not random!

M: Good thinking. Now consider two more examples involving contracted *have*. Tell me if you think they're OK:

> *He's a party every night.*
> *He's had a party every night.*

P: The second sounds fine, but not the first.

M: So what's going on here?

P: I don't know. It's strange. *He has* contracts to *He's* in one but not the other. And you're going to tell me there's a reason, right, Marta?

M: Wrong. <u>You</u>'re going to tell <u>me</u>! What are the two examples <u>without</u> contraction?

P: *He **has** a party* … and *He **has** had a party* …

M: Can you turn them into YES/NO QUESTIONS?

P: Sure … The *has/had* example would be ***Has he had a party*** …? And the other one … let's see … It would be ***Does he have a party*** …?

M: Why the switch to *does* in the second one?

P: Because ***Has he a party*..?** sounds odd. So are we looking at two kinds of ***have***?

M: Maybe <u>more</u> than two. Go back to the *pain in the neck* example. We'll modify it a little. What's the yes/no question version of *He **has** a pain in his neck*?

P: ***Does** he have a pain in his neck*?

M: OK, but can you also form the question by simply inverting *he* and *has*?

P: You mean like ***Has** he a pain in his neck*? I wouldn't say it, Marta, but it's not as bad as ***Has** he a party every night!*

M: Right on! You and I would form the question with ***do/does*** but others can also say ***Has he a pain?*** … So, returning to the matter of contraction with ***have/has***, we used the yes/no question test and came up with the following:

> *He's had a party every night.*   [OK in all dialects]
> *He's a pain in his neck.*   [OK in some dialects]
> *He's a party every night.*   [absent from most dialects]

So what does that tell you about the verb ***have***?

P: That there are three different kinds?

M: Let's just say three different kinds of USAGE. Where in all dialects it freely inverts with the subject in *yes/no* questions we have AUXILIARY ***have***. The other kinds are MAIN VERB ***have***. A kind of POSSESSIVE ***have*** inverts only in some dialects and not in American English. ***Have*** in its other senses—in IDIOMS, for example—doesn't invert at all and we therefore use a form of ***do***.

P: All that patterning with ***have*** … and such a little word.

M: You didn't think it was random and you were right, Patrick! But you use all these forms of ***have*** quite appropriately and without ever thinking <u>about</u> them—till right now, of course!

"Take," "<u>have</u>," and "keep" are pleasant words.

Proverbial

want to & have to

- You <u>wanna</u> go to class?
- No, but I <u>hafta</u>!

▶ M: Shall we look at some more CONTRACTION stuff?

P: You wanna do more? Do we hafta? I thought we wrapped that one up. Why are we gonna do this? And why are you laughing?

M: You can't guess? You really **wanna** know? You really **hafta** be told? You're the one who's really **gonna** laugh!

P: Ha! Guess I'm contracting without realizing. Seems so natural to speak this way.

M: Very natural in speech, Patrick, but not so in writing, no?

P: Yeah. Unless there's a need to represent in writing what's actually spoken, we probably write **want to**, **have to**, **going to**.

M: But it happens sometimes in speaking that we <u>can't</u> use the contracted forms, without it sounding like something's gone wrong. Suppose some guy who's a compulsive fixer at home—call him George—constantly feels that he <u>has</u> to fix something, anything, like say a faucet. So we wonder what it's going to be today. In other words: *What does* … even *What's* …

P: **What's he hafta fix today?** But the **hafta** contraction sounds fine. What are you getting at, Marta?

M: Hold on! Now suppose it <u>is</u> the faucet that George feels compelled to fix but he's looking around for something to use as a tool for the fixing. Would you say this:

What does he hafta fix it? (meaning "What does he have for fixing it?")

P: 'Course not. It would be **What does he have to fix it?**

M: Why? What's wrong with **hafta**?

P: I don't know. Please tell me.

M: Think of it this way. George does have the tool for fixing the faucet, but we don't know what the tool is. It's like "He has *some tool* to fix it" and "some tool" can be questioned with *what*. Of course, we can now form the question as **He has what to fix it?** (More likely as a response of disbelief to someone else saying perhaps *He has a sledge hammer to fix it!*) But in ordinary discourse **what** "moves," so to speak, from inside to the front of the sentence, giving **What does he** … So do you begin to see what's happening, Patrick?

200

P: I'm trying. The **what** moves to the front, and so now it has to be **have to**, not **hafta**?

M: Could be. Can you be more specific?

P: Maybe. It's like you can't contract to **hafta** if something comes between **have** and **to** to start with. That's obvious. But if that something moves out, you still can't contract. Is that what you're driving at?

M: Yes. It's almost as if the movement leaves something behind, like an invisible TRACE, which itself now blocks the contraction.

P: So what about **wanna** and **gonna**? Same thing?

M: Well, let's find out. Take **wanna**. What happens when you form a sentence by moving **what** to the front in these examples:

You want to do <u>what</u>?

You want <u>what</u> to happen?

P: OK. Here's what you get:

What do you want to do?

What do you want to happen?

M: And you know what I'm going to ask next. Right?

P: Yes. What's contractable? No-brainer. It's **What do you wanna do?**

M: And not **What do you wanna happen?**

P: No!

M: All right. Now, what about **Who do they want to teach?** Anything different here?

P: Should be AMBIGUOUS, depending upon whether **who** questions the person to do the teaching or the person to be taught.

M: And **wanna**?

P: You mean **Who do they wanna teach?** Oh, OK. It's not ambiguous any more, 'cause here nothing separated **want** and **to**. Right?

M: Yes! You catch on fast.

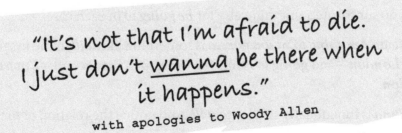

"It's not that I'm afraid to die. I just don't <u>wanna</u> be there when it happens."

with apologies to Woody Allen

gonna & gotta

– You <u>gonna</u> go to class?
– I <u>gotta</u>!

M: So much for *wanna* and *hafta*. Now about **gonna** … This case is a little different.

P: I'm all ears, Marta.

M: I'll ignore that. What's **gonna** a CONTRACTION of?

P: *Going to*, of course. So what makes this case different from the others?

M: Well, let's see. Give me an example of the contracted form.

P: How about ***I'm gonna go to London***? Uncontracted, it would be ***I'm going to go to London***.

M: OK. Now give me a contracted form for ***I'm going to London***.

P: Um … ***I'm gonna London***? Ouch!

M: What's wrong, Patrick? It can't be that something's been lifted from between ***going*** and ***to***, like with ***wanna*** and ***hafta***, because nothing was there to start with.

P: You got me on this one.

M: "Think in other channels," as the sage once said. Is there any difference in the <u>meaning</u> of the two instances of *be going to*:

> ***I'm going to go to London.*** *(or … gonna go …)*

> ***I'm going to London.***

Can you substitute something else for ***be going to*** in each case?

P: Oh. Yeah. ***Am going to*** or ***am gonna*** is something like ***will*** in the first case—***I will go to London***—and ***going to*** is like ***traveling to*** in the second—***I'm traveling to London***.

M: So ***gonna*** is functionally similar to ***will***. And notice the relation of ***to*** to ***going*** in the two cases.

P: OK. In *gonna*, *to* is so close to *going* that both are almost unrecognizable. But in *I'm going to London*, *to* feels like it "goes with" *London* more than with *going*. Big difference.

M: Yes. We can say that *to* "goes with" *London* here or, more formally, is IN CONSTRUCTION WITH it. In other words, *to London* forms a unit or a …

P: Um … oh … CONSTITUENT … yeah. That's important. I gotta do a better job of remembering that stuff.

M: Wonderful! That's another example … what you just said, Patrick.

P: What? You mean "I gotta do a better job"?

M: Yes … Don't you see? What's *gotta*?

P: Hmmm … Never thought about it. Probably *got to*.

M: Yes.

P: So *gotta's* like *gonna* … I mean *got to* in one and *going to* in the other.

M: Really? Try putting them into a sentence.

P: OK. *I gotta go* and *I'm gonna go* … Oh, but it's really *I've gotta go*. So it's <u>not</u> quite the same. I can say *I gotta go* but <u>not</u> *I gonna go*.

M: Me too!

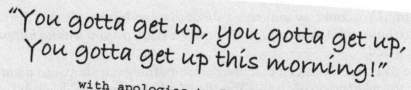

"You gotta get up, you gotta get up, You gotta get up this morning!"

with apologies to Irving Berlin, "Oh! How I Hate to Get up in the Morning" (1918)

Mary, I think, 's happy.

I think ... therefore, I'm.

with apologies to René Descartes

▶ M: Patrick, remember the fascinating time we had examining the *wanna, hafta, gonna* contractions?

P: Please speak for yourself, Marta.

M: Come on now. The contraction stuff gets even <u>more</u> interesting. Tell me if these examples are OK: *Mary's good at ping-pong. She's good at tennis.*

P: Sounds fine to me.

M: OK, now what if we add a simple *as ... as* COMPARATIVE: *Mary's as good at ping-pong as she's at tennis.*

P: Not quite. I'd say *... as she is at tennis.*

M: Why not *she's*?

P: I don't know. That's a tough one.

M: Try some more. Assuming we can say *Fred's tall*, what about *Jim's tall and Fred's too*.

P: No! Has to be *Fred is*.

M: Think about this: If we can say *Mary's happy*, can we say *I wonder <u>how</u> happy Mary's*?

P: Terrible! Has to be *Mary is*.

M: Then what about this? If we (or maybe the Brits) can say *You've a lot of money*, how about *What a lot of money you've*?

P: Stop it, Marta! This is driving me nuts. It's *you have*. But I don't have any idea what's blocking some of these contractions and not others.

M: OK, calm down. It's by no means obvious. Let's take a closer look, and revisit the *wanna* contraction too. Here are a couple of examples to maybe help narrow the focus a bit:

> *Some of us are interested in going to a movie, and ...*
>
> *We wonder if you **want to** as well* → ***wanna** as well (go to a movie)*
> *We wonder if **you are** as well* → ***you're** as well (interested ...)*

P: I don't know what to make of it. But I bet we're gonna see that the contraction constraint here ain't arbitrary!

M: *Ain't*, huh? We could say something about that too, but let's not get distracted. Think back to those awful *wanna* contractions, like *What do you wanna happen?* Again, why is it odd?

P: 'Cause you can't contract if that invisible something stays between *want* and *to* where the *what* originally was—*You want <u>what</u> to happen*? Right?

M: Right. So is the reason that that's odd the same as the reason that, say, *I wonder how happy Mary's* is odd?

P: Can't be ... 'Cause nothing comes between *Mary* and *is*, so nothing gets lifted out.

M: Then <u>why</u> can't we say *I wonder how happy Mary's*? Let me throw in a couple of more examples: *Mary's happy*.

P: Fine, of course.

M: *Mary's, I think, happy*.

P: I don't like it, but I don't know why.

M: Then what about *Mary, I think, 's happy*?

P: This one's OK, but it shouldn't be.

M: Why not?

P: Because now there's a bit of stuff between *Mary* and *is*. So how can there be <u>any</u> contraction?

M: You're assuming that all contraction has to be like *wanna, hafta, gonna*, where *to* contracts with what came before: *want, have, going*.

P: Doesn't <u>have to</u> be to the left; just <u>is</u>. Look at that simple sentence *Mary's happy*.

M: How soon we forget, Patrick! You just told me that *Mary, I think, 's happy* is OK and *Mary's, I think, happy* is <u>less</u> OK. So again, what's the direction of the contraction?

P: You're not going to tell me, are you, that in *Mary's happy* the *'s* gloms onto *happy*, that the contraction goes to the right!

M: Why not?

P: **Look at how it's written!!**

M: It's true that the written form is misleading, but how else can you explain what's going on here?

P: There's got to be a way.

M: Look ... See if you can put aside the written conventions in this case and think about what we actually say, or don't say. You can use some of the examples we've already talked about, like *I wonder how happy Mary is* (not ... *how happy Mary's*).

P: OK, Marta. By your line of reasoning, then, we don't say *I wonder how happy Mary's* because *'s* should contract to the right and there's nothing to attach to.

M: Exactly!

P: Ah, but equally bad would be ... let's see ... OK, *Jim's tall and Fred's too*, where there <u>is</u> something on the right of *'s*: the word *too*.

M: Think again. *Fred is* what?

P: Oh, *tall* ... and <u>that</u>'s what's missing.

M: Isn't that what has to be going on?

P: What a jolt! It's hard to think in new directions when the written form is so misleading.

M: That's not likely to change. But you've just demonstrated how you can discover an organizational principle of your own language.

EVERYBODY'S MIND TO ME A KINGDOM IS
or
A GREAT BIG WONDERFUL WORLD <u>IT'S</u>

Ogden Nash

PS SEVENTEEN The solution to the problem is not working.

We looked at a variety of CONTRACTION possibilities in Days 81 to 85, everything from ordinary *it's* (*it is*) to **wanna** and **gonna** (*want to, going to*) to "forward" CONTRACTION (*Mary, I think, 's happy*). In all those examples where it could occur, contraction was always an option. What then of a situation like the following: Two people are discussing some personal characteristics of a mutual friend—call him "Cecil"—who seems to have the annoying habit of saying one thing but meaning something else. In other words,

> *Cecil's problem <u>is</u> <u>not</u> saying what he means.*

From a purely structural perspective, is contraction of **is not** (**isn't**) a possibility here and, if so, does this now make any sense?

> *Cecil's problem <u>isn't</u> saying what he means.*

If not, why not? Think in terms of CONSTITUENCY. Notice what happens if you <u>reverse</u> the two halves of the original sentence, giving you:

> *<u>Not</u> saying what he means <u>is</u> Cecil's problem.*

What then is the nature of the ambiguity in the following?

> *The solution to the problem <u>is</u> <u>not</u> working.*

What two other versions of this sentence would neutralize the ambiguity? (Hint: one would be the **contracted** form and the other a **reversal** of the two halves of the sentence.)

——

Imagine seeing in operation a complex piece of machinery designed to perform a task that appears to be somewhat baffling. After watching the machinery in operation, you might be inclined to ask any of the following three questions:

> *What'<u>s</u> it do?*
> *What'<u>s</u> it doing?*
> *What'<u>s</u> it done?*

What are the <u>un</u>contracted versions of these three questions? Are all three **contracted** forms possible in the speech of your own dialect?

CHAPTER EIGHTEEN

SPACE, TIME, PERSON

spatial deixis, *coming* and *going*, inclusive and exclusive *we*, aspects of facing, temporal deixis, calendrical deixis, personal deixis, time and space lexicon

---

Day Eighty-six
coming & going

Day Eighty-seven
spatial deixis

Day Eighty-eight
temporal deixis

Day Eighty-nine
time and space

Day Ninety
personal deixis

PS 18
in Hawaii vs. on Hawaii

coming & going
hither and thither

P: Marta, I've been thinking again about some stuff that you brought up here quite a while ago.

M: And what would that be?

P: Oh, the use of **here** and **there**, also the verbs **come** and **go** ... maybe even the verbs **bring** and **take**.

M: Well, there's always much more that we can say about them, Patrick. So?

P: Uh ... I was over at my friend Herb's apartment yesterday and we were talking about maybe having a New Year's Eve party. My place is kind of small so I was wondering where we could have it ... where we could go. Then he says, "Why can't they **go here**?"

M: And?

P: "**Go here**"? It should be **come here**, shouldn't it? I mean, we were at Herb's place when he said that.

M: Right on, Patrick! And if you're still at Herb's but you happen to remind him that your place is larger, then he might say, "Why can't we ..."

P: "Why can't we **go there**?" Not **come there**!

M: Yes! But now what if you're <u>not</u> at Herb's? Let's say he's home but you're talking with him about that party by phone from <u>your</u> home.

P: Ah! Then he <u>could</u> say, "Why can't we **come there**?" ... meaning "Why can't we **come to where you are now**?" (<u>my</u> place). I guess we don't think about all this when we're actually talking and yet when you try to analyze, it comes out looking a bit tricky.

M: OK, so you're talking to Herb and you say, "**Can we come to your place?**" Does it matter whether you're on the phone with him or you're both somewhere else, like on the street?

P: Could be either one.

M: Then who does *we* refer to in these two cases?

P: Refer to? Obviously Herb and me.

M: What! You're asking Herb on the phone if **you and Herb can come to Herb's place**?

P: Wait a minute, Marta! No. If Herb and I are on the street and I say, "**Can we come to your place?**" then *we* refers to Herb and me.

M: And if it's **Can we come to your place?** but you're on the phone with him?

P: Oh, then *we* <u>can't</u> include Herb … has to refer to me and some other person or persons.

M: So, Patrick, what does this tell you about this PERSONAL PRONOUN *we*?

P: Um … that there are two *we*'s?

M: …that *we* can be … *we* can be …

P: AMBIGUOUS!

M: Yes! When *we* includes both the speaker and the person spoken to, we call it INCLUSIVE *we*. But if *we* does <u>not</u> include the person spoken to, then …

P: EXCLUSIVE *we*!

M: *We* are on a roll! Start out with the VERBS **come** and **go** and we wind up with the AMBIGUITY of the PERSONAL PRONOUN *we*. How about that!

Nowhere to <u>go</u> but out,
Nowhere to <u>come</u> but back.

Benjamin Franklin King, Jr. (1857–94),
The Pessimist

spatial deixis

come or go?
left or right?
front or back?
top or bottom?

M: By the way, Patrick, there's a name for the **come** and **go** stuff and AMBIGUITY with the PERSONAL PRONOUN **we** that we talked about last time. It's called "dike-sis," spelled d-e-i-x-i-s, and it derives from the Greek word meaning "to point."

P: "Deixis," huh?

M: Yes, it has to do in general with how and with whom we communicate what we see and hear in the space around us. Call it SPACE DEIXIS. But it takes in a lot more than what we touched on in the last session. For example, what's the meaning of **left** and **right**? Think of the arms on the chair you're sitting in.

P: The arms? Same as my own ... **left** and **right**.

M: So your **left** arm is resting on the **left** arm of the chair?

P: Of course ... and my **right** arm's on the chair's **right** arm.

M: OK, stand up, turn around, face the chair, and tell me now which are its **right** and **left** arms.

P: Oh, I see what you're getting at, Marta. When I **face** the chair, its **left** and **right** arms are the reverse of when I was sitting in it.

M: Very "deictic" of you, Patrick! By the way, look at that photo on the wall: the one showing the president of this college flanked by the provost and the dean of research, the one wearing a hat. How would you identify them in terms of **right** and **left**?

P: Uh, the provost's to the **left** of the president and the dean's to the **right**.

M: And can you describe again what you see, but this time from the <u>president's</u> perspective?

P: OK ... The provost's on the president's **right** and the dean's on her **left**. Wow! It's completely the reverse again ... **left** and **right** from our perspective but **right** and **left** from the perspective of the president, the figure in the middle!

M: So **come** and **go**, **left** and **right** ... Now how about **front** and **back**, **top** and **bottom**? Think of a guided missile ... a missile in its vertical position, before launching, with a **top** and a **bottom** that are obvious. Here, I'll draw one for us: OK, <u>now</u> does it also have a **front** and a **back**?

210

P: Not really, Marta.

M: Then what does it mean to say that here we are standing *in front of* it, not *in back of* it?

P: I guess it means that it does have a *front* and a *back*.

M: Ah … only because we're standing *in front of* it! But think of this guided missile in flight … And again I'll attempt to draw it here. Now does it have a *front* and a *back?*

P: Oh yeah … so I guess that's because it's supposed to be moving.

M: But which end is the *front*, and why?

P: It's where the nose is, because it's moving in that direction. So the fact that it's moving <u>gives</u> it a *front*; right, Marta?

M: Yes, and of course a *back* too. Very nice deductions, Patrick! … and here's one more for you to think about. I'm drawing a diagram of a church here and I want you to think again about the *front* and *back* concept. Imagine you're standing outside. What's the *front?*

P: It's "A," where you enter. You're *in front of* it.

M: OK, so now you enter and someone asks if you want to take a look at the beautiful stained-glass windows in *the front*. What *front* are they talking about?

P: Ah! "B." So it's a <u>different</u> *front* <u>inside</u> … It's where the altar is, where they perform the church service! And then you walk to *the back* of the church, exit through the same door, and immediately you're outside, but in *front !* How about that!

M: Yes! Outside: *in front of* the church or *in back of* it (*behind* it). But inside: it's *in* the *front of* the church or *in* the *back of* it.

P: That's amazing!

Cannon to <u>right</u> of them,
Cannon to <u>left</u> of them,
Cannon in <u>front</u> of them. ....

Alfred, Lord Tennyson, "The Charge
of the Light Brigade"

temporal deixis

"Mommy, I just woke up ... So is it tomorrow now?"

▶ M: Patrick, weren't we supposed to meet here in my office at ten *this morning*?

P: Yes ... and I didn't forget. As a matter of fact, I came here about *an hour ago* and saw the note you left on your door that read BACK IN 30 MINUTES. But "in thirty minutes" starting from when?

M: Oh, for heaven's sake, I can't believe I did that! Of course, you would have no way of knowing. But it's a good example of the kind of language thing I was going to bring up with you anyway.

P: So you did me a favor?

M: I don't know as I'd put it quite that way. We devoted the last couple of sessions to SPATIAL DEIXIS. And the confusing note I left on my door touches on TIME DEIXIS, or TEMPORAL DEIXIS. Suppose, by the way, my note had read BACK AGAIN ON THURSDAY? Would that have been any better?

P: Well, I think I'd find that a bit confusing too, Marta. Today is *Wednesday* but the nearest *Thursday* is tomorrow ... So if that's what you really meant, your note could read BACK AGAIN TOMORROW.

M: But "tomorrow" in reference to when? Wouldn't "back again tomorrow" here be as confusing as "back again on Thursday"? And suppose I had left a note that read BACK AGAIN NEXT FRIDAY, meaning the day after tomorrow? How do you feel about that?

P: Sounds funny ... too close to *Wednesday* to mean "the day after tomorrow." For me it would mean *Friday next week*.

M: Interesting. So then what about BACK AGAIN THIS FRIDAY? How's that?

P: Fine, Marta.

M: Well, what's going on with all this? When does *this Friday* become *next Friday*?

P: I don't know.

M: Yes, you do … You already came up with the example *Friday next week*.

P: Oh … the word *this* changes to *next* when you cross a boundary, which I guess is the *week*. So you say *this Friday* when you're in the same *week* but *next Friday* when it's the *week* after.

M: And <u>*last*</u> *Friday*?

P: Uh, that's in *the week before*.

M: So, when does *last week* become *this week* and *this week* become *next week*? In other words, where does the week begin and end?

P: Well, if "weekend" means *Saturday* and *Sunday*, then I guess the week begins on *Monday*.

M: That's certainly true for the "work week," but how are the days laid out on an ordinary calendar? There's one up there on my wall.

P: Ah hah! *Sunday*'s on the left end and *Saturday*'s on the right! … like *Sunday* through *Saturday*.

M: Yes, and think also about that little trick we play twice a year in this country with "daylight saving time." Somewhere around midnight on a certain day of the week in *March* and another in *September* we set our clocks ahead or back an hour. What day of the week is chosen for that?

P: *Saturday*. The new time starts on *Sunday*, <u>after</u> midnight. Never thought much about this before.

… Striking from the <u>Calendar</u> unborn <u>Tomorrow</u> and dead <u>Yesterday</u>

Edward Fitzgerald, *The Rubáiyát of Omar Khayyám* (1889)

DAY EIGHTY-NINE

time and space

<u>from</u> nine <u>to</u> <u>five</u>
<u>from</u> here <u>to</u> there

▶ P: If we're still on the topic of … what do you call it? … DEIXIS, there's something that struck me, Marta, as I was looking again at your examples.

M: Well, the topic hasn't changed, Patrick, so what are you getting at?

P: Um … it's the expressions like **on Thursday**, **in September**, **at ten**, **after tomorrow** … lots more, but those are what I made a note of.

M: Go on.

P: OK, it's those … I guess … PREPOSITIONS: **on**, **in**, **at**, **after**, and so on; and in the examples I just mentioned it would be … what? Oh, TIME DEIXIS, right?

M: Right you are!

P: But in previous sessions you used examples like **on the arm of the chair**, **in front of the church**, **at Herb's house**, **to your place** …

M: Yes … I remember. We were talking then about SPACE DEIXIS.

P: Well, the same prepositions, or at least some of them, seem to be showing up in both kinds of DEIXIS … Do I have that right?

M: Yes, you do … and a very nice observation, Patrick. Can you think in general of any more?

P: Sure … I've been making notes of what I think are some more since we got started on this. But after writing down a few, I decided to organize them a bit. Here's a copy for you of what I came up with.

M: OK, let's have a look:

Time	Space
<u>from</u> Monday <u>to</u> Friday	<u>from</u> Maine <u>to</u> Florida
warrantee: <u>good for</u> 5 years	warrantee: <u>good for</u> 50,000 miles
<u>ahead of/behind</u> schedule	<u>ahead of/behind</u> the parade
<u>on</u> time	<u>on</u> location
<u>in</u> time	<u>in</u> space
<u>at</u> noon	<u>at</u> Nome

Great! And let me add here a few more that I know of:

ten days <u>before/after</u> Easter	ten miles <u>before/after</u> the exit
no gas <u>till/until</u> tomorrow	no gas <u>till/until</u> Toledo
<u>beyond</u> next Tuesday	<u>beyond</u> the next town
the <u>beginning/end of</u> the concert	the <u>beginning/end of</u> the score
<u>over</u>time	<u>over</u>view

214

P: So does having the same PREPOSITION in these expressions reduce the vocabulary load for everybody, Marta?

M: Never thought of it quite that way, but very likely. What about DEICTIC violations? We saw a little of that in the last session with the confusing note that I left on my office door.

P: But I'm sure we all do it, all the time, accidentally, of course.

M: Yes … and speaking of confusion, here's an example I heard, made up, of course, that should win a prize. A guy out sailing on a small boat sees a bottle floating in the water. He fishes it out, opens it, looks inside, and finds a note. The note reads: ***Would you meet me here in an hour with a stick this big***. How many DEICTIC "violations" in that note can you identify?

P: Hmm … Well, for starters who's ***you*** and who's ***me***? where's ***here***? in an hour from ***when***? … and ***this big*** needs to be accompanied by a gesture of some kind. Wow! So maybe six violations?

M: Bravo!

Forward, the Light Brigade!
Alfred, Lord Tennyson, "The Charge of the Light Brigade"

Backward, turn backward, O Time, in your flight
Elizabeth Akers Allen, "Rock Me to Sleep" (1860)

Astronomy compels the soul to look upward …
Plato, Republic, Book VII

And here face downward in the sun
Archibald MacLeish, "You, Andrew Marvell" (1930)

Half a league, half a league, half a league onward
Alfred, Lord Tennyson, "The Charge of the Light Brigade"

We're homeward bound for New York town
Anonymous, "Good-bye, Fare You Well"

Where the light woods go seaward from the town
Leigh Hunt, The Story of Rimini (1816)

Then westward ho!
Shakespeare, Twelfth Night, Act III, scene i

… and may the outward and inward man be at one.
Plato, Phaedrus

personal
deixis

Now hear this, ye swarthy flock:
All hands on deck at 2 o'clock!

with apologies to Gilbert and Sullivan

▶ M: [*a knock on Marta's office door*] I'm on the phone ... ***Who is it***?

P: ***It's me*** ... Patrick.

M: [*"One of my students is here; I'll have to call you back."*] Come on in, Patrick.

P: Marta, I've brought a friend of mine. Is ***this*** a bad time?

M: No, ***it***'s OK. ***I'm*** Marta Ramirez. And ***you are*** ...?

P: ...***This is*** my friend and fellow student, Eva Silbermann, from Dresden. She's a psychology major.

M: ***Hi***, Eva. I'm ***pleased to meet you***. Have a seat, both of you. That phone call, ***by the way***, was from my brother and I'll need to call him back within the hour.

P: We won't be taking up much of your time, Marta. I've been talking to Eva about our English DEICTIC expressions and she's become interested from a psychological perspective.

M: Good timing, because there's already some interesting DEIXIS ***right now*** in ***this very conversation***.

P: There is?

M: Yes ... the whole ritual of introductions. How many different means of identification have there been in just the few minutes since your knock on the door? For example, I said, ***Who is it?*** not ***Who are you?*** And especially not ***Who are you?***

P: Um ... well, you introduced yourself to Eva by saying ***I'm Marta Ramirez***, followed by ***And you are ...?*** But I'm glad you <u>didn't</u> ask ***Who are you?*** That would sound a bit rude.

M: Yes! So what else? What did <u>you</u> say? How did you introduce Eva to me?

P: Oh ... ***This is my friend, Eva Silbermann***. Guess I could have also said ***I'd like you to meet*** ...

M: OK, and what happened first, after your knock on the door and I said *Who is it?*

P: I said *It's me … Patrick*.

M: And what about, for example: *This is Patrick*, *I'm Patrick*, *My name is Patrick*? Any comments?

P: Well, they seem to get less and less appropriate for our situation here. Maybe *This is Patrick* if I'm telephoning a friend. *I'm Patrick* is OK if I'm introducing myself at a very informal party. *My name is Patrick O'Grady* maybe if I'm applying for a job somewhere, especially by telephone.

M: …And also if your application is by letter … where you can't be seen or heard.

P: By the way, I notice that Eva is really enjoying *this*.

M: So am I, Patrick. One more … How would you introduce yourself on the radio, where you can be heard but not seen? Say you're a newscaster, reporting from London.

P: Hmm … *This is Patrick O'Grady, reporting to you from London*. It's almost like on the telephone, except that there I probably wouldn't be using my last name.

M: Yes … so the different occurrences of the word *this* in all *this* is something for both of you to take away with you and think about.

P: Absolutely! And thanks for talking with us, Marta. I'll see you at the regular time next week.

M: So long, Patrick. *Awfully nice meeting you*, Eva.

"This is London."
Edward R. Murrow,
opening phrase for his broadcasts from London
during World War II

PS EIGHTEEN in Hawaii vs. on Hawaii

in the state of Hawaii
on the island of Hawaii

Consider the following PREPOSITIONAL PHRASES with *in* and *on*. What generalization, if any, can you come up with that could account for the choice of one or the other of these two PREPOSITIONS?

1. **on** 12th Street
2. **on** the Canadian border
3. **in** Times Square
4. **on** the coast
5. **in** the Soho district
6. **in** the swamp
7. **in** a fog
8. **in** the mountains
9. **on** a mountain
10. **on** the summit
11. **in** the valley
12. **on** the island

13. **on** Guam
14. **in** Cuba
15. **in** Australia
16. **on/in** Hawaii
17. **on** edge
18. **in** part
19. **in** the world
20. **on** earth
21. **on** the edge of the earth (*world)
22. **on** the lawn
23. **in** the yard
24. **in/on** time

25. **on** reaching the summit,
26. **on** arriving in Timbuktu,   we sat down and cried
27. **on** realizing that we were lost,
28. **in** waiting for the train,
29. **in** reading your letter,   we fell asleep
30. **in** watching the news

CHAPTER NINETEEN
MODIFICATION

adverbial modification; relative clause: restrictive, non-restrictive, reduced; object and subject relatives; the garden path; cleft sentence and noun complement

Day Ninety-one **adverbials**

Day Ninety-two **relatives**

Day Ninety-three **down the garden path**

Day Ninety-four **noun complement**

PS 19 **the house that Jack built**

Day Ninety-five **non-restrictives**

adverbials

Seated <u>one day at the organ</u>,
I was weary and ill at ease,
And my fingers wandered <u>idly</u>
<u>Over the noisy keys</u>.

Adelaide Anne Procter (1824-64),
"A Lost Chord"

▶ M: Before it's too late, Patrick, we need to turn real attention to *something **that we've touched on*** so far without saying much about it.

P: I can't imagine what that would be, Marta.

M: It's the various kinds of MODIFICATION … How an element in a sentence gets MODIFIED.

P: You mean like **long** *silence,* **high** *mountain,* **tough** *question* … ADJECTIVE plus NOUN?

M: Oh, yes … MODIFICATION of NOUNS. But what about ADJECTIVES?

P: ADJECTIVES? That's **very** *silly,* Marta! It's the ADJECTIVES that <u>do</u> the modifying!

M: Patrick, sometimes you really do put your foot in it. What's **very** *silly* … I mean the construction?

P: Uh, oh! **Silly** *me*! I guess *silly*'s an ADJECTIVE … and that means **very** has to be a MODIFIER … Not **very** *silly* after all!

M: So if *silly's* an ADJECTIVE modified here by **very**, then what's **very**? I mean what PART OF SPEECH is it?

P: Hmmm … ADVERB?

M: Bingo! But of course **very** is hardly the <u>only</u> ADVERB in the language … plenty of others, Patrick. Think of **somewhat** *late,* **a little** *tired,* **right** *on time* … and ADJECTIVE + **-ly**, modifying VERBS and ADJECTIVES. Think of President Theodore Roosevelt's famous foreign policy slogan from the early 1900s.

P: Uh, let's see … Wasn't it something like *Speak* **softly** *and carry a big stick*?

M: Yes! And so, what about larger ADVERBIAL constructions as in *You've been coming to these English sessions with me* **for** *almost four months now*?

P: I don't understand … Isn't the word **for** a PREPOSITION?

M: Yes … good question, Patrick … so the whole construction **for** *almost four months now* is what?

P: What? Oh, a PREPOSITIONAL PHRASE, I guess.

M: Great! … and the <u>meaning</u> of "**for** *almost four months now*" is one of DURATION.

P: Now I'm <u>really</u> confused, Marta.

M: I don't blame you. Let me do this differently. Take the sentence *You've been coming.* I've written it for you here and added some ADVERBIAL complements:

You've been coming <u>here now</u> …   <u>to my office</u>
<u>frequently</u>
<u>for almost four months</u>
<u>on foot, by bicycle</u>
<u>with enthusiasm</u>
<u>on Tuesdays and Thursdays</u>
<u>since the beginning of the semester</u>
<u>whenever we have time</u>
<u>because you want to learn</u>
not   <u>because somebody made you</u>

There. What do you make of the expressions I've listed, Patrick?

P: Well, I'd say that the ones beginning with *to, for, on, by, with,* and *since* are probably PREPOSITIONAL PHRASES. Oh, and the phrases are all MODIFIERS.

M: Yes, ADVERBIAL MODIFIERS … but what <u>kind</u> of ADVERBIAL MODIFIER? We just noted that the phrase headed by *for* is one of DURATION, for example.

P: Well, if that's what you're looking for, then **to** *my office* must be, what, "destination"?

M: Not bad, Patrick; GOAL is the conventional term. And what about **on** *Tuesdays and Thursdays,* **whenever** *we have time,* *frequently* …

P: Uh, FREQUENCY!

M: Sure … and **with** *enthusiasm*? Call it MANNER. MEANS would be what? Think of locomotion …

P: Oh sure … **on** *foot,* **by** *bicycle*!

M: Fine! So now, what about TIME and PLACE?

P: Um … could be **now**, **next** *Friday* for TIME. And PLACE? I don't know, Marta … oh, wait a minute … the word **here**! Maybe **in** *your office,* **on** *the spot* …

M: [*chuckles*] …and those two CLAUSES with **because**?

P: Hmm … REASON?

M: …and also PURPOSE, Patrick? REASON and PURPOSE are not always easy to sort out, by the way. Are you getting the picture in all this? ADVERBIALS come in a variety of different forms: from a single word like **now** (TIME) or **here** (SPACE) to a whole clause like **when** *the cows come home* (TIME) or **where** *the cows come home* (SPACE). Likewise for <u>all</u> ADVERBIALS.

P: You've **really** given me a lot to think about, Marta!

God is more delighted in <u>adverbs</u>
than in nouns.
Hebrew proverb

relatives

Ten Days That Shook the World

John Reed (American journalist),
title of book about the Russian Revolution of 1917

M: Shall we get away for now from MODIFICATION with ADVERBIALS, Patrick?

P: You mean no <u>more</u> MODIFICATION?

M: No! 'Course not. We're just getting started with MODIFICATION in general. And lots of that we've already seen in some of our previous sessions.

P: Like what, Marta?

M: Uh … remember MODIFICATION in the POSSESSIVES: *the title **of the book**, **a good night's** sleep*? … and in the session on COMPOUNDS: ***weight-loss** surgery, **small car mileage** claim*? Remember our conversation about MODIFIERS with a negative PREFIX: ***un**practical person* and ***im**practical solution*? Is that enough for you?

P: OK! OK!

M: Then let's go back to MODIFIERS with NOUNS. Start with the NOUN *cat* … and give me some information about this *cat*.

P: Oh, you mean *that **little black** cat*
             *the cat **on the porch***
             *the cat **that chased the rat** …*
that sort of thing?

M: Yes … good examples. So what <u>kind</u> of MODIFICATION did you just use?

P: Umm … ADJECTIVES: ***little**, **black***? A phrase, ***on the porch*** … PREPOSITIONAL PHRASE! That third one, ***that chased the rat***, is different. I don't know what to call it.

M: The third one <u>is</u> different; it contains the makings of an actual sentence. There's a VERB: *chased* and an OBJECT: *rat*. The whole sequence here—***that chased the rat***— is called a RELATIVE CLAUSE, a *construction **that occurs <u>very</u> frequently***.

P: Your RELATIVE CLAUSE stuff is starting to sound complicated, Marta. Doesn't it involve the words *which* and *who*, even *whom*? … Sentences like *There's the cat **which chased the rat**. Where's the girl **who fed the cat**?*

M: It <u>can</u> involve *which* and *who*, but that's not how <u>you</u> said it a moment ago.

P: Hmm … I guess *There's the cat **that chased the rat*** sounds more natural here.

M: But often we don't even have a choice, Patrick. Let me try something different. I'll write a sentence containing some RELATIVE CLAUSE versions here on the board and ask you to give me your reactions:

> *Here's the example that I was referring to.*   1
> *I was referring to.*   2
> *which I was referring to.*   3
> *to which I was referring.*   4
> *to that I was referring.*   5

P: My reactions … Well, for one thing, they all look OK except for number five. But also I think number four sounds a bit formal. I mean, I can't imagine myself <u>saying</u> it like that. Maybe in writing though.

M: Nice. Those are my feelings too. Let me write two more and add them to the list:

> *Here's the example that interests me.*   6
> *interests me.*   7

Compare six and seven with one and two and tell me what you think.

P: Oh! Number seven … You don't say *Here's the example interests me* … Has to be *the example **that** interests me* or ***which** interests me*!

M: So sentence number two, *Here's the example **I was referring to***, is fine, but number seven, *Here's the example interests me*, is not. Why? What's going on, Patrick? What's the relationship between the RELATIVE CLAUSE and the word it MODIFIES?

P: Um, let's see … in number two, *example* is the <u>OBJECT</u> of ***referring to*** (*referring to the example*) but in number seven *example* is the <u>SUBJECT</u> of ***interests me*** (*the example interests me*).

M: Great! So now can you take the final step? We can see where ***that*** (or ***which***, or ***who***) in a RELATIVE CLAUSE <u>may</u> be left out. But under what condition may they <u>not</u> be left out?

P: I'm not sure, Marta.

M: Yes, you are … You almost said so a minute ago!

P: Oh, OK … I guess you can't leave out the ***that*** or ***who*** or ***which*** when they stand in for the <u>SUBJECT</u> of the RELATIVE CLAUSE.

M: I'm proud of you!

We [English] possess a wonderful richness and variety of <u>modified</u> meanings in our Saxon and Latin quasi-synonymes …

Samuel Taylor Coleridge, 19 August 1832

down the garden path

The horse raced past the barn Friday.
The horse raced past the barn <u>fell</u>.

MacDonald, Pearlmutter, and
Seidenberg (1994)

P: It may just be my imagination, Marta, but we seem to spend time looking at parts of English where things are left out.

M: [*chuckles*] … and just what are you referring to, Patrick?

P: Well, there's that whole bit on CONTRACTIONS a few sessions ago, and COMPARATIVES like **more attractive than Regina (is)**, and the missing *that* in **the movie ___ I saw** … and other stuff that I can't even remember.

M: …and how about MODIFICATION in constructions like *the girl **in the photo***, *the girl **playing the piano***, *the girl **too young to have a driver's license***?

P: I don't get it … What's being left out now?

M: Left out? … *the girl **who's** in the photo*, *the girl **who's** playing the piano* …

P: …and *the girl **who's** too young to have a driver's license*. I see … and how about *I'm the guy **who's** just learned something new*?

M: What!! Fill out the CONTRACTION on that one: ***who's** just learned something* …

P: Sure … *who is* … No, wait. It has to be *who **has** just learned*! So I guess **who is** and **who has** can <u>both</u> CONTRACT to **who's**.

M: Careful, Patrick. It's not so simple. Try a CONTRACTION in **Who has my book?**

P: Um … **Who's my book?** Ouch! I think we had something on this in a recent session … different <u>kinds</u> of *have* … and no CONTRACTION with POSSESSIVE *have*.

M: Nice recollection! But shall we stay with MODIFICATION and your puzzlement over things being left out? That already covers a lot of territory.

P: Fine, Marta.

M: So take a sentence like *Water poured from the faucet* … Simple, no?

P: Sure is!

M: Then extend it to *Water **poured from the faucet** fell into a bucket.*

P: Whoa! That's not grammatical, Marta! There's a missing *and*: ***and** fell into a bucket.*

M: No, Patrick … it's <u>already</u> grammatical. Think of ***poured from the faucet*** as a MODIFIER of ***water***.

P: [*long silence*] Oh … **water <u>that</u> <u>was</u> poured from the faucet** … That's really tricky.

First I hear *water poured from the faucet*, which is already a SENTENCE, and then I get thrown off by what sounds like <u>another</u> SENTENCE with the same SUBJECT, but now the SUBJECT is <u>missing</u>!

M: Yes … you hear *fell into a bucket* and then you have to back up, subconsciously of course, and re-analyze **poured from the faucet** as the remnant of a RELATIVE CLAUSE modifying **water**. That kind of thing happens a lot, even in other languages. It's sometimes referred to as "being led down the garden path." Want another one?

P: Sure.

M: Well, here's something that occurred just the other day. Mr. Freeman is the head football coach here and someone thought he heard the assistant coach say … and I'll write it out for you:

"*Coach Freeman told the players <u>that he saw them leave the field</u>.*"

But what the assistant coach <u>really</u> said was:

"*Coach Freeman <u>told the players that he saw</u> to leave the field.*"

P: …He told two different things!

M: Almost … the first "telling" is a REPORT; the second is a COMMAND. The words in both sentences are almost identical, yet the two are structurally very different. Which of the two has MODIFICATION of the word *players*, by the way?

P: Uh, the second: *the players **that he saw*** … with a RELATIVE CLAUSE!

M: Good, Patrick. And what about the first? What's the VERB PHRASE and what are the CONSTITUENTS?

P: OK … you got the VERB *tell*, what he "told": *that he saw,* etcetera, and who he told it to: *the players.*

M: You got it!

P: You know, Marta, I think I could have some fun trying out this GARDEN PATH thing on a few friends of mine!

"This is the sort of English up with which I will not put."
Attributed to Winston Churchill

"This is the sort of English which I will not put up with interruptions during a lecture on!"
with apologies to Winston Churchill

noun complement

> *– Did you say, "It's a <u>number</u> he never remembers"?*
> *– No … I said, "It's a <u>wonder</u> he ever remembers!"*

▶ M: Ready for some more on MODIFICATION, Patrick?

P: Ready when you are, Marta!

M: OK, tell me again how a NOUN can be modified. Let's use the NOUN *idea*.

P: Well … how about *the **great** idea*? How about *the idea **that I like a lot***?

M: How about *the idea **that I like a lot of help***?

P: Isn't that pretty much what I just said?

M: Not really, Patrick. Try saying the same phrases with *that* replaced by *which*.

P: OK … the *idea **which I like a lot*** … *the idea which I like a lot of help* … No! Wait a minute: ***which I like a lot*** is a RELATIVE CLAUSE. So what happened?

M: You tell <u>me</u>!

P: It has to be *the idea **<u>that</u> I like a lot of help*** … not *which* … but I don't know why.

M: Well, couldn't it be that we're talking about a different construction here? Think of these: *the evidence **that the universe is expanding**; a belief **that the earth is flat**; notions **that poverty is curable*** … The THAT CLAUSE here is a NOUN COMPLEMENT.

P: OK, but it sure <u>looks</u> like a RELATIVE CLAUSE … and it's also a MODIFIER.

M: Right … and of course we can even have <u>both</u> constructions modifying the same NOUN in the same sentence:

> *There's a claim that they make **that the earth is flat**.*

P: …and there's *a feeling that I have **that there's no end to this***!

M: Bravo, Patrick! Funny you should say that. Try making it the FOCUS of still another sentence in which you claim *validation* for your feeling.

P: I don't follow you, Marta.

M: Remember the CLEFT SENTENCE construction we talked about way back when? Sentences like *It's the <u>effort</u> that counts*; *It was a <u>book</u> that I referred to*; *It won't be just <u>money</u> that we lose*.

P: Vaguely.

M: Well, try anyway, Patrick; try to fit your "feeling" sentence into one beginning with *it's the feeling* and ending with *that's now validated*.

P: You gotta be kidding!

M: You're right! It's asking a lot. I'll write it out for you, separating the clauses, so you can see what it looks like:

> *It's the feeling*
> > *<u>that</u> I have*
> > > *<u>that</u> there's no end to this*
> > > *<u>that's</u> now validated.*

Can you identify the three THAT CLAUSES?

P: I guess the big one—*It's the feeling*, etcetera, ***that's*** *now validated*—is probably that CLEFT-SENTENCE thing that you brought up. Oh, and there's the RELATIVE CLAUSE ***that I have***. But what's the middle one?

M: It's what we started out with today: *the idea* ***that I like a lot of help***, *belief* ***that the earth is flat*** …

P: Oh! NOUN COMPLEMENT!

M: Beautiful!

<u>Yikes!</u>
"They provide a useful descriptive framework for the hypothesis presented in this paper—<u>that</u> it is the commonality of features on case values <u>that</u> are given case values <u>that</u> are missing <u>that</u> enables one to make inferences across sentence boundaries."

non-restrictives

Is that the <u>Tom Haines who</u> ran for mayor?
No. That's <u>Tom Baines, who</u> ran for dogcatcher!

▶ M: Patrick, I bet you think that by now we must have exhausted the topic of MODIFICATION of nouns and NOUN PHRASES. Right?

P: Not really, Marta … I know you too well now to believe that!

M: [*laughter*] … and right you are! Let's look again at the RELATIVE CLAUSE. We'll call it RELATIVIZATION, or maybe just RELATIVE. Consider the following sentence and make it number one; I'll write it out for you:

> (1) *The course that I just took was Music History 101.*

Any comments?

P: Sure … RELATIVE: ***that I just took*** … modifies ***course***.

M: Right … so here's another one; call it two:

> (2) *Musicology, which I didn't take, was full.*

Any comments this time, Patrick?

P: Yeah … another RELATIVE: ***which I didn't take*** … modifies ***musicology*** … not much different from number one, except for the commas.

M: All right, then, erase the commas on number two and see what you get.

P: [*erases*] *(2) Musicology which I didn't take was full.*
Hmm … Seems now like it should be, maybe, ***The*** *Musicology which I didn't take* … But then it sounds like there's more than one *Musicology*. So are we looking at maybe more than one kind of <u>RELATIVE</u> here, Marta?

M: Yes! The term for the RELATIVE in number one, with no commas, is RESTRICTIVE RELATIVE. In other words, it "restricts" the MODIFICATION to just ***the course***. So then what would you call the RELATIVE in number two—with the commas, of course?

P: Uh … "<u>un</u>restrictive"?

M: Nice try, Patrick … but no. What's another negative prefix that we looked at some weeks ago … the "<u>non</u>-judgmental" one?

P: Oh … non-restrictive!

M: Yes … and the non-restrictive relative occurs in a range of contexts too. Take your friend, the psychology major, *Eva Silbermann,*

> *whom you introduced me to a couple of weeks ago* or
> *to whom you introduced me* or even
> *who you introduced me to*

but <u>not</u> *that* you introduced me to. And here's another: *You introduced me to your friend Eva, which pleased me*.

P: Shouldn't it be *who pleased me*, Marta? I mean Eva's a person, not a thing!

M: Well, I certainly like Eva, but what was I referring to that I said I found pleasing?

P: Ah, the introduction!

M: …or the whole act of your introducing Eva to me!

P: But in either interpretation, one with *who* and the other with *which*, it's non-restrictive, right?

M: You got it, Patrick!

Busing

The bus <u>that we took</u> is no. 11.

Bus no.10, <u>which we didn't take</u>, doesn't go there.

The first bus <u>(for you)</u> <u>to take</u> is no. 9.

The first bus <u>to come</u> will be no. 8.

The bus <u>arriving late</u> is no. 5.

PS NINETEEN the house that Jack built

This is the farmer sowing the corn,
That kept the cock that crowed in the morn,
That waked the priest all shaven and shorn,
That married the man all tattered and torn,
That kissed the maiden all forlorn,
That milked the cow with the crumpled horn,
That tossed the dog,
That worried the cat,
That killed the rat,
That ate the malt,
That lay in the house that Jack built.

Old nursery rhyme

CHAPTER TWENTY

WORDS, WORDS … AGAIN

internal and external structure of words; modal duality: deontic and epistemic; light verbs; questionable words and phrases

Day Ninety-six
ins & outs of word structure

Day Ninety-seven
the secret life

Day Ninety-eight
Modals must not be difficult.

Day Ninety-nine
the bearable lightness of (certain) verbs

PS 20
to really know a word …

Day One Hundred
strange things said and written

ins & outs of word structure

"Words are the fortresses of thought."

William Hamilton, quoted by Samuel Butler,
The Notebooks of Samuel Butler **(1912)**

▶ M: Patrick, we're nearing the end of all these sessions of ours and I'm thinking that it might be useful now to take another look at what we started out with. Do you remember?

P: How could I forget … <u>words</u>! And what <u>are</u> they?

M: …and what we really "know" when we know a word?

P: That's right … like how it's pronounced, how it's spelled, what it means … oh, and the PART OF SPEECH … NOUN, VERB, ADJECTIVE, PREPOSITION … and so on.

M: …and even more, of course. Take a word like **nationalization**. Does it derive from anything else? In other words, is it somehow "put together"?

P: Yes! Of course! Uh … starting with **nation**, the NOUN; add **-al** and you get **national**, the ADJECTIVE; then add **-ize** and you get **nationalize**, the VERB.

M: …and?

P: Oh! … add **-ation** to **nationalize** and you get **nationalization**: a NOUN again … and a much larger one!

M: Right … so there's a lot that goes into putting together a word like **nationalization**. You can think of all that as its <u>internal</u> structure.

P: Never thought of it that way.

M: Nor do lots of others. But what now about the <u>external</u> part?

P: I don't know what you mean, Marta.

M: Then go back a step and take the VERB **nationalize**. What are examples of some short sentences using that word?

P: Um … "The government **will** nationalize the steel industry." "The government *nationalized* the steel industry."

M: And what are the *-ed* and *will* doing here? What's the relationship of *nationalize* to the rest of the sentence?

P: OK … the verb *nationalize* has a SUBJECT—*the government*—and an OBJECT—the *steel industry* … and *will* puts it into the future and *-ed* puts it in the past.

M: And does any of that change the core <u>make-up</u> of *nationalize*?

P: I guess not … same thing with PRESENT TENSE *nationalizes* … and I think I see what you're getting at.

M: You do?

P: Sure … What surrounds *nationalize* in all your examples—SUBJECT, OBJECT, *-es*, *-ed*, *will*—are <u>external</u> things, right?

M: Yes, Patrick! And does all this tell you anything more about *words* in the language, and VERBS especially?

P: Uh … that they may have an <u>internal</u> structure and everything else is <u>external</u>?

M: Not bad!

Polonius: What do you read, my lord?
Hamlet: Words, words, words.

Shakespeare, Hamlet, Act II, scene ii

the secret life of modals

They <u>must</u> be here tomorrow; they have an obligation.

They <u>must</u> be here now; I can hear their voices.

They <u>must</u> have been here yesterday.

▶ M: One sentence figuring in the last session was *The government **will** nationalize the steel industry*. What's the word ***will*** here, Patrick?

P: I don't know … guess it's one of those MODALS.

M: Yes. It's a PART OF SPEECH that we haven't said much about in all these sessions, and I think it's finally time to turn some attention to it.

P: What do you have in mind, Marta?

M: I'm thinking of the MODALS ***can, will, shall, may, might, could, should, would, must***…

P: Didn't we already do something with them?

M: Only a little bit, and nothing about their <u>duality</u>.

P: Duality?

M: Yes. Take the MODAL ***must***, for example. Suppose you ask me my opinion about the newest Porsche on the market and I say, "Fine; but they're very expensive, so you ***must*** pay a lot if you really want one."

P: You mean, like I'd *have to* pay a lot?

M: Right. But suppose instead I say, "Fine, but you really ***must*** be out of your mind even to think about it."

P: Ah … no obligation here … You ***could*** be … uh … <u>implying</u> that I'm a little crazy to even <u>think</u> about buying one.

234

M: Yes. So what's to conclude about this so far, Patrick?

P: Um … that "must" *must* be AMBIGUOUS? [*chuckles*]

M: It certainly *can* be, though the CONTEXT is likely to suggest one meaning rather than the other, as it probably did here.

P: Well, *can* the other MODALS be AMBIGUOUS too, Marta?

M: You tell me. You just used *can*, so take that, for example. Let's say we were expecting your friend Herb to join us today but you say, "Herb *can't* be here; he's not feeling well," where *can't* here means "is not able to."

P: OK so far.

M: …Yes, but unknown to you, Herb now feels fine and has just arrived and parked his car. You look out the window, see his car, and exclaim, "He *can't* be here; he's sick!" where *can't* means something like "I *can't* believe …"

P: And I heard the MODAL *should* being used something like this in a recent conversation between two people where the use of *should* gave rise to a misunderstanding.

M: That *could* be very interesting, Patrick.

P: Well, I thought it was. A man was talking to his wife as she was leaving to go shopping and he said, "Take Route 4 to avoid the traffic; you *should* be home by five."

M: *Should*, huh? Go on.

P: Well, with his use of *should*, she thought he was telling her to be home by five and resented it.

M: Whereas?

P: Whereas he was only using *should* as a prediction. Seems like MODALS *might* get you in trouble sometimes!

M: Yes, that *can* happen, Patrick. Your example is nice. ▪

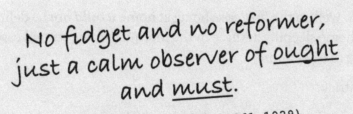

No fidget and no reformer,
just a calm observer of <u>ought</u>
and <u>must</u>.

William Bliss Carman (1861–1929),
The Joy of the Road

Modals must not be difficult.

"A tiny little word _can_ be a clap of thunder."

Proverbial (French)

▶ M: Let's go back to those dualities, Patrick … those AMBIGUITIES we saw last time with **must** and **should**. OK?

P: Fine, Marta … I was going to ask about that anyway.

M: One way to do this **might** be for me to conjure up some MODAL examples and see what you **can** make of them.

P: I **may** have a problem.

M: …If so, you **may** skip to the next one. See! … a duality already. "Possibility" with the first **may**; "permission" with the second.

P: …and maybe even a third? Remember the movie _Star Wars_ and the famous line "**May** the force be with you"?

M: Yes, the use of **may** as a kind of "incantation." You amaze me, Patrick! But let's stay with the duality issue for now. Suppose your friend Herb called you for help at three in the morning; **would** you be home?

P: Yes, of course, I **would**. I'm always home sleeping at that hour.

M: And if he desperately needed you at three in the <u>afternoon</u> and asked you that morning, **would** you be home this time?

P: Well, I have classes in the afternoon, but yes, of course. In this case I**'d** make it a point to be at home.

M: Any difference in meaning between the two **would**s?

P: Hmm … well, in the first case, being at home **would not** be deliberate, since I'm always home sleeping at three in the morning. In the second case, I**'d** be making an <u>effort</u> to be at home.

M: Nice, Patrick.

P: But what difference does it make, Marta? The MODAL **would** or **wouldn't** doesn't change at all in these examples.

M: That's certainly true here, but not everywhere. Consider the MODAL **must** again. Let's say you're planning to play tennis this afternoon with three of your friends, but of course it **mustn't** be raining (or **must not** be raining).

P: OK, so far.

M: But it <u>was</u> raining earlier in the day. You look outside now and don't see any more puddles. So …

P: It **must not** be raining any more?

M: Can you also say "It **mustn't** be raining anymore"?

P: Not unless the "it" refers to some "rain god"!

M: Yes, for some reason the contracted form **mustn't** seems to denote a willful act. "You **mustn't** do that," says a mother to a child.

P: So, Marta, what's behind this mysterious "duality" with the modals?

M: Not so mysterious, Patrick. Take any of the MODALS, say, **may** or **must** or **can** or **should** or **might**. One of their senses is that of permission, obligation, or ability to engage in some action: "You **may/must/can/should** leave," for example. The name often given for this meaning is DEONTIC (from the Greek word meaning "binding" or "needful"). The other sense, or meaning, is one of possibility or necessity: "You **may/must/can/might** be mistaken," for example. The name given for this meaning is EPISTEMIC (from the Greek word meaning "knowledge" or "understanding"). See what you got me into?

P: You're amazing, Marta!

"<u>May</u> you spend eternity roller-skating on cobblestones!"
Charles Fillmore, Lectures on Deixis (1997)

the bearable lightness of (certain) verbs

"Don't <u>make a move</u> without calling [name of moving company]."

M: Many weeks ago, Patrick, we talked about VERBS in sentences like *Put your hat on*, *Look up* that word, *Clean* your desk *out*, *Turn down* the volume … Remember?

P: Yes. You called them … what … PHRASAL VERBS?

M: Good! And where does the <u>meaning</u> lie in PHRASAL VERBS, like *put on*, *look up*, *clean out*, and so on?

P: Well, it's certainly not just in *put*, and *look*, and *clean*. I guess that's why they're called PHRASAL VERBS, Marta.

M: Yes … and in those examples it's VERB + PARTICLE, where the verb alone isn't enough to carry the meaning. So what about other expressions, like *make a claim*, *take a breath*, *have a belief*, *reach a decision* …?

P: Hmm … *make a claim*, *reach a decision* … Well, take any of these verbs: *make*, for example. In *make a claim*, *make* says even <u>less</u> about the meaning.

M: Then what <u>does</u> carry the meaning, Patrick?

P: Oh, *claim*.

M: So could you possibly rephrase a sentence like *Will they **make a claim** of fraud?* <u>without</u> the verb *make*?

P: OK … I guess it would have to be *Will they **claim** fraud?*

M: Yes! And what's the difference between *claim* and *make a claim*?

P: Uh … none; they mean the same thing.

M: …and what about the word *claim*?

P: Oh … it's a VERB by itself, and in *make a claim* I guess it's a NOUN.

M: And you've already noticed that *make* here carries little meaning. The very apt technical term for it, by the way, is LIGHT VERB.

P: But why put the NOUN *claim* with a LIGHT VERB, Marta? Seems like it's just simpler to go with *claim* the VERB.

M: Why? Think! Suppose you run into your friend Herb at the office of your auto insurance company, you ask what he's doing there, and he replies, *I'm making a claim*. Could he have also responded by saying *I'm claiming*?

P: Ah, no! Well, he could have, but it would sound kind of funny.

M: "Funny"? In what way?

P: Well, you can't stop with just *I'm claiming*. You have to *claim* <u>something</u>!

M: Can you think of another way to say this in terms of a <u>property</u> of the VERB *claim*?

P: I guess *claim* has to have an OBJECT, like *claim damages ... to the car*.

M: ...And so if Herb had chosen the LIGHT VERB construction with *claim*, would there also have to be an OBJECT?

P: ...in saying *I'm making a claim*? No ...but if he <u>wanted</u> to elaborate, he could say *I'm making a claim <u>of damages</u>*.

M: So then is it always a <u>choice</u> between LIGHT VERB construction *make a claim* and the VERB *claim*?

P: Guess not. We need them both. ▪

Will someone please <u>make a motion</u> to adjourn this meeting?
Yes ... I <u>move</u> that we adjourn.

<u>make</u> an objection, a suggestion, a move,
object   suggest   move

a guess, a wish, a proposal
guess   wish   propose

<u>reach</u> a decision, a conclusion,
decide   conclude

an understanding, an agreement
understand   agree

<u>have</u> a feeling, a sense,
feel   sense

a belief, doubts,
believe   doubt

<u>do</u> an experiment, an imitation,
experiment   imitate

an impersonation
impersonate

<u>take</u> a bath, a break, a breath, a ride, a walk
bathe   break   breathe   ride   walk

strange things said and written

"The problem is is that people write would of ... should of ... could of ..."

M: This is our final session, Patrick, and you know I'm thinking this time, for once, why don't I let <u>you</u> tell <u>me</u> what we could talk about?

P: Gosh, Marta, I don't know … Well, maybe something about the kinds of mistakes that people make with English. I mean native speakers, of course.

M: OK, but be careful what you call a "mistake." One person's "mistake" usually sounds or looks perfectly fine to the person who makes it. Besides, linguists are not in the habit of telling people what they should or shouldn't say or write. They don't <u>pre</u>scribe; they <u>de</u>scribe. They analyze, form hypotheses, figure out the formal structures that underlie what we hear and see, and form generalizations.

P: You mean anything goes?

M: [*chuckles*] Not really. And we can certainly talk about bits of language that we see or hear that would be hard to fit into the larger grammar picture.

P: I guess it would be helpful to have an example.

M: I was just about to give you one, Patrick. It's really not ***too big of a problem*** to think one up … [*long pause*] Well?

P: Well, what?

M: …***too big of a problem***?

P: Something wrong with it, Marta?

M: Well, a grammar book would have it as ***too big a problem***. I think what happens is maybe an unconscious aversion to having an ADJECTIVE <u>preceding</u> an ARTICLE: ***big a problem*** versus ***a big problem***. So maybe it gets "corrected," mistakenly of course, by insertion of the PREPOSITION ***of***.

P: So I guess I just learned something. Speaking of ***of***, what about writing *should have* as ***should of***, like *He **should of** known better*? I see that all the time.

M: So do I … and *could **of** left, would **of** called, might **of** failed* … Any ideas why people write like this?

P: Hmm … Well, when you actually <u>say</u> them, they sound fine … Oh, and I also see them written as **should've, could've** … Maybe this has something to do with it.

M: You may be right. How could anyone <u>pronounce</u> the final syllable of *should've* without having it sound like *of*?

P: …and if it <u>sounds</u> like *of*, then they think you can <u>write</u> it as *of*.

M: …and *if you* **would have** *asked me, I would have told you*.

P: So, Marta, how about—

M: [*interrupting*] Are you going to let that pass, Patrick?

P: What do you mean?

M: *If you* **would have** *asked me*?

P: Something wrong with that?

M: Well, again, it's quite common, but a grammar book would list them as

> *If you* **asked me**, *I would tell you*.
> *If you* **had asked me**, *I would have told you*.

The problem is **is that** people tend to copy **would have** verb-**ed** in the *if*-clause.

P: I guess I just learned someth—

M: [*interrupting*] Wait a minute! **The problem is is that** …?

P: Ah! Didn't catch that one either: double **is**. Should be **the problem <u>is</u> that** …, right?

M: Right, of course! What's happening here might be tied to the pseudo-cleft construction **<u>What</u> the problem is is that** … where the **what** is simply omitted. Just a guess.

P: Wow! This funny stuff really **gives** you and **I** a lot to talk about.

M: [*pause*] … **gives you and I**, Patrick?

P: Sure … You and I did this, did that, and so on.

M: You're missing the point. Would you say **gives <u>I</u>** *something* …?

P: No! Should be **gives <u>me</u>** …

M: Then why does **me** become **I** after **gives you and** …?

P: Ouch! Should be **you and me**! I wonder why I did that, Marta.

M: Again, very common … and a real violation. The first-person pronoun <u>objects</u> of a verb are **me** and **us**. But it seems that most **people could care less** about all this.

P: I hope you don't think I'm one of them.

M: You didn't catch it, Patrick: **Most people could care less** …

P: What's wrong with that? Everybody says it!

M: It's not the grammar this time, Patrick; it's the meaning: **Most people don't care**.

P: Ah! … So if **most people could care less**, then that means that they do care. If they don't, then it should be **Most people <u>couldn't</u> care less**. Right?

M: Right! … **and the data is pretty clear**.

P: [*silence*] You're setting me up again, aren't you, Marta? I can feel it.

M: Yes … and I'm enjoying it! So what do you notice this time?

P: Nothing!

M: This one's so common that I think it has probably solidified. The word **data** is taken from Latin but it's in the PLURAL form: *the **data** are clear*. Its SINGULAR form is **datum**, which most people don't know and probably **couldn't care less** about anyway. But technically (and maybe a little pompously), a single piece of *data* is a **datum**.

P: Isn't the word **media** also like that, Marta?

M: Like that in what way, Patrick?

P: I think I read somewhere that the word **media** is PLURAL, though all the time I hear it or see it written as **The media <u>is</u> too powerful**, **The media <u>has</u> too much influence**, **The media <u>does</u> this, <u>does</u> that**. And I guess I do it myself.

M: Nice, Patrick! Not many people know that. And what makes it a little different is that we do have the word **medium**—as in **medium of communication** or the ADVERB **medium-rare (roast beef)**—but not in common use as the SINGULAR of a plural **media**. There's a lot more of this sort of thing, but maybe it's enough "correcting," especially for our last day. I think it's probably time now to bring it to a close.

P: Well, I will miss it! These sessions with you have given me so much, Marta. All I can do is give you a big "thank you"!

M: You've been a pleasure to work with, Patrick. You're a very fine student and have become a good friend. So please feel free to stop by my office again … any day, any time!

> "Words should be an intense pleasure, just as leather should be to a shoemaker."
> Evelyn Waugh, New York Times, November 19, 1950

PS TWENTY to really know a word …

Listed in PS1 were a number of properties associated with knowledge of the single word *drink*. Having encountered additional properties in the course of these twenty weeks, we're now in a position to extend that list a bit. The kinds of knowledge entailed in fully "knowing" the English word *drink* would therefore include at least the following:

PRONUNCIATION (drɪŋk)

SPELLING (d-r-i-n-k)

PART OF SPEECH (**verb, noun**)

STRUCTURE (**subject** – *drink* – **object**)

SEMANTICS/SELECTION (**subject** [+animate], **object** [+liquid])

INFLECTION (*drinks, drank / have drunk /*drinked*)

DERIVATIVE (*drinker*)

NEGATIVE (***non-**drinker*)

DERIVED ADJECTIVE, NOUN (***drunk, drunkard***)

COMPARATIVE (*drunker, **more** drunk*)

COMPOUND (***soft drink, coffee drinker, dead drunk***)

AMBIGUITY (*He used to **drink a lot***)

SYNONYMY (***imbibe, libation***)

COLLOCATION (***heavy/**strong drinker**, cf. **strong/**heavy drink***)

IDIOM (***drink in** the scenery*)

METAPHOR/POETRY ("***Drink to me only with thine eyes***")

Examples analogous to many of these can, of course, be drawn for other languages.

ENVOI Sound, Spelling, Meaning

The well-known weekly columnist for the *Los Angeles Times*, Jack Smith, once wrote a piece about how easy it is in writing English to choose the wrong one of a pair of words that sound the same but have different meanings and different spellings, for example, *brake* and *break*. These are what are known as HOMOPHONES. Smith writes that "readers continue to send me examples of misused [homophones] from this newspaper and others. Among the recent crop:

Griffith Park would be adversely <u>effected</u>

the <u>affects</u> of alcohol

the <u>site</u> of so many people in tuxedos

infrared <u>censors</u>

he <u>bares</u> no malice

a backhanded <u>complement</u>

<u>pouring</u> over the numbers

drilling <u>cites</u>

graduates <u>hoards</u> of illiterates"

Smith goes on to cite a reader who says "my mention of *to*, *two*, and *too* moved him to write his first limerick since high school:

> *Three trains to old Kathmandu*
> *Had choices exceedingly few.*
> > *One switched to track One,*
> > *Another to Two;*
> *The third had to go to Two too!*"

Another reader offered the columnist "what he calls the ultimate homophone—a word with four different spellings and meanings and one pronunciation: *right*, *write*, *rite*, and *wright*."

Smith closes his article by calling attention to a reader's observation "that there is no way in the English language to say that there are three *twos*—(tos?, toos?). (We can say there are three words that are pronounced *tew*.)"

(Jack Smith, "On sinking deeper into the mire of past mistakes," *Los Angeles Times*, December 12, 1989. © *Los Angeles Times* 1989. Reprinted with permission.)

ENVOI

Let's carry the homophone idea further. Pairs of words in English can be distinguished according to whether or not they contrast in terms of any combination of three different features: sound, spelling, and meaning. Denoting these pairings, in addition to HOMOPHONES, are other technical names:

HOMOGRAPH (one of a pair of words having the same spelling but different sound and different meaning)

HOMONYM (one of a pair of words having the same spelling and the same sound but different meaning)

SYNONYM (one of a pair of words having the same meaning but different sound and different spelling).

The SAME/DIFFERENT variables yield eight distinct possible kinds of word pairs, although two of them are superfluous. Listed below are the terms for such pairs, together with their characteristics represented as +/- SAME SOUND/SPELLING/MEANING. For each term, write in a pair of English words that exemplifies it. For no.5, write the entries in a phonetic notation of your own devising. For no.6, you might think of spelling contrasts between British and American English.

	Same spelling	Same sound	Same meaning
1. _____ / _____ HOMOGRAPHS	+	−	−
2. _____ / _____ HOMONYMS	+	+	−
3. _____ / _____ HOMOPHONES	−	+	−
4. _____ / _____ SYNONYMS	−	−	+
5. _____ / _____ dialectal pronunciation	+	−	+
6. _____ / _____ dialectal spelling	−	+	+
7. _____ / _____ dictionary lexicon	−	−	−
8. _____ / _____ identical entries	+	+	+

246

A Phonetic Alphabet for American English

CONSONANTS

pʰ	pill	tʰ	till	kʰ	kill
p	spill	t	still	k	skill
b	bill	d	dill	g	gill
f	fill	θ	thin	š	shell
v	villa	ð	then	ž	measure
l	lily	s	sin	č	chill
w	will	z	zebra	ǰ	jelly
m	mill	n	nil	ŋ	sing
r	rent	y	yes	h	hill

VOWELS

i	beat	ə	sofa	u	boot
ɪ	bit	ʌ	but	ʊ	foot
e	bait	aw	cow	o	boat
ɛ	bet	ay	buy	ɔ	long
æ	bat	ɔy	boy	ɑ	pot

NOTES AND SOLUTIONS

Day 4 The Pidgin example is cited in Bickerton and Odo (1976) and the (modified) translation is from Givón (1984). The "bricks and mortar" metaphor is used by Aitchison (1987).

PS 1 The kinds of knowledge entailed in fully "knowing" the English verb *pour* would be at least the following:

PRONUNCIATION (pɔr)

SPELLING (p-o-u-r)

PART OF SPEECH (verb)

STRUCTURE (subject–*pour*–object)

VERB FORMS (*pours / poured / have poured, is pouring*)

HOMOPHONE (*pore*)

SAYING ("*When it rains, it pours.*")

The use of the star in /*drinked, heavy/*strong drinker* and *strong/*heavy drink* is the linguistic convention to indicate ungrammaticality, or non-occurrence, and will be in use elsewhere in the book.

Day 9 The technical term for the constructions under discussion is CLEFT SENTENCE (e.g., *It's the people who said "no"*), where the original (*The people said "no"*) is split in two or "clefted," so to speak, with the focused part (*the people*) assigned the new subject and verb *it is* (*it's*), *it was*, etc., and the residue (*said "no"*) appearing as a *that* (or *who, which*) clause: *who said "no."*

Day 10 The technical term for the FOCALIZED constructions with *what* here is PSEUDO-CLEFT SENTENCE (e.g., *What the people said is "no"*), where the original (*The people said "no"*) is again split in two or (PSEUDO-) "CLEFTED," so to speak, with the focused part ("*no*") given a new verb (*be/is*) and the corresponding wh- form (*what*) attached to the residue (*the people said*).

PS 2 The constituent divisions in question would be the following:

*Elizabeth [3rd **longest reigning queen**]* vs. *[**Elizabeth 3rd**] longest reigning queen*
*surplus [**store owner**]* vs. *[**surplus store**] owner*
*caring [**for hospital director**]* vs. *[**caring for**] hospital director*
*Garden Grove resident naïve, [**foolish judge says**]*
vs. *Garden Grove resident naïve, foolish [**judge says**]*

NOTES AND SOLUTIONS

Day 11   The term MALAPROPISM derives from a character in the play *The Rivals*, by the eighteenth-century English playwright, Richard Brinsley Sheridan. The name of the character, Mrs. Malaprop, is itself a derivative of the adjective "malapropos," meaning "a ludicrous misuse of words, especially in mistaking it for another word resembling it" (*Oxford English Dictionary*), such as "pullet surprise" for "Pulitzer Prize." A good scholarly reference for malapropisms is Fay and Cutler (1977).

Day 13   The term SPOONERISM derives from the Rev. William Archibald Spooner (1844–1930), an Oxford don and educationist with a reputation for SLIPS OF THE TONGUE, or speech errors of the kind cited here. The technical term for the particular error of collapsing two words into one—as in *mud puddle → muddle*—is HAPLOLOGY. Some of the examples used in this session are taken from Fromkin (1973).

Day 14   The term "neologism," meaning literally "new word," is of Greek origin and breaks down into *neo + logos + ism*.

Day 15   The main source of the puns selected for this material is Baron (1989). *WE PRY HARDER* is a pun on the common expression "We **try** harder."

Day 18   There are a few exceptions to the rule that derivational suffixes change the grammatical category of their stems: *pup > puppy, John > Johnny, waiter > waitress, lion > lioness*, etc.

        Answers to the little exercise at the end: The *-en* syllables that are a SUFFIX occur in the following words: *often* (*oft* is archaic), *forgotten* (*forget*), *fallen* (*fall*), *unshaven* (*shave*), *drunken* (= *drunk*), *hidden* (*hide*), *happen* (*hap* is archaic), *tighten* (*tight*), *broken* (*break*). The words *forgotten, fallen, (un) shaven, hidden*, and *broken* are ADJECTIVES derived from PAST PARTICIPLES. The VERB *tighten* is derived from the ADJECTIVE *tight*.

PS 4   If *hogs* is a noun, then *downtown hogs* is a NOUN-COMPOUND functioning as SUBJECT and *grant* is the VERB. If *hogs* is a verb, then *downtown* is the subject and *grant* is a noun within the NOUN-COMPOUND *grant cash*. For more on COMPOUNDS, see Chapter 16.

Day 22   Some of the expressions appearing in this section have been taken from J. Lipton's *An Exaltation of Larks or, The Venereal Game* (1977). The *venereal* here derives from *venery*, having to do with hunting and dates back to the Middle Ages. The first part of the expression *an exaltation of larks* is called a "collective noun," deployed in the realm of venery with such as *a pride of lions, a brace of pheasants, a bevy of quail, a swarm of bees,* etc. But the fun part is where that early imagination begins to take off: *an ostentation of peacocks, a parliament of owls, a crash of rhinoceroses*; and the venereal connection starts to wither: *a herd of harlots, a drift of fishermen, a superfluity of nuns*. Other devices creep in: *a doctrine of doctors, a poverty of pipers* (alliteration); *an embarrassment of twitches, a breach of premises* (punning); *a rascal of boys, a debauchery of bachelors* (behavior); *a goring of butchers, a flush of plumbers, a draught of bottlers, a pummel of masseurs* (occupational). And for more fun in recent times with more plays on words: *a wrangle of philosophers, a conjunction of grammarians, a fumble of checkgrabbers*; some with an occupational twist: *a joint of osteopaths, a rash of dermatologists, a flutter of cardiologists, a corps of anatomists*; others attuned to academia: *a clamber of assistant professors, a tenure of associate professors, an entrenchment of full professors*.

Day 24 The linguistic cover term for *article* (both *definite* and *indefinite*) is *determiner*.

PS 5 A good scan could give you *democratic nations, generic terms, abstract expressions, thought, the operations ..., the mind*. The very nature of de Tocqueville's thesis, articulated throughout his book *Democracy in America*, would seem to give rise to generics.

Day 26 The "missing" final "b" sound in the pronunciation of the nouns *bomb* and *crumb* is somewhat analogous to the missing final "g" sound, for example, in the adjectives *strong* and *young*, where the "g" then is no longer "missing" in the pronunciation of *stronger* and *younger*. An explanation for this in phonological terms can be found in any introductory work on linguistics.

Day 29 In technical terms, the rendition of the same written vowel or the same written consonant in pairs of related words like *sane | sanity, history | historical, medical | medicine, sign | signal* is the MORPHOPHONEMIC spelling. Although the MORPHOPHONEMIC principle underlies most of the English lexicon, there are many examples where the desired pronunciation instead forces application of the PHONOLOGICAL principle (more directly relating sound with letter of the alphabet). The *k/c* alternation for *provoke | provocation* (cf. *provoce*) is a good example of PHONOLOGICAL spelling. A very readable discussion of the regularities in English spelling can be found in Schane (1970). One of the best sources for etymologies is the *Oxford English Dictionary* (OED).

Day 30   Another good resource for word etymology and morphology is the Scripps Spelling Bee website: http://www.spellingbee.com/cctoc.shtml

PS 6   Shaw's "logic" was based on the erroneous assumption that English spelling is PHONOLOGICAL rather than MORPHOPHONEMIC. Furthermore, *gh* as [f] is found only word-finally and only in the words *cough, laugh, enough, tough,* and *trough*.

Day 33   Although the spelling of the *un-* prefix remains constant, unlike the *in-* prefix, the <u>pronunciation</u> of *un-* can vary as *un-* assimilates to the stem: e.g., "*um*believable."

Day 35   Note that there would be little or no assimilation across word boundaries. E.g.

> ...*in possible situations*
> ...*in capable hands*
> ...*in relevant areas*
> ...*in legal terms*

Day 37   It should be obvious that the *'s* inflections illustrated here can represent semantic relations other than just POSSESSIVE. Some examples taken from Brinton (2000), where POSSESSIVE is used in its more literal sense and the term GENITIVE applies to <u>all</u> the *'s* inflections, are the following:

POSSESSIVE GENITIVE:	*Felix's car (Felix has a car)*
SUBJECTIVE GENITIVE:	*the queen's arrival (The queen arrived)*
OBJECTIVE GENITIVE:	*the city's destruction (... destroy the city)*
GENITIVE OF ORIGIN:	*Shakespeare's plays (the plays of Shakespeare)*
GENITIVE OF MEASURE	*an hour's time, a stone's throw*

Notice then the GENITIVE subject-object AMBIGUITY with phrases like the following:

*the judge's appointment (**of** someone) (The judge appointed someone)*
*the judge's appointment (**by** someone) (Someone appointed the judge)*

Day 38   The two kinds of POSSESSION are denoted formally as ALIENABLE (e.g., *key, car, house,* etc.) and INALIENABLE (e.g., *knee, ear, elbow,* etc.).

PS 8   School**s**   Chief'**s**   Viewpoint Evolve**s**
               1   2   3

                   1 is plural s

              2 is possessive s

        3 is third-person singular s

Day 41   Encyclopedias offer pronunciations of *Dnieper* both with and without the *d* sound.

Day 42   The phonetic representation of the consonant spelled as *th* (i.e., a DIGRAPH) is the symbol θ in words like *thin*, *breath*, and the symbol ð in words like *thine* and *breathe*. The other digraphs are *ph* (f), *sh* (š), *ch* (č), *dg* (j), *zh* (ž), *wh* (w or hw).

Day 43   British/American spelling differences with final *-re/-er* such as *centre/ center*, *theatre/theater* are rooted in history, both early and modern. The words themselves were derived centuries ago from French, and British English has retained the French spelling. The American spelling here and elsewhere was proposed in 1806 by Noah Webster in his *Compendious Dictionary of the English Language*.

Day 44   Everything said here about the INFLECTIONAL suffix *-ing* applies as well to the INFLECTIONAL suffix *-ed*: *elóped, shópped, devélóped*.

Day 45   Many of the double-consonant "misspellings" cited here are licensed in the major dictionaries. The double 'l' spelling has a long history, as seen in the Francis Bacon quote. TENSE and LAX correspond roughly to "long" and "short" in primary school teaching.

Other common differences between British and American spelling are the following:

syphon	siphon
pyjamas	pajamas
aluminium	aluminum
programme	program
plough	plow
jewellery	jewelry
tyre	tire
defence	defense
gaol	jail [same pronunciation]

NOTES AND SOLUTIONS

PS 9   *The English indefinite article is <u>an</u> rather than <u>a</u>* **before a word beginning with a <u>syllabic</u>.**

Day 46   Stress marking will be treated with more detail in Chapters 15 and 16.

Day 48   A recently coined term used in reference to the semantic opposites inherent in verbs like *dust* and *seed* is AUTO-ANTONYM. The phenomenon itself would thus be AUTO-ANTONYMY.

Day 49   Barry Scheck and Johnny Cochran were the two famous lawyers for the successful defense in the 1995 murder trial of the American football legend O. J. Simpson.

The DERIVATIONAL SUFFIXES *-ize* and *-ify* exemplified in *humanize* and *humidify* are representative of two classes, each with special properties:

		YES		NO
STRESS SHIFT:	*húman* >	*humán ity* >	*húman ism*
VOWEL CHANGE:	*nátion* >	*nátion al* >	*nátion hood*
	/e/	/æ/	/e/
DEFORMATION OF STEM:	*exámple* >	*exémpl ify*	
	rándom		> *rándom ize*

PS 10   For the record, the geologists and climatologists who coined the terms use *desertification* to refer to natural, climate-driven change, *desertization* to man-induced change. It would be interesting to know if the verbs without their *-ation* suffixation—*desertify* and *desertize*—have also been coined. [N.B. A number of researchers report that it is not possible to distinguish the part of land degradation due to man from the part due to short-term climate changes.]

Day 52   Sentences embodying QUESTION form but with the discourse function of a statement or a DECLARATIVE have been given a name that is a combination of both terms: QUESTION + DECLARATIVE = QUECLARATIVE (Sadock 1971).

Day 53   The stress marks in use here for English are among the standard four: PRIMARY (´), SECONDARY (^), TERTIARY (`), and WEAK (ˇ).

For example: primary, weak: bláckĕn
primary, tertiary: bláckbìrd
secondary, primary: blâck bírd

Day 54 The *Which did who attach … icon preceding the dialogue is, of course, ungrammatical, as indicated by the star (*) convention. A readable source for the multiple **wh-** issue is Quirk *et al.* (1985), section 11.19. Verbs of "saying" that give rise to ambiguity in complex sentences headed by *where*, *when*, *why*, and *how*, as illustrated in the dialogue, are called BRIDGE VERBS.

Consider the "No … why" response to the YES-NO QUESTION at the end of the dialogue and what the word *why* is actually questioning. Obviously, it's not "Why <u>didn't</u> I call you this morning around eleven?" but rather "Why do you ask?" *Why* therefore questions the actual LOCUTION of "asking." See Rutherford (1970).

Day 55 Linguists have traditionally classified the sentence or clause into four basic forms or structural types: DECLARATIVE, INTERROGATIVE, EXCLAMATIVE, IMPERATIVE—each loosely paired with its typical "discourse function" of STATEMENT, QUESTION, EXCLAMATION, DIRECTIVE, respectively. For the sake of convenience, these four discourse functions are what are referred to as "forms" in the dialogue.

PS 11 The suggested solutions would be 2(c), 3(d), 4(j), 5(a), 6(h), 7(f), 8(e), 9(i), 10(g), 11(b).

Day 57 PHRASAL VERBS of the *look up* variety are termed VERB PARTICLE, those of the *look at* variety VERB PREPOSITION.

Repeated here are the two *take off* examples from the airline ad displayed: You *take off* at night. We *take off* 20%. The second *take off* is VERB PREPOSITION; the first is VERB PARTICLE but <u>INTRANSITIVE</u> (no object). Similar INTRANSITIVES might be *look out, look up, come in, go away, fall down*, etc.

Day 58 Some of these metaphors have been taken from Lakoff and Johnson (1980).

Day 59 The come/go analysis and many of the examples are based on material in Clark (1974), where much more is done with the "evaluative" approach. Also discussed by Clark are the related verbs *bring* ("cause to come") and *send* ("cause to go"), where an "evaluative" reading of the contrasting *They* **brought/sent** *the plane down near the lake* mirrors the *came/went* reading at the end of the dialogue.

Day 60 Most of the two-item examples as well as the suggested generalizations are taken from Cooper and Ross (1975).

NOTES AND SOLUTIONS

PS 12   One possible reason why the three-place freezes out of order don't sound right (other than broken habit) could be tied to syllable count: In all but two of the freezes, the pattern is ONE SYLLABLE / ONE SYLLABLE / and MULTI-SYLLABLE, e.g., *this, that, and the other; fair, fat and forty; calm, cool, and collected*. As for the first two items, one might note ALLITERATION (*beg - borrow, signed - sealed, calm - cool, fair - fat*, etc.) or other sound similarities (*lock - stock, this- that*).

Day 61   The two child utterances posted at the top are taken from Bellugi (1967).

Day 63   The two examples with *"in not many years ..."* have been drawn from Klima (1964).

Day 65   The sources for many of these quotes are the *Oxford English Dictionary, Bartlett's Familiar Quotations* (2002), and *Words on Words* (Crystal and Crystal, 2000).

PS 13   The source for most of these examples is *Bartlett's Familiar Quotations*, 17th edition (2002), Little, Brown and Company, Inc.

Day 68   "Until recently, *farther* was preferred of physical distance, *further* in figurative contexts, but *further* is now usual in all contexts" (*Oxford English Dictionary*). Only *further* occurs as a verb, however: *A little help could further his career.*

Day 69   These examples were inspired by another four-way ambiguous example from the great early-twentieth-century Danish linguist, Otto Jespersen, in his seven-volume *A Modern English Grammar on Historical Principles*: "He had known more attractive women than Annie."

Day 71   Stress within the English word can vary with affixation, as we saw earlier with *pérson ~ persónify ~ personificátion*, for example, where the main stress falls successively on three adjacent syllables. Similarly with *phótograph ~ photógraphy ~ photográphic*, although here -*ic* and -*y* are each attached to *photograph* independently, whereas in the previous example first -*ify* was attached to *pérson* and then –*(c)ation* attached to *person**ify***.

Day 72   The following (on the next page) are some other possible pairing contrasts of stress levels 2 and 3, letting standard accent marks stand in here for all three levels.

	V		N		N
Compare:	cŏnvíct	/	cónvìct	with	vérdĭct
	èxpórt	/	éxpòrt	with	éffŏrt
	prŏgréss	/	prógrèss	with	tígrĕss
	pĕrmít	/	pérmìt	with	hérmĭt
also:	prŏtést	/	prótèst	with	módĕst [adj]
	tòrmént	/	tórmènt	with	dórmănt [adj]

We can also look again at stress in words from Day 71. Consider the syllables that do <u>not</u> carry main stress in sets like *photograph ~ photography ~ photographic*. Phonetically, assigning stress levels 1 to 3, we might represent the word *photograph* as

fotəgræf
1 3 2

Photographic would then be   fotəgræf with attached *-ic*
                                                      2 3 1

and *photography* would be   fətagrəf with attached *-y*
                                                    3 1 3

Day 73 These observations concerning the spelling of one- and two-syllable words that contain a pair of vowels are one part of a larger statistical study of the relationship between such words and part of speech (noun, verb, adverb, etc.) in Dolby and Resnikoff (1964).

Attention needs also to be called to the fact that spoken syllabification concerning adjacent vowels will sometimes vary depending on dialect. For example, *dial, liar, giant*, etc. are <u>one</u>-syllable words [dæl, lær, jænt] in some dialects ranging over the southeastern United States.

Day 74 O'Neil has "orthography" instead of "spelling."

PS 15 Possible but presumably non-occurring words (except for two!):
- measurement of humans *anthropómetry*
- measure of human (adjective) *anthropométric(al)*
- a device for measuring small things *micrómeter*
- a message book *bíbliogram*
- knowledge of god (adjective) *theológic(al)*
- the sound of heat *thermóphony*
- aiming at the mind *psychóscopy*

What is listed is only a sample of roots of Greek origin that can be found in English. There are many more. A good source for these would be the *Oxford English Dictionary*.

Day 78 A number of the compound examples have been taken from Gleitman and Gleitman (1970).

Day 79 The notion that the rightmost element of derivations is the HEAD (Williams 1981) is not quite accurate, however, since English does have a few words like the VERBS *dethrone* (*de + throne*), *debone* (*de + bone*), *enrich* (*en + rich*), *empower* (*en/em + power*), etc., where rightmost *throne*, *bone*, and *power* are, of course, NOUNS and *rich* is an ADJECTIVE, as noted by Beard (1995).

It is perhaps worth mentioning that in German the GENDER of a COMPOUND is the GENDER of the rightmost element. For example, "coffee" and "house" are *Der Kaffee* and *Das Haus*. The compound "coffeehouse" is therefore ***Das Kaffeehaus***. Add "music" (*Die Musik*) to the end ("coffeehouse music") and the compound is now ***Die Kaffeehausmusik***.

Day 80 For a useful and readable discussion of the different types of compound in a variety of languages, see Fabb (1998).

PS 16 Consider *Danube steamship journey company captain's cabin key*, with perhaps the possessive necessarily thrown in.

Day 81 The possessive NEUTER form *its* entered the language in the early 1600s, centuries later than the other third-person singular possessives *his* and *her(s)*.

The contraction of *it is* to *it's* came into use in the seventeenth century as a replacement for *'tis*, likewise a contraction of *it is*. Thus, the earlier *'tis* is a contraction of the pronoun *it*; the later *it's* is a contraction of the verb *is*. See also the Note for Day 85.

Day 82 The difference between the use of *have* in the second and third of the three examples was described by the linguist Arnold Zwicky (1970: 329) in the following way. Examples like *He **has** a pain in his neck, She **had** a lot of courage, They **have** a house in the country*, etc., show "main-verb *have* in its central senses of possession, location, availability, and the like." Examples like *He **has** a party every night, She **had** me on the ropes, They **have** their friends pick them up*, etc., show main-verb *have* "in various restricted, idiomatic, or derived usages."

Day 83   Marta's question, *Who do they want to teach?*, if interpreted formally, is not AMBIGUOUS in strictly grammatical terms, since the *wh-* word questioning the <u>object</u> of *teach* would then need to be *whom*, not *who*.

Day 84   In addition to the **hafta, wanna, gonna, gotta** examples, contraction of a certain kind is evident also in conversational uses of **useta** [yustə] (*used to*), as in **I useta go home early**.

Day 85   The more technical term for the "contraction" looked at in Days 81 to 85 is CLITICIZATION; contraction to the preceding word (e.g., *want ← to = wanna*) would be ENCLITICIZATION, and to the following word (e.g., *is → here = 's here*) PROCLITICIZATION (Lasnik, 1989; Lightfoot, 1991). The item being attached (e.g., *to, is*) is the CLITIC. It's therefore interesting to note that the two contractions for *it is*—namely, *it's* and the historically earlier *'tis*—are both examples of PROCLITICIZATION, the PROCLITIC in the earlier *'tis* being *'t* (*it*), in the later *it's* being *'s* (*is*).

PS 17   Resolution of the ambiguity of the sentence

The solution to the problem is not working.

can be either of the following:

CONTRACTION: *The solution to the problem isn't working* (i.e., doesn't solve it).

INVERSION: *Not working* (i.e., not to work) *is the solution to the problem.*

The **un**contracted versions of the three sentences illustrated would be :

What <u>does</u> it do?
What <u>is</u> it doing?
What <u>has</u> it done?

Contraction of *does* would seem to be less frequent.

Day 86   The material on DEIXIS presented in much of this chapter (Days 86–90) draws from the work of Charles Fillmore (1997).

Day 87   Many of the insights here are attributable to Kimball (1974).

PS 18   Most of the examples are taken from Ross (1973), an article with the title "On edge, in part." It suggests that **on** (but not **in**) occurs as head of a PREPOSITIONAL PHRASE whose meaning has an "edge" sense to it: *coast, earth, border, mountain*, etc., versus *swamp, fog, world, yard*, etc. Thus, **in** *the world*, but **on** *earth*; **in** *Hawaii* (the state), but **on** *Hawaii* (the island); even **in** *time* (loose), but **on** *time* (punctual). The extension of the contrast to PREPOSITIONAL PHRASES containing a verbal element is quite radical and perhaps somewhat controversial.

Day 93 A good source for the garden-path phenomenon in English would be some of the papers in Clifton *et al.* (1994). See also Bever (1970)

Day 94 The NOUN COMPLEMENT construction is also called APPOSITIVE CLAUSE, in helpful contrast perhaps to RELATIVE CLAUSE. See Quirk *et al.* (1985), section 17.26.

Day 96 In the words of the linguist Alec Marantz (2008): "Words are grammatical entities with <u>internal</u> structures and <u>external</u> characteristics. To learn words, therefore, means to acquire these grammatical characteristics."

Day 97 The MODAL is often referred to in grammar books as AUXILIARY.

Day 98 Historically, the EPISTEMIC sense of MODALS <u>derived</u> from the DEONTIC. A good source for this would be Traugott (1989). A good source for English MODALS in general is Quirk *et al.* (1985).

Day 99 Note that the verb *move* can be ambiguous, as revealed in its corresponding noun forms: *make a **move*** vs. *make a **motion***.

Day 100 It has been suggested that the occasional tendency to say things like *They asked he and I to do something* instead of the correct *him and me* (sometimes labeled HYPER-CORRECTION) can arise from the common admonition of parents to children not to say *me and Emily did this, me and him did that*, etc.

Envoi Possible entries for this exercise might be as follows:

		Same spelling	Same sound	Same meaning
1. *bow / bow*	HOMOGRAPHS	+	−	−
2. *rose / rose*	HOMONYMS	+	+	−
3. *flour / flower*	HOMOPHONES	−	+	−
4. *hard / difficult*	SYNONYMS	−	−	+
5. [vez] / [vaz]	dialectal pronunciation	+	−	+
6. *center / centre*	dialectal spelling	−	+	+
7. *scat / cat*	dictionary lexicon	−	−	−
8. *arrive / arrive*	identical entries	+	+	+

Note: The *bow/bow* pair in no.1 would be pronounced [baw] / [bo]. Similar pairs could be *row/row* [raw] / [ro], *sow/sow* [saw] / [so]. The *rose/rose* pair in no.2 would be the flower *rose* and the past tense of the verb *rise*. Others could be *saw* [V] / *saw* [N], *fast* [V] / *fast* [ADJ], etc. Other entries for no.3 could be *red/read, no/know, serial/cereal*, etc.; for no.4 *book/tome, frail/fragile*, etc.; for no.5 *láboratory/labóratory, garáge/gárage*, etc.; for no.6 *color/colour, traveling/travelling, jail/gaol*, etc. No.7 would be any two distinct and unrelated dictionary entries, and no.8 any entry simply repeated. The second of the pairs in nos. 5 and 6 is the British pronunciation or spelling.

REFERENCES

Aitchison, J. 1987. *Words in the Mind: An Introduction to the Mental Lexicon.* Oxford: Blackwell.

Bartlett's Familiar Quotations, 17th edn. New York: Little, Brown & Company.

Baron, D. 1989. *Declining Grammar and Other Essays on the English Vocabulary.* Urbana, IL: National Council of Teachers of English.

Beard, R. 1995. *Lexeme-Morpheme Base Morphology: A General Theory of Inflection and Word Formation.* Albany: State University of New York Press.

Bellugi, U. 1967. "The Acquisition of Negation," unpublished doctoral dissertation, Harvard University.

Bever, T. 1970. The cognitive basis for linguistic structures. In John R. Hayes (ed.), *Cognition and the Development of Language.* New York: Wiley.

Bickerton, D., and C. Odo. 1976. *Change and Variation in Hawaiian English*, vol. 1, *The Pidgin.* Final Report on NSF Grant No. GS-39748. University of Hawaii.

Binnick, R. I. 1971. Bring and come. *Linguistic Inquiry*, 2:260–5.

Bolinger, D. 1968. *Aspects of Language.* New York: Harcourt, Brace & World.

Bresnan, J. 1973. Syntax of the comparative clause construction in English. *Linguistic Inquiry*, 4:276–343.

Brinton, L. 2000. *The Structure of Modern English: A Linguistic Introduction.* Amsterdam: John Benjamins.

Chomsky, N., and M. Halle. 1968. *The Sound Pattern of English.* New York: Harper & Row.

Clark, E. 1974. Normal states and evaluative viewpoints. *Language*, 50:316–32.

Clifton, C., L. Frazier, and K. Rayner (eds). 1994. *Perspectives on Sentence Processing.* Hillsdale, NJ: Lawrence Erlbaum Associates.

Cook, G. 2000. *Language Play, Language Learning.* Oxford: Oxford University Press.

Cooper, W., and J. Ross. 1975. World order. In R. Grossman, L. San, and T. Vance (eds), *Papers from the Parasession on Functionalism.* Chicago: Chicago Linguistic Society.

Crystal, D. 1997. *The Cambridge Encyclopedia of the English Language.* Cambridge: Cambridge University Press.

Crystal, D. 1998. *Language Play.* Chicago: University of Chicago Press.

Crystal, D. 2006. *The Fight for English: How Language Pundits Ate, Shot, and Left.* Oxford: Oxford University Press.

Crystal, D., and H. Crystal. 2000. *Words on Words: Quotations about Language and Languages.* Chicago: Chicago University Press.

Denham, K. 2006. Linguistics in a one-room schoolhouse. Paper presented at the K-12 Linguistics Materials Workshop, Linguistics Society of America, Albuquerque, NM.

Denham, K, and A. Lobeck. 2005. *Language in the Schools: Integrating Linguistic Knowledge into K-12 Teaching.* Mahwah, NJ: Erlbaum.

Dolby, J., and H. Resnikoff. 1964. On the structure of written English words. *Language*, 40:167–96.

Downing, P. 1977. On the creation and use of English compound nouns. *Language*, 53:810–42.

Fabb, N. 1998. "Compounding," in Andrew Spencer and Arnold Zwicky (eds), *The Handbook of Morphology*, chap. 3. Oxford: Blackwell.

REFERENCES

Fay, D., and A. Cutler. 1977. Malapropisms and the structure of the mental lexicon. *Linguistic Inquiry*, 8:505–20.

Fillmore, C. 1997. *Lectures on Deixis*. Stanford, CA: CSLI Publications.

Fillmore, C., and B. Atkins (1992). "Toward a frame-based lexicon: The semantics of RISK and its neighbors," in A. Lehrer and E. Kittay (eds), *Frames, Fields, and Contrasts*. Hillsdale, NJ: Lawrence Erlbaum Associates.

Freire, P. 2000. *Pedagogy of the Oppressed*. London: Continuum. (First published in English in 1970.)

Fromkin, V. (ed.). 1973. *Speech Errors as Linguistic Evidence*. The Hague: Mouton.

Gallas, K. 1995. *Talking Their Way into Science: Hearing Children's Questions and Theories, Responding with Curricula*. New York: Teachers College Press.

Givón, T. 1984. "Universals of discourse structure and second language acquisition," in W. Rutherford (ed.), *Language Universals and Second Language Acquisition*. Amsterdam: Benjamins.

Gleason, H. 1964. What grammar? *Language and Learning*. A special issue of *Harvard Educational Review*, 34:267–81.

Gleitman, L., and H. Gleitman. 1970. *Phrase and Paraphrase: Some Innovative Uses of Language*. New York: Norton.

Haegeman, L., and J. Guéron. 1999. *English Grammar: A Generative Perspective*. Oxford: Blackwell.

Hall, Rich. 1984. *Sniglets*. New York: Macmillan.

Honda, M. 1994. *Linguistic Inquiry in the Science Classroom*. MIT Working Papers in Linguistics.

Honda, M., and W. O'Neil. 1993. "Triggering science-forming capacity through linguistic inquiry," in K. Hale and S. Keyser (eds), *The View from Building 20: Essays in Linguistics in Honor of Sylvain Bromberger*. Cambridge, MA: MIT Press.

Honda, M., and W. O'Neil. 2006. Problem-set based linguistics for fifth-graders and beyond. Paper presented at the K-12 Linguistics Materials Workshop, Linguistics Society of America, Albuquerque, NM.

Hudson, R. 1992. *Teaching Grammar: A Guide for the National Curriculum*. Oxford: Blackwell.

Jespersen, O. 1954. *A Modern English Grammar on Historical Principles*. London: Allen and Unwin.

Joos, M. 1964. Language and the school child. *Language and Learning*. A special issue of *Harvard Educational Review*, 34:203–10.

Kavanagh, J., and I. Mattingly (eds). 1972. *Language by Eye and by Ear*. Cambridge, MA: MIT Press.

Keyser, S. 1970. The role of linguistics in the elementary school curriculum. *Elementary English*, 47:39–45.

Kimball, J. 1974. *The Grammar of Facing*. Bloomington: Indiana University Linguistics Club.

Kirkpatrick, B. 2006. *Clichés: Over 1500 Phrases Explored and Explained*. New York: St. Martin's Griffin.

Klein, S. 2006. Fourth graders discovering language. Paper presented at the K-12 Linguistics Materials Workshop, Linguistics Society of America, Albuquerque, NM.

Klein, S., S. Hendricks, and J. Fodor. 2006. "The Virtual Museum of Language and Linguistics." Proposed project presented at Linguistics Society of America, Albuquerque, NM, January 2006.

Klima, E. 1964. "Negation in English," in J. Fodor and J. Katz (eds), *The Structure of Language: Readings in the Philosophy of Language*. Englewood Cliffs, NJ: Prentice Hall.

Klima, E. 1972. "How alphabets might reflect language," in Kavanagh and Mattingly (1972).

Kövecses, Z., and P. Szabó. 1996. Idioms: A view from cognitive semantics. *Applied Linguistics*, 17:326–55.

Lakoff, G., and M. Johnson. 1980. *Metaphors We Live By*. Chicago: Chicago University Press.

Larson, R. 2010. *Grammar as Science*. Cambridge, MA: MIT Press.

Lasnik, H. 1989. "On certain substitutes for negative data," in R. Matthews and W. Demopoulos (eds), *Learnability and Linguistic Theory*. Dordrecht: Kluwer.

Lipton, J. 1977. *An Exaltation of Larks or, The Venereal Game*. Harmondsworth: Penguin Books.

MacDonald, M., D. Pearlmutter, and M. Seidenberg. 1994. "Syntactic ambiguity resolution as lexical ambiguity resolution," in C. Clifton, L. Frazier, and K. Rayner (eds), *Perspectives on Sentence Processing*. Hillsdale, NJ: Lawrence Erlbaum Associates.

Marantz, Alec. 2008. Words. Unpublished paper.

McLellan, V. 1996. *The Complete Book of Practical Proverbs & Wacky Wit*. Wheaton, IL: Tyndale House Publishers.

Nickerson, R. 1986. "Reasoning," in R. Dillon and R. Sternberg (eds), *Cognition and Instruction*. Orlando, FL: Academic Press.

Nystrand, M. 1997. *Opening Dialogue: Understanding the Dynamics of Language and Learning in the English Classroom*. New York: Teachers College Press.

O'Neil, W. 1969. Foreword to N. R. Catell, *The New English Grammar: A Descriptive Introduction*. Cambridge, MA: MIT Press.

O'Neil, W. 1980. "English orthography," in T. Shopen (ed.), *Standards and Dialects in English*. Cambridge, MA: Winthrop Publishers.

Payne, T. 2006. The linguistics challenge: Challenging future generations. Paper presented at the K-12 Linguistics Materials Workshop, Linguistics Society of America, Albuquerque, NM.

Quirk, R., S. Greenbaum, G. Leech, and J. Svartvik. 1985. *A Comprehensive Grammar of the English Language*. London: Longman.

Ross, J. 1973. On edge, in part. *Foundations of Language*, 10:329.

Rutherford, W. 1970. Some observations concerning subordinate clauses in English, *Language*, 46:97–115.

Rutherford, W. 1972. English in a low key: grammar instruction based on knowledge the student already possesses. *California English Journal*, 8:36–46.

Rutherford, W. 1973. *Sentence Sense*. New York: Harcourt Brace Jovanovich.

Rutherford, W. 1998. *Workbook in the Structure of English: Linguistic Principles and Language Acquisition*. Oxford: Blackwell.

Sadock, J. 1971. Queclaratives. In *Papers from the Seventh Regional Meeting*. Chicago: Chicago Linguistics Society.

REFERENCES

Schane, S. 1970. Linguistics, spelling, and pronunciation. *TESOL Quarterly*, 4:137–41.

Strevens, P. 1972. *British and American English*. London: Collier-Macmillan.

Taylor, K. 2003. *Reference and the Rational Mind*. Stanford: CSLI Publications.

Thomas, M. 2004. Two proposals for the extra-linguistic value of the study of language: Eighteenth century *ideologues* and modern generative grammarians. Paper presented at the annual meeting of the North American Association for the History of the Language Sciences, Boston.

Traugott, E. 1989. On the rise of epistemic modals in English: An example of subjectification in semantic change. *Language*, 65:31–55.

Venezky, R. 1970. *The Structure of English Orthography*. The Hague: Mouton.

Williams, E. 1981. On the notions 'Lexically related,' and 'Head of a Word.' *Linguistic Inquiry*, 12:245–74.

Zwicky, A. 1970. Auxiliary reduction in English. *Linguistic Inquiry*, 1:323–36.

INDEX OF TECHNICAL TERMS

Numbers in parentheses ( ) indicate the Day(s) in which the term was highlighted (used in small capital letters). Numbers in square brackets [ ] indicate the PS in which the term was featured. Numbers in braces { } are the Day or PS reference in the Notes. (E) indicates Envoi.